Frommer's®

PORTABLE
San Diego

4th Edition

D0907405

Here's what critics say about Frommer's:

"Amazingly easy to use. Very portable, very complete."
—*Booklist*

"Detailed, accurate, and easy-to-read information for all price ranges."
—*Glamour Magazine*

WILEY

Wiley Publishing, Inc.

Published by:

WILEY PUBLISHING, INC.
111 River St.
Hoboken, NJ 07030-5774

ISBN-13: 978-0-7645-9662-9
ISBN-10: 0-7645-9662-4

Editor: Caroline Sieg
Production Editors: M. Faunette Johnston, Lindsay Thompson
Photo Editor: Richard Fox
Cartographer: Tim Lohnes
Production by Wiley Indianapolis Composition Services

For information on our other products and services or to obtain technical support, please contact our Customer Care Department within the U.S. at 800/762-2974, outside the U.S. at 317/572-3993 or fax 317/572-4002.

Wiley also publishes its books in a variety of electronic formats. Some content that appears in print may not be available in electronic formats.

Manufactured in the United States of America

5   4   3   2   1

Contents

List of Maps

AN INVITATION TO THE READER

In researching this book, we discovered many wonderful places—hotels, restaurants, shops, and more. We're sure you'll find others. Please tell us about them, so we can share the information with your fellow travelers in upcoming editions. If you were disappointed with a recommendation, we'd love to know that, too. Please write to:

Frommer's Portable San Diego, 4th Edition
Wiley Publishing, Inc. • 111 River St. • Hoboken, NJ 07030-5774

AN ADDITIONAL NOTE

Please be advised that travel information is subject to change at any time— and this is especially true of prices. We therefore suggest that you write or call ahead for confirmation when making your travel plans. The authors, editors, and publisher cannot be held responsible for the experiences of readers while traveling. Your safety is important to us, however, so we encourage you to stay alert and be aware of your surroundings. Keep a close eye on cameras, purses, and wallets, all favorite targets of thieves and pickpockets.

FROMMER'S STAR RATINGS, ICONS & ABBREVIATIONS

Every hotel, restaurant, and attraction listing in this guide has been ranked for quality, value, service, amenities, and special features using a **star-rating system.** In country, state, and regional guides, we also rate towns and regions to help you narrow down your choices and budget your time accordingly. Hotels and restaurants are rated on a scale of zero (recommended) to three stars (exceptional). Attractions, shopping, nightlife, towns, and regions are rated according to the following scale: zero stars (recommended), one star (highly recommended), two stars (very highly recommended), and three stars (must-see).

In addition to the star-rating system, we also use **seven feature icons** that point you to the great deals, in-the-know advice, and unique experiences that separate travelers from tourists. Throughout the book, look for:

Finds	Special finds—those places only insiders know about
Fun Fact	Fun facts—details that make travelers more informed and their trips more fun
Kids	Best bets for kids and advice for the whole family
Moments	Special moments—those experiences that memories are made of
Overrated	Places or experiences not worth your time or money
Tips	Insider tips—great ways to save time and money
Value	Great values—where to get the best deals

The following **abbreviations** are used for credit cards:

AE	American Express	DISC	Discover	V	Visa
DC	Diners Club	MC	MasterCard		

FROMMERS.COM

Now that you have the guidebook to a great trip, visit our website at **www. frommers.com** for travel information on more than 3,000 destinations. With features updated regularly, we give you instant access to the most current trip-planning information available. At Frommers.com, you'll also find the best prices on airfares, accommodations, and car rentals—and you can even book travel online through our travel booking partners. At Frommers.com, you'll also find the following:

- Online updates to our most popular guidebooks
- Vacation sweepstakes and contest giveaways
- Newsletter highlighting the hottest travel trends
- Online travel message boards with featured travel discussions

The Best of San Diego

Best known for its benign climate and fabulous beaches, San Diego is one big outdoor playground. With 70 miles of sandy coastline—plus pretty, sheltered Mission Bay—you can choose from swimming, snorkeling, windsurfing, kayaking, bicycling, skating, and tons of other fun in or near the water. The city is also home to top-notch attractions, including three world-famous animal parks and splendid Balboa Park, a cultural and recreational jewel that's one of the finest urban parks in the country.

1 Frommer's Favorite San Diego Experiences

- **Driving over the Bridge to Coronado:** The first time or the fiftieth, there's always an adrenaline rush as you follow this engineering marvel's dramatic curves and catch a glimpse of the panoramic view to either side. See "Orientation," p. 16, for more about the city's neighborhoods.
- **Riding on the San Diego Trolley to Mexico:** The trip from downtown costs a mere $3, takes only 40 minutes, and the clean, quick, bright red trolleys are fun in their own right. See "Getting Around," p. 23.
- **Taking the Ferry to Coronado:** The 15-minute ride gets you out into San Diego Harbor and provides some of the best views of the city. See "Getting Around," p. 23.
- **Escaping to Torrey Pines State Reserve:** This state park is set aside for the rarest pine tree in North America. See p. 126.
- **Drinking Coffee at Sidewalk Cafe:** San Diego offers a plethora of coffee shops beyond the ubiquitous Starbucks: some of my favorites include **Peet's,** 350 University Ave., Hillcrest (© **619/296-5995**), **Gargoyle Gallery and Café,** 1845 India St., Little Italy (© **619/234-1344**), the **Pannikin,** 7467 Girard Ave., La Jolla (© **858/454-5453**), and the various branches of **Living Room Coffeehouse** (p. 84).
- **Watching the Sun Set over the Ocean:** It's a free and memorable experience. See "San Diego's Beaches," p. 105.

Watching the Seals at the Children's Pool: This tiny La Jolla cove was originally named for the toddlers who could safely frolic behind a man-made seawall. These days, the sand is mostly off-limits to humans, but you can get surprisingly close, and it's a truly mesmerizing sight. See "San Diego's Beaches," p. 105.

• **Renting Bikes, Skates, or Kayaks in Mission Bay:** Landscaped shores, calm waters, paved paths, and friendly neighbors make Mission Bay an aquatic playground like no other. See "Outdoor Pursuits," p. 137.

• **Strolling Through the Gaslamp Quarter:** Victorian commercial buildings that fill a 16½-block area will make you think you've stepped back in time. See "Gaslamp Quarter Historical Foundation," p. 135.

Listening to Free Sunday Organ Recitals in Balboa Park: Even if you usually don't like organ music, you might enjoy these outdoor concerts and the crowds they draw—San Diegans with their parents, their children, and their dogs. See "Attractions in Balboa Park," p. 110.

• **Listening to Live Music Outdoors at Humphrey's:** An intimate, palm-fringed venue located on the water at Shelter Island, Humphrey's has name acts from mid-May to October and puts those impersonal summer concert "sheds" found in other cities to shame. See "The Club & Music Scene," p. 162.

• **Running with the Grunion:** These tiny fish spawn on San Diego beaches between April and June, and the locals love to be there. See the "Running with the Grunion" box on p. 171.

2 Best Hotel Bets

• **Best Historic Hotel:** The **Hotel del Coronado,** 1500 Orange Ave. (© **800/HOTEL-DEL** or 619/435-6611), positively reeks of history. Meticulous restoration has enhanced this glorious landmark, whose early days are well chronicled in displays throughout the hotel. See p. 63.

• **Best for a Romantic Getaway:** The **Lodge at Torrey Pines,** 11480 North Torrey Pines Rd. (© **800/656-0087** or 858/453-4420), the city's only AAA five-diamond hotel, sits next to the Torrey Pines Golf Course, San Diego's top links. You can enjoy a fireplace in your room, sunset ocean views from your balcony, and superb meals at the hotel's A.R. Valentine restaurant. See p. 58.

The Best of San Diego Online

Here are my favorite helpful planning and general information sites.

- **www.sandiegoartandsol.com** is the link for cultural tourism, also overseen by the Convention and Visitors Bureau.
- **www.sandiego-online.com**, the *San Diego* magazine website, features abbreviated stories from the current month's issue, plus dining and events listings.
- **www.sdreader.com**, the site of the free weekly *San Diego Reader*, is a great source for club and show listings, plus edgy topical journalism.
- **www.signonsandiego.com** is where CitySearch teams up with the *San Diego Union-Tribune*, catering as much to locals as to visitors.
- **www.digitalcity.com/sandiego** is a lifestyle guide targeted at locals, and therefore yields occasional off-the-beaten-tourist-path recommendations.
- **www.sandiegoinsider.com** is a well-rounded online guide containing bar, club, and movie reviews. Searching this site can be tedious, but the articles are generally rewarding.

- **Best for Families:** The **Paradise Point Resort & Spa,** 1404 Vacation Rd. (© **800/344-2626** or 858/274-4630), is a tropical playground offering enough activities to keep family members of all ages happy. See p. 50.
- **Best Moderately Priced Hotel:** The **Gaslamp Plaza Suites,** 520 E St. (© **800/874-8770** or 619/232-9500), is an elegant landmark full of creature comforts that belie its superfriendly rates. You'll also be smack-dab in the heart of the trendy Gaslamp Quarter. See p. 42.
- **Best Budget Hotel:** In San Diego's Little Italy, **La Pensione Hotel,** 606 W. Date St. (© **800/232-4683** or 619/236-8000), feels like a small European hotel and offers tidy lodgings at bargain prices. See p. 42.
- **Best Bed & Breakfast:** The picture-perfect **Heritage Park Bed & Breakfast Inn,** 2470 Heritage Park Row (© **800/995-2470**

or 619/299-6832), is an exquisitely maintained Victorian house, with lively and gracious hosts who delight in creating a pampering and romantic ambience. See p. 47.

- **Best Place to Stay on the Beach:** Although the Hotel del Coronado operation takes the cake, a more moderate landing is found at La Jolla's **The Sea Lodge,** 8110 Camino del Oro (© **800/237-5211** or 858/459-8271), where you can walk right onto the wide beach and frolic amid great waves. See p. 60.
- **Best Hotel Pool:** The genteel pool at **La Valencia,** 1132 Prospect St. (© **800/451-0772** or 858/454-0771), is oh-so-special, with its spectacular setting overlooking Scripps Park and the Pacific. See p. 58.

3 Best Dining Bets

- **Best Spot for a Business Lunch: Dakota Grill & Spirits,** 901 Fifth Ave., in the Gaslamp Quarter (© **619/234-5554**), has a great location, appropriate atmosphere, and excellent food—but without prices that scream "power lunch." See p. 72.
- **Best View:** Many restaurants overlook the ocean, but only from **Brockton Villa,** 1235 Coast Blvd., La Jolla (© **858/454-7393**), can you see sublime La Jolla Cove. Diners with a window seat will feel as if they're looking out on a gigantic picture postcard. See p. 92.
- **Best Value:** The word "huge" barely begins to describe the portions at **Filippi's Pizza Grotto,** 1747 India St. (© **619/232-5095**), where a salad for one is enough for three, and an order of lasagna must weigh a pound. See p. 75.
- **Best Chinese Cuisine: Emerald Restaurant,** 3709 Convoy St., Kearny Mesa (© **858/565-6888**), is in the most unromantic of locations, yet the culinary wizardry that transpires in the kitchen draws the Chinese community citywide for Hong Kong–style seafood, much of it plucked from live fish tanks. See p. 98.
- **Best Seafood:** At **Star of the Sea,** 1360 N. Harbor Dr. (© **619/232-7408**), you'll find the city's best package of fresh seafood, graceful presentation, and memorable views from the edge of San Diego Bay. See p. 71.
- **Best New-American Cuisine:** Chef Deborah Scott's menu at **Indigo Grill,** 1536 India St. in Little Italy (© **619/234-6802**), cleverly fuses the flavors of the Pacific Coast from Mexico to

Mexican [handwritten annotation]

Alaska. The results create the city's most adventurous menu, and one of its most delicious. See p. 73.

- **Best Mexican Cuisine:** Rather than the "combination plate" fare that's common on this side of the border, **El Agave Tequileria,** 2304 San Diego Ave., Old Town (© **619/220-0692**), offers a memorable combination of freshly prepared recipes from Veracruz, Chiapas, Puebla, and Mexico City—along with an impressive selection of boutique and artisan tequilas. See p. 82.

- **Best Pizza:** For gourmet pizza from a wood-fired oven, head for **Sammy's California Woodfired Pizza,** a local institution with several locations, including 770 Fourth Ave., in the Gaslamp Quarter (© **619/230-8888**). For the traditional Sicilian variety, line up for **Filippi's Pizza Grotto,** 1747 India St., (© **619/232-5095**) See p. 79 and 75, respectively.

- **Best Desserts:** You'll forget your diet at **Extraordinary Desserts,** 2929 Fifth Ave., Hillcrest (© **619/294-7001**). Heck, it's so good you might forget your name! Proprietor Karen Krasne has a *Certificate de Patisserie* from Le Cordon Bleu in Paris, and makes everything fresh on the premises daily. See p. 78.

(Lindsay) [handwritten annotation]

- **Best Fast Food:** Fish tacos from the burgeoning local chain **Rubio's,** 4504 E. Mission Bay Dr. (© **619/272-2801**), and other locations, are legendary in San Diego. Sounds strange? Taste one and you'll know why there's a line. See "Baja Fish Tacos" on p. 82.

- **Best Picnic Fare:** Pack a superb sandwich from the **Bread & Cie.,** 350 University Ave. (© **619/683-9322**), where the hearty breads are the toast of the city. See p. 79. Or head to one of several locations of **Whole Foods,** in Hillcrest at 711 University Ave. (© **619/294-2800**), and in La Jolla at 8825 Villa La Jolla Dr. (© **858/642-6700**). See p. 76.

2

Planning Your Trip to San Diego

This chapter contains all the practical information and logistical advice you need to make your travel arrangements a snap, from deciding when to go to finding the best airfare.

1 Visitor Information

Start your homework by contacting the **International Visitor Information Center,** 11 Horton Plaza, San Diego, CA 92101 (✆ **619/236-1212;** www.sandiego.org). Ask for the *San Diego Vacation Planning Kit* which includes the *Visitors Planning Guide,* featuring information on accommodations, activities, and attractions, and excellent maps. The *San Diego Travel Values* insert is full of discount coupons for hotels at all price levels, restaurants, attractions, cultural and recreational activities, and tours.

You can also find information in advance of your trip online at the following websites: **www.infosandiego.com**, for general information; **www.gaslamp.org**, for information about the Gaslamp's history and revival; **www.coronadohistory.org**, for details about Coronado; and **www.sandiegonorth.com**, for information on excursion areas in northern San Diego County, including Del Mar, Carlsbad, Escondido, Julian, and Anza-Borrego Desert State Park. For more helpful websites, see "The Best of San Diego Online," on p. 3.

2 When to Go

San Diego is blessed with a mild climate, low humidity, good air quality, and welcoming blue skies through much of the year. In fact, *Pleasant Weather Rankings,* published by Consumer Travel, ranked San Diego's weather number two in the world. Indeed, is it difficult to convince yourself that you want to vacation in a place where that the afternoon high will most likely be 82°F (27°C)?

Although the temperature can change 20°F to 30°F between day and evening, it rarely reaches a point of extreme heat or cold—daytime highs above 100°F (37°C)are usually limited to two or three a year, and the mercury dropping below freezing can be counted in mere hours once or twice each year. San Diego receives very little precipitation (9½ in. of rainfall in an average year); what rain does fall comes primarily between November and April, and by July our hillsides start to look brown and parched. It's not unusual for the city to go without measurable precipitation for as long as 6 months in the summer and fall.

My favorite weather in San Diego is in the fall. October and November are ideal months to visit—daytime temperatures are warm, the skies are clearest, and water temps are still comfortable for swimming. February and March are often beautiful periods when the landscapes are greenest and flowers at their peak, but most of us find it's still too cold for ocean swimming. Beach bunnies should note tanning sessions from mid-May through mid-July are often compromised by a local phenomenon called June Gloom—a layer of low-lying clouds or fog along the coast that sometimes doesn't burn off till noon or later and returns before sunset. Use days like these to explore inland San Diego, where places like the Wild Animal Park are probably warm and clear.

San Diego is most crowded between Memorial Day and Labor Day. The kids are out of school and *everyone* wants to be by the seashore; if you visit in summer, expect fully booked hotels, crowded family attractions, and full parking lots at the beach. Along the beaches the week of the July 4th holiday is a zoo—you'll love it or hate it. But San Diego's popularity as a convention destination and its year-round weather keep the tourism business steady the rest of the year, as well. The only slow season is from Thanksgiving through early February—hotels are less full, and the beaches are peaceful and uncrowded.

Average Monthly Temperatures & Rainfall (in.)

	Jan	Feb	Mar	Apr	May	June	July	Aug	Sept	Oct	Nov	Dec
High (°F)	65	66	66	68	70	71	75	77	76	74	70	66
(°C)	18	19	19	20	21	21	24	25	25	23	21	19
Low (°F)	46	47	50	54	57	60	64	66	63	58	52	47
(°C)	7	9	10	12	14	15	17	19	17	15	10	8
Rainfall	1.88	1.48	1.55	0.81	0.15	0.05	0.01	0.07	0.13	0.34	1.25	1.73

SAN DIEGO CALENDAR OF EVENTS

January

Whale-Watching. Mid-December through mid-March is the eagerly anticipated whale-watching season. Scores of graceful yet gargantuan California gray whales make their annual migration to warm breeding lagoons in Baja, then return with their calves to springtime feeding grounds in Alaska. See "Whale-Watching," p. 136.

San Diego Marathon. The course begins in Carlsbad and stretches 26¼ miles, mainly along the coast. It's a gorgeous run, and spectators don't need tickets. For more information, call ⓒ **858/792-2900.** For an entry application, send a self-addressed stamped envelope to In Motion, 511 S. Cedros, Suite B, Solana Beach, CA 92075. Third Sunday in January.

Nations of San Diego International Dance Festival. Founded in 1993, this festival is Southern California's largest ethnic dance showcase, featuring over 200 dancers from different cultures and dance groups and companies. Performances are at the Mandeville Auditorium at the UCSD Campus. Call ⓒ **619/220-TIXS.** Mid-January.

February

Buick Invitational, Torrey Pines Golf Course, La Jolla. This PGA Tour men's tournament, an annual event since 1952, draws more than 100,000 spectators each year. It features 150 of the finest professionals in the world. For information, call ⓒ **800/888-BUICK** or 619/281-4653; or write Buick Invitational, 3333 Camino Del Rio S., Suite 100, San Diego, CA 92108. Early to mid-February.

March

Kiwanis Ocean Beach Kite Festival. The late-winter skies over the Ocean Beach Recreational Center get a brilliant shot of color. Learn to make and decorate a kite of your own, participate in an all-ages flying contest, take part in all types of food and entertainment, and finish up with the grand finale—a parade down to the beach. For more information, call ⓒ **619/531-1527.** First weekend in March.

Flower Fields in Bloom at Carlsbad Ranch. One of the most spectacular sights in North County is the yearly blossoming of a gigantic sea of bright ranunculuses during March and April, creating a striped blanket that's visible from the freeway. Visitors are welcome to view and tour the fields, which are off Interstate 5 at the Palomar Airport Road exit (adults $7). For more information, call ℂ **760/431-0352.**

April

Del Mar National Horse Show, Del Mar Fairgrounds. The first event in the Del Mar racing season takes place from late April into early May at the famous Del Mar Fairgrounds. The field at this show includes Olympic-caliber and national championship horse-and-rider teams; there are also Western fashion boutiques and artist displays and demonstrations. For more information, call ℂ **858/792-4288,** or visit www.sdfair.com.

Adams Avenue Roots Festival, Normal Heights. Vintage blues, folk, bluegrass, and international music held on six stages at 35th and Adams are free to the public, and there's food, a beer garden, and arts and crafts vendors. Check it out by calling ℂ **619/282-7329** or stop by www.gothere.com/adamsave. Late April.

Day at the Docks, Harbor Drive and Scott Street, Point Loma. This sportfishing tournament and festival features food, entertainment, and free boat rides. Call ℂ **800/994-FISH,** or see www.sportfishing.org. Usually the last weekend of April or the first weekend in May.

May

Cinco de Mayo Celebration, Old Town. Uniformed troops march and guns blast to mark the 1862 triumph of Mexican soldiers over the French. Festivities include a battle reenactment with costumed actors, mariachi music, and margaritas galore. Free admission. For further details, call ℂ **619/296-3236,** or visit www.fiestacincodemayo.com. Weekend closest to May 5.

June

Indian Fair, Museum of Man, Balboa Park. Native Americans from the southwestern United States gather to demonstrate tribal dances and sell arts, crafts, and ethnic food. Call ℂ **619/239-2001.** Mid-June.

Twilight in the Park Concerts, Spreckels Organ Pavilion, Balboa Park. These free concerts held on Tuesday, Wednesday, and Thursday evenings have been held since 1979 and run from mid-June through August. For information, call ℂ **619/235-1105.** The Spreckels Organ Society also holds free organ concerts on Mondays at 7:30pm in summer (ℂ **619/702-8138;** www.serve.com/sosorgan).

San Diego County Fair. More than 1.1 million visitors attend this annual fair at the Del Mar Fairgrounds. Livestock competitions, thrill rides, flower and garden shows, gem and mineral exhibits, food and craft booths, carnival games, home arts exhibits, and concerts by name performers dominate the event. The fair lasts 3 weeks, from mid-June to early July. For details, call © **858/793-5555,** or check www.sdfair.com.

San Diego Symphony Summer Pops. The symphony's summer pops series features lighter classical, jazz and other vocalists, opera, and Broadway and show tunes, all performed under the stars and sometimes capped by fireworks. Held most weekends, late June through August, at the Navy Pier, Broadway and Harbor Dr. For details, call © **619/235-0804** or www.sandiegosymphony.com.

July

World Championship Over-the-Line Tournament, Mission Bay. This popular tournament is a San Diego original. The beach softball event dates from 1953 and is renowned for boisterous, beer-soaked, anything-goes behavior. It's a heap of fun for the open-minded, but a bit much for small kids. It takes place on two consecutive weekends in mid-July, on Fiesta Island in Mission Bay, and the admission is free. For more details, call © **619/688-0817,** or visit www.ombac.org.

Thoroughbred Racing Season. The "turf meets the surf" in Del Mar from mid-July to mid-September during the Thoroughbred racing season at the Del Mar Race Track. Post time is 2pm most days; the track is dark on Tuesdays. For this year's schedule of events, call © **858/792-4242** or 858/755-1141.

U.S. Open Sandcastle Competition, Imperial Beach Pier. Here's the quintessential beach event: There's a parade and children's sand castle contest on Saturday, followed by the main competition Sunday. Past years have seen creations of astounding complexity, but note that the castles are usually plundered right after the award ceremony. Late July. For further details, call © **619/424-6663.**

August

Surfing Competitions. Oceanside's world-famous surfing spots attract numerous competitions, including the **World Bodysurfing Championships** and **Longboard Surf Club Competition.** The Longboard Competition takes place in mid-August at the Oceanside pier, and includes a trade show and gala awards presentation with music and dancers. For further details, call the Oceanside Visitors Bureau at © **800/350-7873** or 760/722-1534, or visit www.oceansidelongboardsurfingclub.org.

September

Street Scene, Gaslamp Quarter. This 3-day, 25-block extravaganza fills the historic streets of downtown's Gaslamp Quarter and East Village with music, food, dance, and international character. Twelve separate stages are erected to showcase jazz, blues, reggae, rock, and soul music all weekend. Attendees must be 21 or over for Friday and Saturday events—Sunday is all-ages day. For ticket and show information, call ✆ **800/260-9985,** or visit www.street-scene.com. Weekend after Labor Day.

La Jolla Rough Water Swim, La Jolla Cove. The country's largest rough-water swimming competition began in 1916 and features masters, men's and women's swims, a junior swim, and an amateur swim. All are 1-mile events except the junior swim and gator-man 3-mile championship. For recorded information, call ✆ **858/456-2100.** For an entry form, send a self-addressed stamped envelope to Entries Chairman, La Jolla Sports Group, P.O. Box 46, La Jolla, CA 92038. Sunday after Labor Day.

October

Underwater Pumpkin Carving Contest, La Jolla. The rules are relaxed, the panel of judges is serendipitous (one year it was the staff of a local dive shop, the next year five kids off the beach), and it's always a fun party. Spectators can hang out and wait for triumphant artists to break the surface with their creations. For details, call ✆ **858/565-6054.** Weekend before Halloween.

November

Carlsbad Fall Village Faire. Billed as the largest 1-day street fair in California, this festival features more than 800 vendors on 24 city blocks. Items for sale include ceramics, jewelry, clothing, glassware, and plants. Mexican, Italian, Japanese, Korean, Indonesian, and other edible fare is sold at booths along the way. The epicenter is the intersection of Grand Avenue and Jefferson Street. Call ✆ **760/945-9288,** or visit www.carlsbad.org. First Sunday in November.

Fall Flower Tour and the **Poinsettia Festival Street Fair,** Encinitas. Like its close neighbor Carlsbad, Encinitas is a flower-growing center—90% of the world's poinsettia plants get their start here. These two events celebrate the quintessential holiday plant and other late-flowering blooms. The 1-day Street Festival takes place in late November. For the Flower Tour, make reservations by early October; the nursery tours take place early December. For information, call the Encinitas Visitors Center at ✆ **800/953-6041** or 760/753-6041.

December

Balboa Park December Nights, Balboa Park. San Diego's fine urban park is decked out in holiday splendor for a weekend of evening events. A candlelight procession, traditional caroling, and baroque music ensembles are just part of the entertainment. The event is free and lasts from 5 to 9pm both days; the park's museums are free during those hours. For more information, call ✆ **619/239-0512,** or check www.balboapark.org. First weekend in December.

Whale-Watching. The season starts in mid-December; see the January listing earlier in this section.

Mission Bay Boat Parade of Lights, from Quivira Basin in Mission Bay. Held on a Saturday, the best viewing is around Crown Point, on the east side of Vacation Island, or the west side of Fiesta Island; it concludes with the lighting of a 320-foot tower of Christmas lights at SeaWorld. Call ✆ **858/488-0501.** For more vessels dressed up like Christmas trees, the **San Diego Boat Parade of Lights** is held in San Diego Bay on a Sunday, with a route starting at Shelter Island and running past Seaport Village and the Coronado Ferry Landing Marketplace. Visit www.sd paradeoflights.org for more information. Mid-December.

3 Specialized Travel Resources

TRAVELERS WITH DISABILITIES

San Diego is one of the most accessible cities in the country. Most of the city's major attractions are wheelchair friendly, including the walkways and museums of Balboa Park, the zoo (which has bus tours to navigate the steep canyons), and downtown's Gaslamp Quarter. Old Town and the beaches require a little more effort, but are generally accessible.

Obtain more specific information from **Accessible San Diego** (✆ **858/279-0704;** www.accessandiego.com), the nation's oldest center for information for travelers with disabilities. The center has an info line that helps travelers find accessible hotels, tours, attractions, and transportation. Ask for the annual *Access in San Diego* pamphlet, a citywide guide with specifics on which establishments are accessible for those with visual, mobility, or hearing disabilities (a nominal donation is requested). Another organization providing info and referrals is **Access Center of San Diego** (✆ **619/293-3500**). In the San Diego Convention & Visitors Bureau's *Dining* *and Accommodations* guide, a wheelchair symbol designates places that are accessible to persons with disabilities.

GAY & LESBIAN TRAVELERS

Despite the sometimes conservative local politics, San Diego is one of America's gay-friendliest destinations, boasting the first openly gay district attorney in the U.S., Bonnie Dumanis. Gay and lesbian visitors might already know about Hillcrest, the trendy part of town near Balboa Park that's the city's most prominent "out" community. In the 1990s, the community's residential embrace spread west to Mission Hills, and east along Adams Avenue to Kensington.

The **Lesbian and Gay Men's Community Center** is located at 3909 Centre St. in Hillcrest (© **619/692-2077**; www.thecentersd. org). It's open Monday through Friday from 9am to 10pm and Saturday from 9am to 7pm. Community outreach and counseling are offered.

The **Annual San Diego Lesbian and Gay Pride Parade, Rally, and Festival** is held on the third or fourth Saturday in July, and a weekend-long festival follows. For more information, call © **619/ 297-7683**; www.sdpride.org.

The free *San Diego Gay and Lesbian Times,* published every Thursday, is available at the gay and lesbian **Obelisk** bookstore, 1029 University Ave., Hillcrest (© **619/297-4171**), along with other gay-friendly businesses in Hillcrest and neighboring communities. And check out the **San Diego Gay & Lesbian Chamber of Commerce** online at www.gsdba.org, which boasts a large directory of gay-friendly businesses.

SENIOR TRAVEL

Nearly every attraction in San Diego offers a senior discount; age requirements vary, and prices are discussed in chapter 6 with each individual listing. Public transportation and movie theaters also have reduced rates. Don't be shy about asking for discounts, but always carry identification, such as a driver's license, that shows your date of birth. San Diego's special senior citizens referral and information line is © **619/560-2500.**

Members of **AARP** (formerly known as the American Association of Retired Persons), 601 E St. NW, Washington, DC 20049 (© **888/ 687-2277**; www.aarp.org), get discounts on hotels, airfares, and car rentals. AARP offers members a wide range of benefits, including *AARP: The Magazine* and a monthly newsletter. Anyone over 50 can join.

Many reliable agencies and organizations target the 50-plus market. **Elderhostel** (© **877/426-8056;** www.elderhostel.org) arranges study programs for those ages 55 and over (and a spouse or companion of any age) in the U.S. and in more than 80 countries around the world. Most courses last 5 to 7 days in the U.S., and many include airfare, accommodations in university dormitories or modest inns, meals, and tuition; there is an Elderhostel program in the San Diego area, at the Point Loma Youth Hostel.

FAMILY TRAVEL

You can find good family-oriented vacation advice on the Internet from sites like the **Family Travel Network** (www.familytravel network.com) and **Family Travel Files** (www.thefamilytravelfiles. com), which offers an online magazine and a directory of off-the-beaten-path tours and tour operators for families. Other resources include *The Unofficial Guide to California with Kids* (Wiley Publishing, Inc.), and *How to Take Great Trips with Your Kids* (The Harvard Common Press), which is full of good general advice that can apply to travel anywhere.

Family Travel Times is published six times a year (© **888/822-4388** or 212/477-5524; www.familytraveltimes.com), and includes a weekly call-in service for subscribers. Subscriptions are $39 a year, $49 for 2 years.

4 Getting There

BY PLANE

Flights arrive at San Diego International Airport/Lindbergh Field (airport code: SAN), which is named after aviation hero Charles Lindbergh. It's located close to downtown San Diego and is served by most national and regional air carriers as well as Aeroméxico, Air Canada, and British Airways from Mexico, Canada, and England.

Airlines flying into San Diego include: **Aeroméxico** (© 800/237-6639; www.aeromexico.com), **Alaska Airlines** (© 800/252-7522; www.alaskaair.com), **America West** (© 800/235-9292; www.america west.com), **American Airlines** (© 800/433-7300; www.aa.com), **Continental Airlines** (© 800/525-0280; www.continental.com), **Delta Airlines** (© 800/221-1212; www.delta.com), **Frontier Airlines** (© 800/432-1359; www.frontierairlines.com), **Hawaiian Airlines** (© 800/367-5320; www.hawaiianair.com), **Independence Air** (© 800/359-3594; www.flyi.com), **JetBlue** (© 800/538-2583;

www.jetblue.com), **Northwest Airlines** (© 800/225-2525; www. nwa.com), **Southwest Airlines** (© 800/435-9792; www.southwest. com), **United Airlines** (© 800/241-6522; www.united.com), and **US Airways** (© 800/428-4322; www.usairways.com). The Commuter Terminal, located a half-mile from the main terminals, is used by regional carriers **American Eagle** and **United Express.**

BY CAR

Visitors driving to San Diego from Los Angeles and points north do so via coastal route I-5. From points northeast, take I-15 and link up with Hwy. 163 South as you enter Miramar (use I-8 West for the beaches). From the east, use I-8 into the city, connecting to Highway 163 South for Hillcrest and downtown. Entering the downtown area, Highway 163 turns into 10th Avenue. Try to avoid arriving during weekday rush hours, between 7 and 9am and 3 and 6pm. If you are heading to Coronado, take the San Diego–Coronado Bay Bridge from I-5. Maximum speed in the San Diego area is 65 mph, and many areas are limited to 55 mph.

San Diego is 130 miles (2–3 hr.) from **Los Angeles;** 149 miles from **Palm Springs,** a 2½-hour trip; and 532 miles, or 8 to 9 hours, from **San Francisco.**

BY TRAIN

Trains from all points in the United States and Canada will take you to Los Angeles, where you'll need to change trains for the 2-hour, 40-minute journey to San Diego. You'll arrive at San Diego's striking, mission-style Santa Fe Station, built in 1914 and located downtown at Broadway and Kettner Boulevard. A few hotels are found within walking distance. The San Diego Trolley station is across the street. For price and schedule information, call **Amtrak** (© **800/ USA-RAIL;** www.amtrak.com).

BY BUS

Greyhound buses serve San Diego from downtown Los Angeles, Phoenix, Las Vegas, and other southwestern cities, arriving at the downtown terminal, located at 120 W. Broadway (© **800/231-2222** or 619/239-8082; www.greyhound.com). Several hotels, Horton Plaza, and the Gaslamp Quarter are within walking distance. Buses from Los Angeles are as frequent as every 30 minutes, take about 2½ hours for the journey, and the round-trip fare is $25 (one-way is $15).

3

Getting to Know San Diego

San Diego is laid out in an easy-to-decipher manner, so learning the lay of the land is neither confusing nor daunting. Most San Diegans welcome visitors and are eager to answer questions and provide assistance; you'll feel like a local before you know it.

1 Orientation

ARRIVING

BY PLANE

We have a love-hate relationship with our **San Diego International Airport** (© 619/231-2100; www.san.org), or Lindbergh Field. The facility is conveniently located just 2 miles northwest of downtown, and the landing approach is right at the edge of the central business district. Pilots thread a passage between high-rise buildings and Balboa Park on their final descent to the runway—you'll get a great view on either side of the plane. But it's also a small facility for today's travel demands.

Planes land at Terminal 1 or 2, though most flights to and from Southern California airports use the Commuter Terminal, a half-mile away; the "red bus" provides free service from the main airport to the Commuter Terminal, or there's a footpath. General **information desks** with visitor materials, maps, and other services are located near the baggage claim areas of both Terminal 1 and 2. You can exchange

---

Tips Need a Lift into Town?

When you're thinking about airport transfers, remember to ask your hotel whether it has an **airport shuttle.** It's common for hotels to offer this service—usually free, sometimes for a nominal charge—and some also offer complimentary shuttles from the hotel to popular shopping and dining areas around town. Make sure the hotel knows when you're arriving, and get precise directions on where the driver will pick you up.

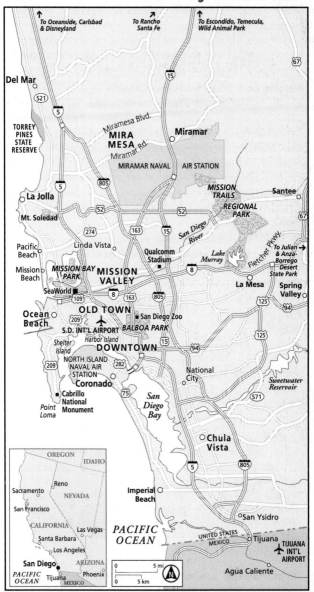

17

foreign currency at **Travelex America** (© **619/295-1501;** www. travelexusa.com), in Terminal 1 across from the United Airlines ticket counter, or in Terminal 2 on the second level (*inside* the security area, near the gates). **Hotel reservation** and **car-rental courtesy phones** are located in the baggage-claim areas of Terminals 1 and 2.

Getting into Town from the Airport

BY BUS The **Metropolitan Transit System (MTS)** (© **619/ 233-3004;** www.sdcommute.com) operates the San Diego Transit Flyer—bus Route no. 992—providing service between the airport and downtown San Diego, running along Broadway. Bus stops are located at each of Lindbergh Field's three terminals. The one-way fare is $2.25, and exact change is required. Request a transfer if you're connecting to another bus or San Diego Trolley route downtown. The ride takes about 15 minutes and buses come at 10- to 15-minute intervals.

BY TAXI Taxis line up outside both terminals and the trip to a downtown location, usually a 10-minute ride, is about $10 (plus tip); budget $20 to $22 for Coronado or Mission Beach, and about $30 to $35 for La Jolla.

BY SHUTTLE Several airport shuttles run regularly from the airport to points around the city; you'll see designated pick-up areas outside each terminal. The shuttles are a good deal for single travelers; two or more people traveling together might as well take a taxi. The fare is about $5 per person to downtown hotels; Mission Valley and Mission Beach are $8 to $10; La Jolla and Coronado are around $12. One company that serves all of San Diego county is **Cloud 9 Shuttle** (© **800/9-SHUTTLE** or 858/9-SHUTTLE; www.cloud9shuttle.com).

BY CAR If you're driving to downtown from the airport, take Harbor Drive south to Broadway, the main east-west thoroughfare, and turn left. To reach Hillcrest or Balboa Park, exit the airport toward I-5, and follow the signs for Laurel Street. To reach Mission Bay, take I-5 north to I-8 west. To reach La Jolla, take I-5 north to the La Jolla Parkway exit, bearing left onto Torrey Pines Road. For complete information on rental cars in San Diego, see "Getting Around," below.

BY TRAIN

San Diego's **Santa Fe Station** is located at the west end of Broadway, between Front Street and First Avenue, within a half-mile of most downtown hotels and the Embarcadero. Taxis line up outside the main door, the trolley station is across the street, and a dozen local bus routes stop on Broadway or Pacific Highway, 1 block away.

BY BUS

Greyhound buses from Los Angeles, Phoenix, Las Vegas, and other points in the southwest U.S. arrive at the station in downtown San Diego at 120 W. Broadway. Local buses stop in front and the San Diego Trolley line is nearby.

VISITOR INFORMATION

There are staffed information booths at airport terminals, the train station, and the cruise-ship terminal.

In downtown San Diego, the Convention & Visitors Bureau's **International Visitor Information Center** (© 619/236-1212; www.sandiego.org) is downtown at 11 Horton Plaza, at First Avenue and F Street. The glossy *Official Visitors Pocket Guide* includes information on accommodations, dining, activities, attractions, tours, and transportation, and be sure to ask for the *San Diego Travel Values* pamplet, which is full of money-saving coupons for hotels, restaurants, and attractions. The center is open Monday through Saturday from 8:30am to 5pm year-round and Sunday from 11am to 5pm, June through August; it is closed major holidays. There is also a walk-up only facility at the **La Jolla Visitor Center,** 7966 Herschel Ave., near the corner of Prospect Street. This office is open daily in summer, 10am to 7pm; mid-September through mid-June the center is open Thursday through Tuesday, from 10am to 5pm.

San Diego has two major print publications. The daily *San Diego Union-Tribune* is a rah-rah booster of all things local, especially when it involves spectator sports or pouring cement for the local teams. The leading "alternative" publication, the *San Diego Weekly Reader,* is alternative only in the sense that it rains on most any parade, especially if it involves the *Union-Tribune.* But for local nightlife and entertainment, comprehensive listings are found in the *Reader,* free and published on Thursdays and available all over the city at bookstores, cafes, liquor stores, and other outlets. The *Union-Tribune* publishes a weekly entertainment supplement called "Night and Day," also on Thursdays.

For websites with up-to-the-minute information, see "The Best of San Diego Online," p. 3.

CITY LAYOUT
MAIN ARTERIES & STREETS

It's not hard to find your way around downtown San Diego. Most streets run one-way, in a grid pattern. First through Twelfth avenues run north and south; A through K streets alternate running east and west. Broadway (the equivalent of D St.) runs both directions, as do Market Street and Harbor Drive. North of A Street the east-west streets bear the names of trees, in alphabetical order: Ash, Beech, Cedar, Date, and so on. Harbor Drive runs past the airport and along the waterfront, which is known as the Embarcadero. Ash Street and Broadway are the downtown arteries that connect with Harbor Drive.

I-5 north leads to Old Town, Mission Bay, La Jolla, and North County coastal areas. Balboa Park (home of the San Diego Zoo), Hillcrest, and uptown areas lie north of downtown San Diego. The park and zoo are easily reached by way of Twelfth Avenue, which turns into Park Boulevard and leads to the parking lots. Highway 163, which heads north from Eleventh Ave., leads into Mission Valley.

DOWNTOWN   The major thoroughfares are Broadway (a major bus artery), Fourth and Fifth avenues (which run south and north, respectively), C Street (the trolley line), and Harbor Drive, which curls along the waterfront and passes the Maritime Museum, Seaport Village, the Convention Center, and PETCO Park.

HILLCREST   Get here by taking Highway 163 to the Washington, University, or Sixth Avenue exit. The main streets are University Avenue and Washington Street (both two-way, running east and west), and Fourth and Fifth avenues.

LA JOLLA   Most easily reached from I-5 north via the La Jolla Parkway exit, the main avenues are Prospect and Girard, which are perpendicular to each other.

PACIFIC BEACH   From the I-5, take I-8, or Grand or Garnet avenues west. Mission Boulevard is the main north-south drag, parallel to and 1 block in from the beach, and perpendicular to it are Grand and Garnet avenues and Pacific Beach Drive. East and West Mission Bay drives encircle most of the bay and Ingraham Street cuts through the middle of it.

CORONADO   The Coronado Bay Bridge leading to Coronado is accessible from I-5 just south of downtown. The main streets are Orange Avenue, where most of the hotels and restaurants are clustered, and Ocean Drive, which follows Coronado Beach.

THE NEIGHBORHOODS IN BRIEF

In this guidebook, San Diego is divided into six main areas, where most visitors spend the bulk of their visit.

Downtown   The business, shopping, dining, and entertainment heart of the city, the downtown area encompasses Horton Plaza, the Gaslamp Quarter, the Embarcadero (waterfront), and the Convention Center, sprawling over eight individual "neighborhoods." Visitors with business in the city center would be wise to stay downtown, and it's also the most convenient area for those attending meetings at the Convention Center. The **Gaslamp Quarter** is the center of a massive redevelopment kicked off in the mid-1980s with the opening of the Horton Plaza shopping complex; now, the once-seedy area is jam-packed with trendy boutiques, restaurants, and nightspots. Immediately southeast of the Gaslamp is the brand-new **PETCO Park,** home of the San Diego Padres. Also undergoing a renaissance is **Little Italy,** a small neighborhood along India Street between Cedar and Fir at the northern edge of downtown, and a great place to find gelato, espresso, pizza, and pasta.

Hillcrest & Uptown   At the turn of the 20th century, the "uptown" neighborhoods north of downtown were home to San Diego's white-collar elite—Hillcrest was the city's first self-contained suburb in the 1920s. Despite the cachet of being close to Balboa Park (home of the San Diego Zoo and numerous museums), the area fell into neglect in the 1960s. However, starting in the late 1970s, legions of preservation-minded residents—particularly its lively gay community—restored Hillcrest's charms, making it the local equivalent of a West Hollywood or SoHo. Centrally located and brimming with popular restaurants and avant-garde boutiques, Hillcrest also offers less expensive and more personalized accommodations than any other area in the city. Other Uptown neighborhoods of interest are **Mission Hills** to the west of Hillcrest, and **University Heights, Normal Heights, North Park,** and **Kensington** to the east.

Old Town & Mission Valley   These two busy areas wrap around the neighborhood of Mission Hills. On one end is the Old Town State Historic Park (where California "began"), Presidio Park, Heritage Park, and numerous museums that recall the turn of the 20th-century and the city's beginnings. There's shopping and dining here, too, aimed largely at tourists. Not far from Old Town lies the vast suburban sprawl of Mission Valley, home to gigantic shopping centers. Hotel Circle is an elongated loop road paralleling the I-8, where a string of moderately priced and budget hotels offer an alternative to the ritzier neighborhoods. In recent years several major hotel and convention complexes have opened in Mission Valley, and 1990s condo developments have made the valley a residential area.

Mission Bay & the Beaches   Here's where they took the picture on the postcard you'll send home. Mission Bay is a watery playground perfect for water-skiing, sailing, and windsurfing. The adjacent communities of **Ocean Beach, Mission Beach,** and **Pacific Beach** are known for their wide stretches of sand, active nightlife, and casual dining. Many single San Diegans live here, and once you've visited you'll understand why. The boardwalk, which runs from South Mission Beach to Pacific Beach, is a popular place for in-line skating, bike riding, people-watching, and sunsets. This is the place to stay if you are traveling with beach-loving children or want to walk barefoot on the sand.

La Jolla   With an atmosphere that's somewhere between Rodeo Drive and a Mediterranean village, this seaside community is home to an inordinate number of wealthy folks who could live anywhere. They choose La Jolla, surrounded by the beach, the **University of California, San Diego,** outstanding restaurants, both pricey and traditional shops, and some of the world's best medical facilities. Tourists who bed down here can take advantage of the community's attributes without having to buy its high-priced real estate, though all share in La Jolla's problematic parking and traffic snarls. There are really two La Jollas: the so-called "village" is the original seaside community, while residential and business areas that have sprouted along La Jolla Village Drive east of I-8 are of less interest to visitors. Incidentally, the name is a compromise between Spanish and American Indian, as is the pronunciation (la *hoy*-ya); it has come to mean "the jewel."

Coronado   You may be tempted to think of Coronado as an island, as San Diegans once called it. Coronado does have an isolated, resort ambience and is most easily accessed by ferry or sweeping bridge, but the city of Coronado is actually on a bulbous peninsula connected to the mainland by a narrow sand spit, the **Silver Strand.** The northern portion of the peninsula is home to the **U.S. Naval Air Station,** in use since World War I. The southern sector has a history as an elite playground for snow birds and represents a charming suburban community. Quaint shops line the main street, Orange Avenue, and you'll find several resorts, including the landmark **Hotel del Coronado** (p. 63).

Coronado has a lovely duned beach (one of the area's finest), fine restaurants, and its "downtown" is reminiscent of a small Midwestern town; it's also home to more retired admirals than any other community in the country.

2 Getting Around

San Diego has many walkable neighborhoods, from the historic downtown area, to Hillcrest and nearby Balboa Park, to the Embarcadero, to Mission Bay Park. You get there by car, bus, or trolley, and your feet do the rest.

BY CAR

We complain of increasing traffic, but San Diego is still easy to navigate by car. Most downtown streets run one way, in a grid pattern. However, outside downtown, canyons and bays often make streets indirect. Finding a parking space can be tricky in the Gaslamp, Old Town, Mission Beach, and La Jolla, but parking lots are often centrally located. Rush hour on the freeways is generally concentrated from 7 to 9am and from 4:30 to 6:30pm. Be aware that San Diego's gas prices are often among the highest in the country.

RENTALS

All the major car rental firms have an office at the airport and several in larger hotels. Some of the national companies include **Alamo** (© 800/462-5266; www.alamo.com), **Avis** (© 800/230-4898; www.avis.com), **Budget** (© 800/527-0700; www.budget.com), **Dollar** (© 800/800-3665; www.dollar.com), **Enterprise** (© 800/736-8222; www.enterprise.com), **Hertz** (© 800/654-3131; www.hertz.com), **National** (© 800/227-7368; www.nationalcar.com), and **Thrifty** (© 800/847-4389; www.thrifty.com). Avis and several other companies will allow their cars into Mexico as far as Ensenada, but other rental outfits won't allow you to drive south of the border.

Demystifying Renter's Insurance

Before you drive off in a rental car, be sure you're insured. Hasty assumptions about your personal auto insurance or a rental agency's additional coverage could end up costing you tens of thousands of dollars, even if you are involved in an accident that was clearly the fault of another driver.

If you already hold a **private auto insurance** policy, you are most likely covered in the United States for loss of or damage to a rental car and liability in case of injury to any other party involved in an accident. Be sure to find out whether you are covered in the area you are visiting, whether your policy extends to everyone who will be driving the car, how much liability is covered in case an outside party is injured in an accident, and whether the type of vehicle you are renting is included under your contract. (Rental trucks, sport-utility vehicles, and luxury vehicles or sports cars may not be covered.)

Most **major credit cards** (especially gold and platinum cards) provide some degree of coverage as well, provided they're used to pay for the rental. Terms vary widely, however, so be sure to call your credit card company directly before you rent.

If you are **uninsured,** your credit card will probably provide primary coverage as long as you decline the rental agency's insurance and as long as you rent with that card. This means that the credit card will cover damage or theft of a rental car for the full cost of the vehicle. (In a few states, however, theft is not covered; ask specifically about state law where you will be renting and driving.) If you already have insurance, your credit card will provide secondary coverage, which basically covers your deductible.

Note: Though they may cover damage to your rental car, *credit cards will not cover liability,* or the cost of injury to an outside party, damage to an outside party's vehicle, or both. If you do not hold an insurance policy, you may seriously want to consider purchasing additional liability insurance from your rental company, even if you decline collision coverage. Be sure to check the terms, however. Some rental agencies cover liability only if the renter is not at fault; even then, the rental company's obligation varies from state to state.

The basic insurance coverage offered by most car-rental companies, known as the **Loss/Damage Waiver (LDW)** or **Collision Damage Waiver (CDW),** can cost as much as $20 a day. It usually covers the full value of the vehicle with no deductible if an outside party causes an accident or other damage to the rental car. Liability coverage varies according to the company policy and state law, but the minimum is usually at least $15,000. If you are at fault in an accident, you will be covered for the full replacement value of the car, but not for liability. Some states allow you to buy additional liability coverage for such cases. Most rental companies will require a police report to process any claims you file, but your private insurer will not be notified of the accident.

Saving Money on a Rental Car

Car-rental rates vary even more than airline fares. Prices depend on the size of the car, where and when you pick it up and drop it off, the length of the rental period, where and how far you drive it, whether you buy insurance, and a host of other factors. A few key questions could save you hundreds of dollars:

- Are weekend rates lower than weekday rates? Ask if the rate is the same for pickup Friday morning, for instance, as it is for Thursday night.
- Does the agency assess a drop-off charge if you don't return the car to the same location where you picked it up?
- Are special promotional rates available? If you see an advertised price in your local newspaper, be sure to ask for that specific rate; otherwise you may be charged the standard cost.
- Are discounts available for members of AARP, AAA, frequent-flyer programs, or trade unions?
- How much tax will be added to the rental bill? Local tax? State tax?
- How much does the rental company charge to refill your gas tank if you return with the tank less than full? Though most rental companies claim these prices are competitive, fuel is almost always cheaper in town.

PARKING

Metered parking spaces are found in downtown, Hillcrest, and the beach communities, but demand outpaces supply. Posted signs indicate operating hours—generally from 8am to 6pm, even on Saturdays. Be prepared with several dollars in change—you'll burn through quarters faster than a laundromat. Most unmetered areas have signs restricting street parking to 1 or 2 hours; count on vigilant chalking and ticketing during the regulated hours. Three-hour meters line Harbor Drive opposite the ticket offices for harbor tours; even on weekends, you have to feed them. If you can't find a metered space, there are plenty of hourly lots downtown. Parking in Mission Valley is usually within large parking structures and free, though congested on weekends and particularly leading up to Christmas.

The first pitch has yet to be thrown as we go to press, but I predict downtown parking will be tougher on evenings when Padres games are scheduled with the opening of PETCO Park.

DRIVING RULES

San Diegans are relatively respectful drivers, although admittedly we often speed and sometimes we lose patience with those who don't know their way around. California has a seat-belt law for both drivers and passengers, so buckle up before you venture out—children under the age of 6 and weighing less than 60 pounds must be in a car seat.

You may turn right at a red light after stopping unless a sign says otherwise. Likewise, you can turn left on a red light from a one-way street onto another one-way street after coming to a full stop. Keep in mind that pedestrians have the right of way at all times, not just in cross walks—stop for pedestrians who have stepped off the curb. Penalties in California for drunk driving are among the toughest in the country. Speed limits on freeways, particularly Highway 8 through Mission Valley, are aggressively enforced after dark, partly as a pretext for nabbing drivers who might have imbibed.

BY PUBLIC TRANSPORTATION
BY BUS

San Diego has an adequate bus system that will get you to where you're going—eventually. Most drivers are friendly and helpful. The system encompasses more than 100 routes in the greater San Diego area. Bus stops are marked by rectangular blue signs every other block or so on local routes, farther apart on express routes. More than 20 bus routes pass through the downtown area. Most **bus fares** are $2.25; a few express routes are $2.50. Buses accept dollar bills, but the driver can't give change. You can request a free transfer as long as you continue on a bus with an equal or lower fare (if it's higher, you pay the difference). Transfers must be used within 90 minutes, and you can return to where you started.

The **Transit Store,** 102 Broadway, at First Avenue (© **619/234-1060**), dispenses passes, tokens, timetables, maps, brochures, and lost-and-found information. It issues ID cards for seniors 60 and older, and for travelers with disabilities, all of whom pay $1 per ride. Request a copy of the useful brochure *Way to Go to See the Sights,* which details the city's most popular tourist attractions and the buses that will take you to them. The office is open Monday through Friday from 9am to 5pm. There is also a small **kiosk** staffed during the day located at the northwest corner of Fifth Avenue and University Avenue in Hillcrest—they have maps and schedules and can sell bus and trolley passes. If you know your route and just need schedule information—or automated answers to FAQs—call **Info Express** (© **619/685-4900**) from any touch-tone phone, 24 hours a day.

Some of the most popular tourist attractions served by bus and rail routes are Balboa Park (Rte. 1, 3, 7, 7A, 7B, and 25); the San Diego Zoo (Rte. 7, 7A, and 7B); the Convention Center and Gaslamp

✳ Tips   Money-Saving Bus & Trolley Passes

The **Day Tripper pass** allows unlimited rides on MTS (bus) and trolley routes. Passes are good for 1, 2, 3, and 4 consecutive days, and cost $5, $9, $12, and $15, respectively. Day Trippers are for sale at the Transit Store and all trolley station automatic ticket vending machines; call ✆ **619/685-4900** for more information.

Quarter (San Diego Trolley's Orange Line); Coronado (Rte. 901); Horton Plaza (most downtown bus routes and the San Diego Trolley's Blue and Orange Lines); Old Town (San Diego Trolley's Blue Line); Cabrillo National Monument (Rte. 26 from Old Town Transit Center); Seaport Village (Rte. 7 and the San Diego Trolley's Orange Line); SeaWorld (Rte. 9 from the Old Town Transit Center); Qualcomm Stadium (San Diego Trolley's Blue Line); and Tijuana (San Diego Trolley's Blue Line to San Ysidro).

When planning your route, note that schedules vary and most buses do not run all night. Some stop at 6pm, while other lines continue to 9pm, midnight, and 2am—ask your bus driver for more specific information. On Saturdays some routes run all night.

BY TROLLEY

Although the system is too limited for most San Diegans to utilize for work commutes, the San Diego Trolley is great for visitors, particularly if you're staying downtown or plan to visit Tijuana. There are three routes. The **Blue Line** is the one that is the handiest for most visitors: It travels from the Mexican border north through downtown and Old Town, with some trolleys continuing into Mission Valley. The **Orange Line** runs from downtown east through Lemon Grove and El Cajon. The **Green Line** runs from Old Town through Mission Valley to Qualcomm Stadium, San Diego State University, and on to Santee. The trip to the border crossing takes 40 minutes from downtown; from downtown to Old Town takes 10 to 15 minutes. For a route map, see the inside backcover of this guide.

Trolleys operate on a self-service fare-collection system; riders buy tickets from machines in stations before boarding. The machines list fares for each destination (ranging from $1.25 for anywhere within downtown, to $3 for the longest trips) and dispense change. Tickets are valid for 2 hours from the time of purchase, in any direction.

Fare inspectors board trains at random to check tickets. A round-trip ticket is double the price, but is valid all day between the origination and destination points.

The lines run every 15 minutes during the day and every 30 minutes at night; during peak weekday rush hours the Blue Line runs every 10 minutes. Trolleys stop at each station for only 30 seconds. To open the door for boarding, push the lighted green button; to open the door to exit the trolley, push the lighted white button.

For recorded transit information, call ✆ **619/685-4900.** To speak with a customer service representative, call ✆ **619/233-3004** (TTY/TDD 619/234-5005) daily from 5:30am to 8:30pm. For wheelchair lift info call ✆ **619/595-4960.** The trolley generally operates daily from 5am to about midnight; the Blue Line provides limited but additional service between Old Town and San Isidro throughout the night from Saturday evening to Sunday morning; check the website for details.

BY TAXI

Half a dozen taxi companies serve the area. Rates are based on mileage, and can add up quickly in sprawling San Diego—a trip from downtown to La Jolla, for example, will cost about $35. Other than in the Gaslamp Quarter after dark, taxis don't cruise the streets as they do in other cities, so you have to call ahead for quick pickup. If you are at a hotel or restaurant, the front-desk attendant or concierge will call one for you. Among the local companies are **Orange Cab** (✆ 619/291-3333), **San Diego Cab** (✆ 619/226-TAXI), and **Yellow Cab** (✆ 619/234-6161). The **Coronado Cab Company** (✆ 935/435-6211) serves Coronado. In La Jolla, use **La Jolla Cab** (✆ 858/453-4222).

BY TRAIN

San Diego's express rail commuter service, the **Coaster,** travels between the downtown Santa Fe Depot station and the Oceanside Transit Center, with stops at Old Town, Sorrento Valley, Solana Beach, Encinitas, and Carlsbad. Fares range from $3.50 to $4.75 each way, depending on how far you go, and can be paid by credit card at vending machines at each station. Eligible seniors and riders with disabilities pay half price. The scenic trip between downtown San Diego and Oceanside takes just under an hour. Trains run Monday through Friday about once an hour, with four trains each direction on Saturday; call ✆ **800/COASTER** for the current schedule, or log on to **www.sdcommute.com.**

Amtrak (© **800/USA-RAIL;** www.amtrakwest.com) trains run between San Diego and downtown Los Angeles, about 11 times daily each way. Trains to Los Angeles depart from the Santa Fe Depot and stop at Solana Beach, Oceanside, San Juan Capistrano, and Anaheim (Disneyland). The travel time from San Diego to Los Angeles is about 2 hours, 45 minutes (for comparison, driving time can be as little as 2 hr., or as much as 4 hr. during rush hour). A one-way ticket to Los Angeles is $24 ($48 round-trip), or $36 each way in business class. One-way to Solana Beach is $7, to Oceanside $9.50, to San Juan Capistrano $12, and to Anaheim $17.

BY WATER

BY FERRY   There's regularly scheduled ferry service between San Diego and Coronado (© **619/234-4111** for information). Ferries leave from the Broadway Pier (1050 N. Harbor Dr., at the intersection of Broadway) on the hour from 9am to 9pm Sunday through Thursday, and until 10pm Friday and Saturday. They return from the Old Ferry Landing in Coronado to the Broadway Pier every hour on the half-hour from 9:30am to 9:30pm Sunday through Thursday and until 10:30pm Friday and Saturday. The ride takes 15 minutes. The fare is $2 each way (50¢ extra if you bring your bike). Buy tickets at the Harbor Excursion kiosk on Broadway Pier or at the Old Ferry Landing in Coronado.

BY WATER TAXI   Water taxis (© **619/235-TAXI**) will pick you up from any dock around San Diego Bay, and operate daily between noon and 10pm, with extended hours in summer. If you're staying in a downtown hotel, this is a great way to reach the beaches of Coronado. Boats are sometimes available spur of the moment, but reservations are advised. Fares are just $5 per person to most locations.

BY BICYCLE

San Diego is ideal for exploration by bicycle, and many roads have designated bike lanes. Bikes are available for rent in most areas; see "Outdoor Pursuits," in chapter 6 for suggestions.

The San Diego Ridelink publishes a comprehensive map of the county detailing bike *paths* (separate rights-of-way for bicyclists), bike *lanes* (alongside motor vehicle ways), and bike *routes* (shared ways designated only by bike-symbol signs). The **San Diego Region Bike Map** is available at visitor centers; to receive a copy in advance, call © **619/231-BIKE.**

If you want to take your two-wheeler on a city bus, look for bike-route signs at the bus stop. The signs mean that the buses that stop here have bike racks. Let the driver know you want to stow your bike on the front of the bus, then board and pay the regular fare. With this service, you can bus the bike to an area you'd like to explore, do your biking there, then return by bus. Not all routes are served by buses with bike racks; call ✆ **619/233-3004** for information.

The San Diego Trolley has a **Bike-N-Ride** program that lets you bring your bike on the trolley for free. Bikers must board at the back of each trolley car, where the bike-storage area is located; cars carry two bikes except during weekday rush hours, when the limit is one bike per car. Several trolley stops connect with routes for buses with bike racks. For more information, call the **Transit Information Line** (✆ **619/233-3004**).

Bikes are permitted on the ferry connecting San Diego and Coronado.

FAST FACTS: San Diego

American Express A full-service travel office is located in La Jolla at 1020 Prospect St. (✆ **858/459-4161**).

Area Codes San Diego's main area code is **619,** used primarily by downtown, uptown, Mission Valley, Point Loma, Coronado, La Mesa, and El Cajon. The area code **858** is used for northern and coastal areas, including Mission Beach, Pacific Beach, La Jolla, Del Mar, Rancho Sante Fe, and Rancho Bernardo. Use **760** to reach the remainder of San Diego County, including Encinitas, Carlsbad, Oceanside, Escondido, Ramona, Julian, and Anza-Borrego.

Babysitters **Marion's Childcare** (✆ **619/582-5029**) has bonded babysitters available to come to your hotel room. **Panda Services** (✆ **858/292-5503**) is also available.

Business Hours Banks are open weekdays from 9am to 4pm or later, and sometimes Saturday morning. Shops in shopping malls tend to stay open until about 9pm weekdays and until 6pm weekends.

Dentists For dental referrals, contact the **San Diego County Dental Society** at ✆ **800/201-0244,** or call ✆ **800/DENTIST**.

Doctors **Hotel Docs** (✆ **800/468-3537**) is a 24-hour network of physicians, dentists, and chiropractors. They accept credit cards, and their services are covered by most insurance policies. In a life-threatening situation, dial ✆ **911**.

Drugstores Long's, Rite-Aid, and Sav-On sell pharmaceuticals and non-prescription products. Look in the phone book to find the one nearest you. If you need a pharmacy after normal business hours, the following branches are open 24 hours: **Sav-On Drugs**, 8831 Villa La Jolla Dr., La Jolla (℃ 858/457-4390), and 313 E. Washington St., Hillcrest (℃ 619/291-7170); and **Rite-Aid**, 535 Robinson Ave., Hillcrest (℃ 619/291-3703). Local hospitals also sell prescription drugs.

Emergencies Call ℃ **911** for fire, police, and ambulance. The main police station is at 1401 Broadway, at 14th Street (℃ **619/531-2000**, or 619/531-2065 for the hearing impaired).

Eyeglass Repair **Optometric Expressions**, 55 Horton Plaza (℃ 619/544-9000), is at street level near the Westin Hotel; it's open Monday through Saturday from 9:30am to 6pm. **Optometry on the Plaza**, on the second level of Horton Plaza (℃ 619/239-1716), is open Monday through Saturday from 10am to 6pm. Both can fill eyeglass prescriptions, repair glasses, and replace contact lenses. The major shopping centers in Mission Valley also have eyeglass stores that can fill prescriptions and handle most repairs.

Hospitals Near downtown San Diego, **UCSD Medical Center–Hillcrest**, 200 W. Arbor Dr. (℃ 619/543-6400), has the most convenient emergency room. In La Jolla, **Thornton Hospital**, 9300 Campus Point Dr. (℃ 858/657-7600), has a good emergency room, and you'll find another in Coronado, at **Coronado Hospital**, 250 Prospect Place, opposite the Marriott Resort (℃ 619/435-6251).

Hot Lines HIV Hot Line ℃ 619/236-2352. Alcoholics Anonymous ℃ 619/265-8762. Debtors Anonymous ℃ 619/525-3065. Mental Health Access & Crisis Line ℃ 800/479-3339. Traveler's Aid Society ℃ 619/231-7361.

Liquor Laws The drinking age in California is 21. Beer, wine, and hard liquor are sold daily from 6am to 2am and are available in grocery stores.

Newspapers & Magazines The *San Diego Union-Tribune* is published daily, and its entertainment section, "Night & Day," is in the Thursday edition. The free *San Diego Weekly Reader* is published Thursdays and is available at many shops, restaurants, theaters, and public hot spots; it's the best source for up-to-the-minute club and show listings. *San Diego* magazine is filled with dining listings for an elite audience (which explains all the ads for face-lifts and tummy tucks). *San Diego Home-Garden Lifestyles* magazine highlights the city's homes and gardens, and includes a monthly calendar of events and some savvy articles about the restaurant scene. Both magazines are published monthly and sold at newsstands.

Police   The downtown police station is at 1401 Broadway (✆ 619/531-2000). Call ✆ 911 in an emergency.

Post Office   San Diego's main post office is located at 2535 Midway Dr., just west of Old Town; it is open Monday through Friday from 8am to 5pm, and Saturday from 8am to 4pm. Post offices are located downtown, at 815 E St. and at 51 Horton Plaza, next to the Westin Hotel. There is a post office in the Mission Valley Shopping Center, next to Macy's. These branch offices are generally open Monday through Friday during regular business hours, plus Saturday morning; for specific branch information, call ✆ 800/ASK-USPS or log on to **www.usps.gov**.

Restrooms   Horton Plaza and Seaport Village downtown, Balboa Park, Old Town State Historic Park in Old Town, and the Ferry Landing Marketplace in Coronado all have well-marked public restrooms. In general, you won't have a problem finding one. The restrooms in most fast-food restaurants are usually clean and accessible.

Safety   Of the 10 largest cities in the United States, San Diego historically has had the lowest incidence of violent crime, per capita. Still, it never hurts to take precautions. Virtually all areas of the city are safe during the day. Caution is advised in Balboa Park, in areas not frequented by regular foot traffic. Homeless transients are common—especially downtown, in Hillcrest, and in beach areas. They are rarely a problem, but can be unpredictable when inebriated. Downtown areas to the east of PETCO Park are sparsely populated after dusk, and poorly lighted. Neighborhoods that are usually safe on foot at night include the Gaslamp Quarter, Hillcrest, Old Town, Mission Valley, La Jolla, and Coronado.

Smoking   Smoking is prohibited in all indoor public places, including theaters, hotel lobbies, and enclosed shopping malls. In 1998, California enacted legislation prohibiting smoking in all restaurants and bars, except those with outdoor seating.

Taxes   Sales tax in restaurants and shops is 7.75%. The hotel tax is 10.5.

Time Zone San Diego, like the rest of the West Coast, is in the Pacific Standard Time zone, which is 8 hours behind Greenwich (mean) time. Daylight saving time is observed. To check the time, call ✆ **619/853-1212.**

Transit Information Call ✆ **619/233-3004** (TTY/TDD 619/234-5005). If you know your route and just need schedule information, call ✆ **619/685-4900.**

Useful Telephone Numbers For the latest San Diego arts and entertainment information, call ✆ **619/238-0700;** for half-price day-of-performance tickets, call ✆ **619/497-5000;** for a beach and surf report, call ✆ **619/221-8824.**

Weather Call ✆ **619/289-1212.**

4

Where to Stay

San Diego offers a variety of places to stay that range from pricey high-rise hostelries to spa- and golf-blessed resorts, from inexpensive cookie-cutter motels to out-of-the-ordinary B&Bs.

High season is vaguely defined as the summer period between Memorial Day and Labor Day—some hotels inch rates higher still in July and August. However, as San Diego has grown into a convention destination, you'll find that rates for the larger downtown hotels and a few of the Mission Valley hotels are largely determined by the ebb and flow of conventions in town—weekend and holiday rates can offer good bargains. On the other hand, leisure-oriented hotels along the coast and in Mission Valley are generally busier on weekends, especially in summer, so mid-week deals are easier to snag. (Here's an idea to maximize your discounts: Spend the weekend at a downtown high-rise and duck into a beach bungalow on Monday.)

TIPS FOR SAVING ON YOUR HOTEL ROOM

A hotel's "rack rate" is the official published rate—I use these prices to help you make an apples-and-apples comparison. The truth is, hardly anybody pays rack rates, and you can nearly always do better. *Always* peruse the category above your target price—you might just find the perfect match, especially if you follow the advice below.

- **Ask about special rates or other discounts.** You may qualify for corporate, student, military, senior, or other discounts. Mention membership in AAA, AARP, frequent-flier programs, or trade unions, and find out the hotel's rates for children.
- **Dial direct.** When booking a room in a chain hotel, you'll often get a better deal by calling the individual hotel's reservation desk than at the chain's main number.
- **Book online.** Many hotels offer Internet-only discounts, or supply rooms to Priceline, Hotwire, Orbitz, Travelocity, or Expedia at discounted rates.

- **Look into group or long-stay discounts.** If you come as part of a large group, or are planning a long stay, you should be able to negotiate a bargain rate, because the hotel can then guarantee occupancy in a number of rooms.
- **Avoid excess charges and hidden costs.** Check ahead about parking charges; use your own cellphone, pay phones, or prepaid phone cards instead of dialing direct from expensive hotel phones; don't be tempted by the room's minibar offerings; and ask about any service charges ahead of time.
- **Book an efficiency.** A room with a kitchenette allows you to shop for groceries and cook your own meals.
- **Investigate reservation services.** These outfits usually work as consolidators, buying up or reserving rooms in bulk, and then dealing them out to customers at a profit: **San Diego Hotel Reservations** (© 800/SAVE-CASH; www.sandiegohotelres. com); **Hotel Locators** (© 800/423-7846; www.hotellocators. com); **Accommodations Express** (© 800/950-4685; www. accommodationsexpress.com); **Hotel Discounts** (© 800/715-7666; www.hoteldiscount.com); and **Quikbook** (© 800/789-9887, includes fax-on-demand service; www.quikbook.com).

Note: Rates given in this chapter do not include the hotel tax, which is an additional 10.5%. Also, many San Diego hotels provide a free shuttle to and from the airport, so before you pony up for a taxi, check to see what your hotel offers.

BED & BREAKFASTS
Travelers who seek bed-and-breakfast accommodations will be pleasantly surprised by the variety and affordability of San Diego B&Bs; for more information, try the **San Diego Bed & Breakfast Guild** (© 619/523-1300; www.bandbguildsandiego.org).

HOSTELS
Those in search of less expensive accommodations should check in to San Diego's small collection of hostels. Downtown, you'll find **USAHostels** (© 800/438-8622 or 619/232-3100; www.usahostels. com), located in the heart of the Gaslamp Quarter at 726 Fifth Ave., in a historic building; double rooms cost $50 and dorm rooms run $21 per person. Also in the Gaslamp is **HI Downtown Hostel** (© 800/909-4776, ext. 43 or 619/525-1531; www.sandiegohostels. com), 521 Market St.; doubles cost $44 to $55 and dorm rooms run $18 to $25. Hostelling International (formerly American Youth

Hostels) also has a 60-bed location in **Point Loma** (© **800/909-4776,** ext. 44 or 619/223-4778), which is about 2 miles inland from Ocean Beach; rates run $15 to $18 per person.

1 Downtown

Compared to many American cities, San Diego's downtown is a good place for leisure travelers to be based. The nightlife and dining in the Gaslamp Quarter and Horton Plaza shopping are at hand, Balboa Park, Hillcrest, Old Town, and Coronado are less than 10 minutes away by car, and beaches aren't much farther. And of course, the downtown area is very convenient for business travelers.

Conventions are big business, and the high-rise hotels cater primarily to the meet-and-greet crowd. While they don't offer much personality for leisure travelers, it's not hard to get rooms for 25% to 40% off the rack rates when a convention hasn't wiped out all the availability. Although their *rack* rates start in the high-$300s, three chain operations are a good place to test your wheelin'-and-dealin' skills. Start with **Embassy Suites Hotel San Diego Bay Downtown** 🐟🐟, 601 Pacific Hwy. (© **800/EMBASSY** or 619/239-2400; www.embassysuites.com), an all-suite property that throws in full breakfast and an afternoon cocktail. The city's biggest hotel is the 1,625-room **Manchester Grand Hyatt San Diego** 🐟🐟, 1 Market Place (© **800/233-1234** or 619/232-1234; www.hyatt.com), a two-towered behemoth with a 40th-floor cocktail lounge with sweeping views of the city and the bay. Then there's the 1,408-room **San Diego Marriott Marina** 🐟🐟, 333 W. Harbor Dr. (© **800/228-9290** or 619/234-1500; www.marriott.com), the convention hotel that started the waterfront boom—at least it boasts a tropical swimming pool and marina. You might also check out newcomer **Hotel Solamar** 🐟🐟 (© **877/230-0300,** www.hotelsolamar.com). This 235-room, stylishly urban Kimpton Hotels property also draws non-guests to revel in its restaurant and bar.

In the budget category, the 260-room **500 West,** 500 W. Broadway (© **619/234-5252**), offers small but comfortable rooms for $69 to $89 a night in a seven-story building dating to 1924. It offers contemporary style, history, and a good location, but bathrooms are down the hall.

VERY EXPENSIVE

US Grant Hotel At press time, this historic hotel was slated to reopen in late 2005 as part of Starwood Hotels & Resorts

Downtown San Diego Accommodations & Dining

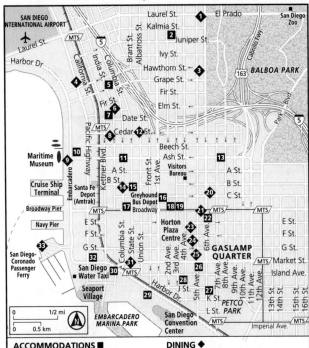

ACCOMMODATIONS ■

Best Western Bayside Inn **11**
Bristol Hotel **16**
Comfort Inn-Downtown **13**
Embassy Suites Hotel San Diego Bay-
    Downtown **32**
500 West **17**
Gaslamp Plaza Suites **22**
HI Downtown Hostel **26**
Holiday Inn on the Bay **10**
Horton Grand **28**
Hotel Solamar **27**
Keating House **2**
Manchester Grand Hyatt San Diego **30**
La Pensione Hotel **7**
Little Italy Hotel **5**
San Diego Marriott Marina **29**
USA Hostels **25**
U.S. Grant Hotel **19**
Westgate Hotel **18**
W San Diego **15**

DINING ◆

Café Lulu **20**
Chive **24**
Croce's **24**
Dakota Grill and Spirits **21**
Extraordinary Desserts **1, 12**
Fat City **4**
Fifth & Hawthorn **3**
Filippi's Pizza Grotto **6**
The Fish Market/Top of the Market **33**
Indigo Grill **8**
Kansas City Barbecue **31**
Karl Strauss Brewery and Grill **14**
Lilo's **20**
Sammy's Woodfired Pizza **23**
Star of the Sea **9**

Worldwide's prestigious Luxury Collection after undergoing a huge ($26 million is the current estimate) renovation. The comprehensive restoration includes overhauling guest rooms, food and beverage facilities, lobby areas, and meeting space with a focus on returning the property to an ambience and atmosphere true to its 1910 origins.

326 Broadway (at 4th Ave.), San Diego, CA 92101. (€ 619/232-3121. www. usgrant.net. 285 units. Call for rates. Trolley: Gaslamp Quarter. **Amenities:** Restaurant; bar; health club; Jacuzzi; concierge; room service (6:30am–midnight); laundry service; dry cleaning. *In room:* A/C, TV w/pay movies, dataport, coffeemaker, hair dryer.

The Westgate Hotel ★★★   Legend has it that local banker C. Arnholt Smith was challenged by President Eisenhower to build a better hotel for San Diego. Smith's wife toured Europe collecting pieces to furnish the public spaces, including Louis XVI period antiques and Baccarat crystal chandeliers, and when the Westgate opened, it was downtown's first new hotel in 35 years. Accusations of *"nouveau riche"* were flung and, ultimately, the Westgate became a money pit, leading to its sale to the Holding family in 1975. They in turn spent years nurturing a profile for the white elephant, eventually establishing a standard of luxury that today holds great appeal to visiting celebrities and dignitaries.

Despite the plain, modern exterior of this high-rise, the lobby appears straight out of 18th-century France. Afternoon tea is conducted daily here with great aplomb. The once-dowdy rooms were thoroughly gutted and upgraded in 2003—old-world decadence remains, but they feature DVD players, Italian armoires, and new marble finishings. At 400 square feet, standard rooms are the largest of any downtown hotel, and the harbor and city views are splendid. The Westgate has a fine jewel-box restaurant, **Le Fontainebleau**, noted for its French-California-Asian fusion cuisine, live piano music, silver place settings, and Saturday-night dinner dancing. Yes, it's more prissy-formal than the convention-centric Marriott or Hyatt down the street, but the Westgate is actually a bit cheaper, and you get a bigger room—a good bet for anyone thinking of packing fancy duds.

1055 Second Ave. (between Broadway and C St.), San Diego, CA 92101. (€ 800/ 221-3802 or 619/238-1818. Fax 619/557-3604. www.westgatehotel.com. 223 units. $239–$349 double; from $490 suite. Children 18 and under stay free in parent's room. AE, DC, DISC, MC, V. Underground valet parking $18. Bus: All Broadway routes. Trolley: Civic Center. **Amenities:** 3 restaurants; bar; fitness center; concierge; business center; barbershop; 24-hr. room service; laundry service; dry cleaning. *In room:* A/C, TV/DVD w/pay movies, dataport, minibar, hair dryer, safe.

W San Diego 🌟🌟   This W is hands-down San Diego's hippest scene to beat. Its swanky nightlife means on Friday and Saturday evenings there's a line to get in to the packed lobby. But if you hold a reservation, go to the front of the line and let one of the many black-clad *Friends* castoffs that work here lead you past the velvet rope to the front desk, where check-in can be accomplished by shouting above the din. Fortunately, your room is bright and cheery—like a mod beach cabana beamed into downtown, replete with sexy shower. *Nouveau nautique* is the theme, with elegant aqua and sand tones accenting the whites, a window seat (great idea) for gazing down on this languid corner of downtown, and a beach ball–shaped pillow, which should be the only exclamation point needed to remind you that this hotel is supposed to be fun.

So, go downstairs and sample the restaurant, **Rice,** and enjoy its adjoining bar, where cocktail waitresses clad in leather hot pants and fishnets serve blue-tinged cotton-candy treats that float through the room like tiny psychedelic clouds. A DJ spins here, another mixes in the Living Room—i.e., the lobby. Here, the path leading to the bathrooms is a catwalk with see-through plexi portholes underfoot. Then there's the Beach, up on the third floor, where the developers got really creative: The open-air bar has a sand floor (heated at night), a fire pit, and cabanas—drinks are served in plastic, allowing you to safely roam the terrace barefoot. Shoe check, please. The cacophony mostly dies down by Sunday, when the contingent of mostly Los Angelenos departs, and for a few days the W is the very model of a proper business hotel—albeit one with a (tiny) pool, a 24-hour open-air gym, and a bank of 18 video screens glowing with an idealized landscape of bubbles floating heavenward. Look closely and you'll notice that each bubble has a floating W logo within it. Self-absorbed? To the max. Fun? Check me in.

421 West B St. (at State St.), San Diego, CA 92101. ☎ 888/625-5144 or 619/231-8220. Fax 619/231-5779. www.whotels.com/sandiego. 261 units. $389–$439 double; $700 suite. AE, DC, DISC, MC, V. Valet parking $23. Bus: All Broadway routes. Trolley: American Plaza or Civic Center. **Amenities:** Restaurant; 3 bars; 24-hr. concierge; 24-hr. room service; laundry service; dry cleaning. *In room:* A/C, TV/VCR/DVD, CD player, dataport, minibar, coffeemaker, hair dryer, iron.

EXPENSIVE

Holiday Inn on the Bay 🌟🌟 *Kids*   This better-than-average Holiday Inn is reliable and nearly always offers great deals. The three-building high-rise complex is located on the Embarcadero across from the harbor and the Maritime Museum; this scenic spot is only

1½ miles from the airport (you can watch planes landing and taking off), and 2 blocks from the train station and trolley. Rooms, while basic, always seem to sport clean, modern furnishings and plenty of thoughtful comforts. Although rooms are identical inside, choose carefully; the bay views are astounding, while city views can be depressing (you're looking at utilitarian older office buildings). In either case, request the highest floor possible.

1355 N. Harbor Dr. (at Ash St.), San Diego, CA 92101-3385. © **800/HOLIDAY** or 619/232-3861. Fax 619/232-4924. 600 units. $199–$219 double; from $400 suite. Children under 18 stay free in parent's room. AE, DC, MC, V. Self-parking $15. Bus: All Pacific Highway routes. Trolley: American Plaza. Pets accepted with $25 fee and $100 deposit. **Amenities:** 4 restaurants; bar; outdoor heated pool; exercise room; concierge; business center; limited room service (6–11am and 5–11pm); babysitting; laundry service; coin-op laundry. *In room:* A/C, TV w/pay movies, dataport, coffeemaker, hair dryer, iron.

MODERATE

Best Western Bayside Inn ⌖   This high-rise, representative of reliable Best Western, offers quiet downtown lodgings. Although calling it "bayview" would be more accurate than "bayside," rooms in the 14-story hotel reveal nice city and harbor views. Rooms and bathrooms are basic chain-hotel issue, but are well maintained and all have balconies overlooking the bay or downtown (ask for the higher floors). The accommodating staff makes this a mecca for budget-minded business travelers, and this Best Western is also close to downtown's tourist sites. It's an easy walk to the Embarcadero, a bit farther to Horton Plaza, and just 5 blocks to the train station. Best of all, there's no charge for parking—almost unheard of among downtown hotels.

555 W. Ash St. (at Columbia St.), San Diego, CA 92101. © **800/341-1818** or 619/ 233-7500. Fax 619/239-8060. www.baysideinn.com. 122 units. $189 double. Extra person $10. Children under 12 stay free in parent's room. Rates include continental breakfast. AE, DC, DISC, MC, V. Free covered parking. Bus: 5 or 16. Trolley: Little Italy. **Amenities:** Restaurant (lunch daily, dinner Mon–Fri only); outdoor pool; Jacuzzi; laundry service; dry cleaning. *In room:* A/C, TV w/pay movies, dataport, fridge, microwave, coffeemaker, hair dryer, iron.

Bristol Hotel ⌖ *Value*   If you're looking for a basic business hotel with a sunny splash of style, you can do no better than the economical Bristol, which boasts a boxy, IKEA-esque geometric decor accented by energetic primary colors and an admirable collection of late-20th-century pop art from Warhol, Kandinsky, Lichtenstein, and Haring. Though it doesn't offer many on-site amenities to keep you around during the day, and the staff could be warmer, these brightly modern rooms are fun to come home to. Each morning a nice breakfast spread is laid out in the downstairs Daisies Bistro, which offers all-day dining and a cozy, after-work bar.

1055 First Ave. (between Broadway and C St.), San Diego, CA 92101. ℂ 800/662-4477 or 619/232-6141. Fax 619/232-1948. www.thebristolsandiego.com. 102 units. $179–$199 double. Children under 18 stay free in parent's room. AE, DC, DISC, MC, V. Valet parking $18. Bus: All Broadway routes. Trolley: Civic Center. **Amenities:** Restaurant; bar; concierge; laundry service; dry cleaning. *In room:* A/C, TV w/pay movies, Web TV, CD player, dataport, minibar, coffeemaker, hair dryer, iron.

Horton Grand 🐾   A cross between an elegant hotel and a charming inn, the Horton Grand combines two hotels that date from 1886—the Horton Grand (once an infamous red-light establishment) and the Brooklyn Hotel (which for a time was the Kahle Saddlery Shop). Both were saved from demolition, moved to this spot, and connected by an airy atrium lobby filled with white wicker. The facade, with its graceful bay windows, is original.

Each room is utterly unique—but all boast vintage furnishings, gas fireplaces, and business-savvy features—and bathrooms are lush with reproduction floor tiles, fine brass fixtures, and genteel appointments. Rooms overlook either the city or the fig tree–filled courtyard; they're divided between the clubby and darker "saddlery" side and the pastel-toned and Victorian "brothel" side. The suites (really just large studio-style rooms) are located in a newer wing; choosing one means sacrificing historic character for a sitting area/sofa bed and minibar with microwave. With all these offerings, there's a room that's right for everyone, so query your reservationist on the different features. The Palace Bar serves afternoon tea Saturdays from 2:30 to 5pm. My only qualm about this property is a lackadaisical staff that doesn't rise to the potential of this place.

311 Island Ave. (at Fourth Ave.), San Diego, CA 92101. ℂ 800/542-1886 or 619/544-1886. Fax 619/239-3823. www.hortongrand.com. 132 units. $169–$189 double; $279 suite. Extra person $20. Children under 18 stay free in parent's room. AE, DC, MC, V. Valet parking $20. Bus: 1, 4, 5, 16, or 25. Trolley: Convention Center. **Amenities:** Restaurant (Fri–Sat dinner and Sun brunch only); bar. *In room:* A/C, TV, dataport, hair dryer.

INEXPENSIVE

Comfort Inn–Downtown   In the northern corner of downtown, this value is popular with business travelers without expense accounts, and vacationers who just need reliable, safe accommodations. This humble chain motel must be surprised to find itself in a gentrified part of town: The Comfort Inn is smartly designed so rooms open onto exterior walkways surrounding the drive-in entry courtyard, lending an insular feel in this once-dicey corner of town. There are few frills here, but coffee is always brewing in the lobby. The hotel operates a free shuttle to the airport and the train and bus stations. *Note:* The hilltop location gives thighs a workout on the walk to and from the Gaslamp Quarter.

719 Ash St. (at Seventh Ave.), San Diego, CA 92101. © 619/232-2525. Fax 619/687-3024. www.comfortinnsandiego.com. 67 units. $89–$139 double. Extra person $15. Children under 18 stay free in parent's room. Rates include continental breakfast. AE, DISC, MC, V. Free parking. Bus: 1, 3, 25, or 992. **Amenities:** Jacuzzi; laundry service. *In room:* A/C, TV, dataport, coffeemaker.

Gaslamp Plaza Suites 🎔🎔 *Value*   You can't get closer to the center of the vibrant Gaslamp Quarter than this impeccably restored late Victorian. At 11 stories, it was San Diego's first skyscraper, built in 1913. Crafted (at great expense) of Australian gumwood, marble, brass, and exquisite etched glass, this splendid building originally housed San Diego Trust & Savings. Various other businesses (jewelers, lawyers, doctors, photographers) set up shop here until 1988, when the elegant structure was placed on the National Register of Historic Places and reopened as a boutique hotel.

You'll be surprised at the timeless elegance, from the dramatic lobby and wide corridors to guest rooms furnished with European flair. Each bears the name of a writer (Emerson, Swift, Zola, Shelley, Fitzgerald, and so on). Most rooms are spacious and offer luxuries rare in this price range, like pillow-top mattresses and premium toiletries; microwaves and dinnerware; and impressive luxury bathrooms. Beware of the cheapest rooms on the back side—they are uncomfortably small (although they do have regular-size bathrooms) and have no view. The higher floors boast splendid city and bay views, as do the rooftop patio, Jacuzzi, and breakfast room. Despite the welcome addition of noise-muffling windows, don't be surprised to hear a hum from the street below, especially when the Quarter gets rockin' on the weekends.

520 E St. (corner of Fifth Ave.), San Diego, CA 92101. © 800/874-8770 or 619/232-9500. Fax 619/238-9945. www.gaslampplaza.com. 64 units. $95–$189 double; from $199 suite. Rates include continental breakfast. AE, DC, DISC, MC, V. Valet parking $18. Bus: 1, 3, or 25. Trolley: Fifth Ave. **Amenities:** Rooftop Jacuzzi; limited room service (lunch and dinner). *In room:* A/C, TV w/VCR, dataport, fridge, microwave, coffeemaker, hair dryer, iron, safe.

La Pensione Hotel 🎔 *Value*   This place has a lot going for it: modern amenities, remarkable value, a convenient location within walking distance of the central business district, a friendly staff, and free parking (a premium for small hotels in San Diego). The four-story Pensione is built around a courtyard and feels like a small European hotel. The decor throughout is modern and streamlined, with plenty of sleek black and metallic surfaces, crisp white walls, and modern wood furnishings. Guest rooms, while not overly large, make the most of their space and leave you with room to move around. Each room offers a ceiling fan and minifridge; some have a small balcony. Try for a bay or city view rather than the concrete courtyard view. La Pensione is in San Diego's Little Italy and within walking distance of eateries (mostly Italian) and nightspots; there are two restaurants directly downstairs.

606 W. Date St. (at India St.), San Diego, CA 92101. ℂ **800/232-4683** or 619/236-8000. Fax 619/236-8088. www.lapensionehotel.com. 80 units. $75 double. AE, DC, DISC, MC, V. Limited free underground parking. Bus: 5 or 16. Trolley: Little Italy. **Amenities:** Self-service laundry. *In room:* TV, dataport, fridge.

Little Italy Hotel   Little Italy's newest addition, a renovated 1910 property, is a boutique bed-and-breakfast located right in the heart of San Diego's Italian cultural village, just steps from quaint bakeries, delightful eateries, and hip boutiques, and a few blocks from the historic Gaslamp Quarter and Balboa Park. While preserving the building's historic architecture, they have added the latest in guest comforts, including a secluded courtyard pool (a rare treat in Little Italy) and European-style continental breakfast each morning. Wide hallways lead into a variety of unique rooms featuring luxury touches like bay views, Jacuzzi tubs, oversize closets, wood floors, and spacious baths with plush bathrobes. Upgraded conveniences include free HBO, wireless Internet access, and free local calls.

505 West Grape St. (at India St.), San Diego, CA 92101. ℂ **800/518-9930** or 619/230-1600. Fax 619/230-0322. www.littleitalyhotel.com. 23 units. From $79 double; from $149 suite. Rates include breakfast. AE, DC, MC, V. *In room:* A/C, TV.

2 Hillcrest/Uptown

Although they're certainly no longer a secret, the gentrified historic neighborhoods north of downtown are still something of a bargain. They're convenient to Balboa Park and offer easy access to the rest of town. Filled with casual and upscale restaurants, eclectic shops, and upbeat nightlife, the area is also easy to navigate. All of the following accommodations cater to the mainstream market and attract a gay and lesbian clientele, as well.

MODERATE

Crone's Cobblestone Cottage Bed & Breakfast ⋆ *Finds*

After just 1 night at this magnificently restored Craftsman bungalow, you'll feel like an honored guest rather than a paying customer.
Artist Joan Crone lives in the architectural-award-winning addition
to her 1913 home, which is a designated historical landmark.
Guests have the run of the entire house, including a book-filled,
wood-paneled den and antique-filled living room. Both cozy guest
rooms have antique beds, goose-down pillows and comforters, and
eclectic bedside reading. They share a full bathroom; the Eaton
Room also has a private half bathroom. You can rent the entire
house (two bedrooms plus the den) to sleep five or six, for $285.
Bookmaker Crone lends a calm and craftsman aesthetic to the surroundings, aided by a pair of cats, who peer in from their side of the
house. Mission Hills, the neighborhood a half-mile west of Hillcrest, is one of San Diego's treasures, and lots of other historic
homes can be explored along quiet streets.

1302 Washington Place (4 blocks west of Goldfinch St. at Ingalls St.), San Diego, CA
92103. ℅ 619/295-4765. www.cobblestonebandb.com. 2 units. $125 double.
Rates include continental breakfast. Minimum 2 nights. No credit cards (checks
accepted). From I-5, take Washington St. exit east uphill. Make a U-turn at
Goldfinch, then keep right at Y intersection onto Washington Place. Bus: 3. *In room:*
No phone.

Sommerset Suites Hotel ⋆

This all-suite hotel on a busy street
was originally built as apartment housing for interns at the hospital
nearby. It retains a residential ambience and unexpected amenities
such as huge closets, medicine cabinets, and fully equipped kitchens
in all rooms (executive suites even have dishwashers). Poolside barbecue facilities encourage warm-weather mingling. The hotel has a
personal, welcoming feel, from the friendly, helpful staff to the
snacks, soda, beer, and wine served each afternoon. You'll even get a
welcome basket with cookies and microwave popcorn. Rooms are
comfortably furnished, and each has a private balcony. Be prepared
for noise from the nearby restaurants, shops, and multiplex cinema.
Guest services include a courtesy van to the airport, SeaWorld, the
zoo, and other attractions within a 5-mile radius.

606 Washington St. (at Fifth Ave.), San Diego, CA 92103. ℅ 800/962-9665 or 619/
692-5200. Fax 619/692-5299. www.sommersetsuites.com. 80 units. $139–$329 double. Children under 12 stay free in parent's room. Rates include continental breakfast
and afternoon refreshments. AE, DC, DISC, MC, V. Free covered parking. Take Washington St. exit off I-5. Bus: 1, 3, 7, 11, or 25. **Amenities:** Outdoor pool; Jacuzzi; coin-
op laundry. *In room:* A/C, TV, dataport, kitchen, coffeemaker, hair dryer, iron.

INEXPENSIVE

Balboa Park Inn 🏡 Insiders looking for unusual accommodations head straight for this small pink inn at the northern edge of Balboa Park. It's a cluster of four Spanish colonial–style former apartment buildings in a mostly residential neighborhood a half-mile east of Hillcrest proper. The hotel is popular with gay travelers drawn to Hillcrest's hip restaurants and clubs, but note that all of these are at least 4 blocks away. All the rooms and suites are tastefully decorated; the specialty suites, however, are over-the-top. There's the "Tara Suite," as in *Gone With the Wind;* the "Nouveau Ritz," which employs every Art Deco cliché, including mirrors and Hollywood lighting; and the "Greystoke" suite, a jumble of jungle, safari, and tropical themes with a completely mirrored bathroom and Jacuzzi tub. From here, you're close enough to walk to the San Diego Zoo and other Balboa Park attractions.

3402 Park Blvd. (at Upas St.), San Diego, CA 92103. ℂ **800/938-8181** or 619/298-0823. Fax 619/294-8070. www.balboaparkinn.com. 26 units. $99 double; $119–$199 suites. Extra person $10. Children under 12 stay free in parent's room. Rates include continental breakfast. AE, DC, DISC, MC, V. Parking available on street. From I-5, take Washington St. east, follow signs to University Ave. E. Turn right at Park Blvd. Bus: 7 or 7A/B. *In room:* TV, fridge, coffeemaker.

The Cottage Built in 1913, this B&B at the end of a residential cul-de-sac is surrounded by a secret garden, and features a private hideaway—"the cottage"—tucked behind a homestead-style house. There's an herb garden in front, birdbaths, and a walkway lined with climbing roses. The cottage has a king-size bed, a living room with a wood-burning stove and a queen-size sofa bed, and a charming kitchen with a coffeemaker. The guest room in the main house features a king-size bed. Both accommodations are filled with fresh flowers and antiques put to clever uses, and each has a private entrance. Owner Carol Emerick (she used to run an antiques store—and it shows!) serves a scrumptious breakfast, complete with the morning paper. Guests are welcome to use the dining room and parlor in the main house, where they sometimes light a fire and rev up the 19th-century player piano. The Cottage is located 5 blocks from the cafes of Mission Hills and Hillcrest, and a short drive from Balboa Park.

3829 Albatross St. (off Robinson Ave.), San Diego, CA 92103. ℂ **619/299-1564.** Fax 619/299-6213. www.sandiegobandb.com/cottage.htm. 2 units. $75 double; $99 cottage. Extra person in cottage $10. 2-night minimum stay. Rates include continental breakfast. AE, DISC, MC, V. Take Washington St. exit off I-5, take University Ave. exit; right on First Ave., right on Robinson Ave. Bus: 3 or 11. *In room:* TV, fridge, hair dryer.

Keating House ⭐⭐ *Finds*   This grand 1880s Bankers Hill mansion, located between downtown and Hillcrest and 4 blocks from Balboa Park, has been meticulously restored by two energetic innkeepers with a solid background in architectural preservation. Doug Scott and Ben Baltic not only know old houses, but are also neighborhood devotees filled with historical knowledge. Authentic period design is celebrated throughout, even in the overflowing gardens that bloom on four sides of this local landmark. The house contains a comfortable hodgepodge of antique furnishings and appointments; three additional rooms are in the restored carriage house opening onto an exotic garden patio. The downstairs entry, parlor, and dining room all have cozy fireplaces; bathrooms—all private—are gorgeously restored with updated period fixtures. Breakfast is served in a sunny, friendly setting; special dietary needs are cheerfully considered. In contrast to many B&Bs in Victorian-era homes, this one eschews dollhouse frills for a classy, sophisticated approach. The inn draws guests ranging from Europeans to business travelers avoiding the cookie-cutter ambience of chain hotels.

2331 Second Ave. (between Juniper and Kalmia sts.), San Diego, CA 92101. © 800/ 995-8644 or 619/239-8585. Fax 619/239-5774. www.keatinghouse.com. 9 units. $95–$155 double. Rates include full breakfast. AE, DISC, MC, V. Bus: 1, 3, 11, or 25. From the airport, take Harbor Dr. toward downtown; turn left on Laurel St., then right on Second Ave. *In room:* Hair dryer, no phone.

Park Manor Suites ⭐ *Value*   Popular with actors appearing at the Old Globe Theatre in neighboring Balboa Park, this eight-story hotel was built as a full-service luxury hotel in 1926 on a prime corner overlooking the park. One of the original investors was the family of child actor Jackie Coogan. The Hollywood connection continued— the hotel became a popular stopping-off point for celebrities headed for Mexican vacations in the 1920s and 1930s. Although dated, guest rooms are huge and very comfortable, featuring full kitchens, dining rooms, living rooms, and bedrooms with a separate dressing area. A few have glassed-in terraces; request one when you book. The overall feeling is that of a prewar East Coast apartment building, complete with steam heat and lavish moldings. Park Manor Suites does have its weaknesses, particularly bathrooms that have mostly original fixtures and could use some renovation. But prices are quite reasonable for Hillcrest; there's a darkly old-world restaurant on the ground floor, laundry service is also available, and a simple continental breakfast buffet is served in the penthouse banquet room (the view is spectacular). In fact, the penthouse bar becomes a bustling social scene on Friday evenings, drawing a horde—the single elevator gets a real workout that night.

525 Spruce St. (between Fifth and Sixth aves.), San Diego, CA 92103. © 800/874-2649 or 619/291-0999. Fax 619/291-8884. www.parkmanorsuites.com. 74 units. $99–$129 studio; $139–$179 1-bedroom suite; $199–$229 2-bedroom suite. Extra person $15. Children under 12 stay free in parent's room. Rates include continental breakfast. AE, DC, DISC, MC, V. Free parking. Bus: 1, 3, or 25. Take Washington St. exit off I-5, right on Fourth Ave., left on Spruce. **Amenities:** Restaurant/bar; access to nearby health club ($5); coin-op laundry and laundry service; dry cleaning. *In room:* TV, dataport, kitchen, coffeemaker, hair dryer, iron.

3 Old Town & Mission Valley

This is the spot for chain restaurants and shopping malls, not gardens or water views. But it caters to convention groups, families visiting the University of San Diego or San Diego State University, and leisure travelers drawn by the lower prices and competitive facilities.

Room rates at properties on Mission Valley's Hotel Circle are significantly cheaper than those in most other parts of the city. The chain hotels and motels include **Best Western Seven Seas** (© 800/421-6662 or 619/291-1300), **Mission Valley Travelodge** (© 800/255-3050 or 619/297-2271), **Ramada Plaza** (© 800/532-4241 or 619/291-6500), and **Vagabond Inn–Hotel Circle** (© 800/522-1555 or 619/297-1691).

MODERATE

Heritage Park Bed & Breakfast Inn 𝕲𝕲   This exquisite 1889 Queen Anne mansion is set in a Victorian park—an artfully arranged cobblestone cul-de-sac lined with historic buildings saved from the wrecking ball and assembled here, in Old Town, as a tourist attraction. Most of the inn's rooms are in the main house, with a handful of equally appealing choices in an adjacent 1887 Italianate companion. Owner Nancy Helsper is an amiable and energetic innkeeper with an eye for every necessary detail; she's always eager to share tales of these homes' fascinating history and how they crossed paths with Nancy and her husband, Charles. A stay here is about surrendering to the pampering of afternoon tea, candlelight breakfast, and a number of romantic extras (champagne and chocolates, dear?) available for special celebrations. Like the gracious parlors and porches, each room is outfitted with meticulous period antiques and luxurious fabrics; the small staff provides turndown service and virtually anything else you might require. Although the fireplaces are all ornamental, some rooms have whirlpool baths. In the evenings, vintage films are shown in the Victorian parlor.

2470 Heritage Park Row, San Diego, CA 92110. © 800/995-2470 or 619/299-6832. Fax 619/299-9465. www.heritageparkinn.com. 12 units. $120–$250 double. Extra person $20. Rates include full breakfast and afternoon tea. AE, DC, DISC, MC, V. Free parking. Take I-5 to Old Town Ave., turn left onto San Diego Ave., then turn right onto Harney St. Bus: 5. Trolley: Old Town. *In room:* A/C, hair dryer, iron.

Holiday Inn Express–Old Town ☆   Just a couple of easy walking blocks from the heart of Old Town, this Holiday Inn has a Spanish colonial exterior that suits the neighborhood's theme. Inside you'll find better-than-they-have-to-be contemporary furnishings and surprising small touches that make this hotel an affordable option favored by business travelers and families alike. There's nothing spectacular about the adjacent streets, so the hotel is smartly oriented toward the inside; request a room whose patio or balcony opens onto the pleasant courtyard. Rooms are thoughtfully and practically appointed, with extras like microwaves and writing tables. The lobby, surrounded by French doors, features a large fireplace, several sitting areas, and a TV. The hotel entrance, on Jefferson Street, is hard to find but definitely worth the search.

3900 Old Town Ave., San Diego, CA 92110. © 800/451-9846 or 619/299-7400. Fax 619/299-1619. www.hiexpress.com/ex-oldtown. 125 units. $139–$169 double. Extra person $10. Children under 18 stay free in parent's room. Rates include continental breakfast. AE, DC, DISC, MC, V. Free parking. Take I-5 to Old Town Ave. exit. Bus: 5. **Amenities:** Outdoor pool; Jacuzzi; laundry service; dry cleaning. *In room:* A/C, TV, fridge, microwave, coffeemaker.

Red Lion Hanalei Hotel ☆   My favorite hotel along Mission Valley's Hotel Circle has a Polynesian theme and comfort-conscious sophistication that sets it apart from the rest of the pack. Most rooms are split between two eight-story towers, set back from the freeway and cleverly positioned so that the balconies open onto the tropically landscaped pool courtyard or the attractive links of a golf club. A few more rooms are found in the Presidio Building, which is too close to the freeway for my comfort. The heated outdoor pool is large enough for any luau, as is the oversize Jacuzzi beside it. The hotel boasts an unmistakable 1960s vibe and Hawaiian ambience; the restaurant and bar have over-the-top kitschy decor, with waterfalls, outrigger canoes, and more. But guest rooms are outfitted with contemporary furnishings and conveniences; some have microwaves and fridges. Services include a free shuttle to Old Town and the Fashion Valley Shopping Center, plus meeting facilities; golf packages are available.

2270 Hotel Circle North, San Diego, CA 92108. © **800/RED-LION** or 619/297-1101. Fax 619/297-6049. www.redlion.com. 416 units. $159 double; $275–$375 suite. Extra person $10. AE, DISC, MC, V. Parking $8. From I-8, take Hotel Circle exit, follow signs for Hotel Circle N. Bus: 6. Pets accepted with $50 deposit. **Amenities:** 2 restaurants; bar; outdoor pool; nearby golf course; fitness center; Jacuzzi; game room; activities desk; 24-hr. business center; limited room service (6am–10pm); coin-op laundry and laundry service; dry cleaning. *In room:* A/C, TV w/pay movies, dataport, coffeemaker, hair dryer, iron.

INEXPENSIVE

Motel 6 Hotel Circle Yes, it's a Motel 6, so you know the drill: No mint on the pillow and you have to trundle down to the front desk to retrieve a cup of coffee in the morning. On the other hand, these budget hotels—now part of the mammoth Accor chain, the world's third-largest hotel company—know how to provide a consistent product at dependably inexpensive rates, and this one is very central to San Diego's sightseeing. The modern, four-story motel sits at the western end of Hotel Circle. Rooms are sparingly but adequately outfitted, with standard motel furnishings; bathrooms are perfunctory. Stay away from the loud freeway side—rooms in the four-story structure in back overlook a scenic 18-hole golf course and river. The hotel doesn't have a restaurant, but a fair steakhouse is across the street.

2424 Hotel Circle N., San Diego, CA 92108. © **800/4-MOTEL6** or 619/296-1612. Fax 619/543-9305. www.motel6.com. 204 units. $66–$80 double. Extra person $3. Children under 18 stay free in parent's room. AE, DC, DISC, MC, V. Free parking. From I-8, take Taylor St. exit. Bus: 6. **Amenities:** Outdoor pool; coin-op laundry. *In room:* A/C, TV.

4 Mission Bay & the Beaches

If the beach and aquatic activities are front-and-center in your San Diego agenda, this part of town may be just the ticket. Some hotels are right on Mission Bay, San Diego's water playground; they're usually good choices for families. Ocean Beach is more neighborhood oriented and easygoing, while Mission Beach and Pacific Beach provide a taste of the transient beach-bum lifestyle—they can be a bit raucous at times, especially on summer weekends, and dining options are largely limited to chain eateries. If you're looking for a more refined landing, head to La Jolla or Coronado. Even though the beach communities are far removed in atmosphere, downtown and Balboa Park are only a 15-minute drive away.

VERY EXPENSIVE

Pacific Terrace Hotel 🐾🐾 The best modern hotel on the boardwalk swaggers with a heavy-handed South Seas–meets–Spanish colonial ambience. Rattan fans circulate in the lobby and hint at the sunny Indonesian-inspired decor in guest rooms, which are named after Caribbean islands. Hands-on owners kicked up the luxury factor (and prices) following a renovation, resulting in a more upscale atmosphere than most of the casual beach pads nearby are able to muster, and the staff is friendly and accommodating. Located at the north end of the Pacific Beach boardwalk, the surfer contingent tends to stay a few blocks south.

Large, comfortable guest rooms each come with balconies or terraces and fancy wall safes; bathrooms, designed with warm-toned marble and natural woods, have a separate sink/vanity area. About half the rooms have kitchenettes, and top-floor rooms in this three-story hotel enjoy particularly nice views—you'll find yourself mesmerized by the rhythmic waves and determined surfers below. Management keeps cookies, coffee, and iced tea at the ready throughout the day; the lushly landscaped pool and hot tub overlook a relatively quiet stretch of beach. Five nearby restaurants allow meals to be billed to the hotel, but there's no restaurant on the premises.

610 Diamond St., San Diego, CA 92109. ✆ **800/344-3370** or 858/581-3500. Fax 858/274-3341. www.pacificterrace.com. 75 units. $260–$385 double; suites from $435. Rates include continental breakfast. AE, DC, DISC, MC, V. Parking $8; limited free parking in off-street lot. Take I-5 to Grand/Garnet exit and follow Grand or Garnet west to Mission Blvd., turn right (north), then left (west) onto Diamond. Bus: 30 or 34. **Amenities:** Pool; access to nearby health club ($5); Jacuzzi; bike rental nearby; activities desk; limited room service (11am–10:30pm); in-room massage; coin-op laundry and laundry service; dry cleaning. *In room:* A/C, TV w/pay movies, dataport, minibar, coffeemaker, hair dryer, iron.

Paradise Point Resort & Spa 🌟🌟 *(Kids)*   Smack dab in the middle of Mission Bay, this hotel complex is almost as much a theme park as its closest neighbor, SeaWorld (a 3-min. drive). Single-story accommodations are spread across 44 tropically landscaped acres of duck-filled lagoons, lush gardens, and swim-friendly beaches; all have private lanais and plenty of thoughtful conveniences. The resort was recently updated to keep its low-tech 1960s charm but lose tacky holdovers—rooms now have a refreshingly colorful beach cottage decor. And despite daunting high-season rack rates, there's usually a deal to be had here. There's an upscale waterfront restaurant, Baleen (fine dining in a contemporary, fun space), and a stunning Indonesian-inspired spa that offers cool serenity and aroma-tinged Asian treatments—this spa is a vacation in itself!

Accommodations & Dining in Mission Bay & the Beaches

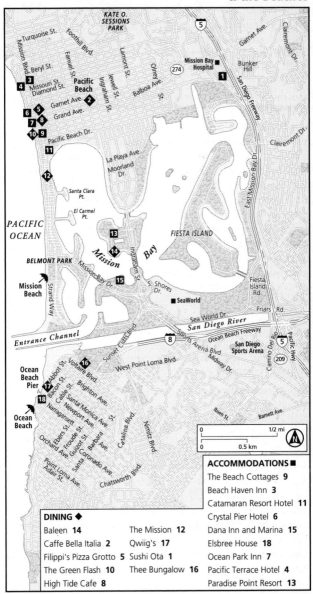

ACCOMMODATIONS ■

The Beach Cottages **9**
Beach Haven Inn **3**
Catamaran Resort Hotel **11**
Crystal Pier Hotel **6**
Dana Inn and Marina **15**
Elsbree House **18**
Ocean Park Inn **7**
Pacific Terrace Hotel **4**
Paradise Point Resort **13**

DINING ◆

Baleen **14**
Caffe Bella Italia **2**
Filippi's Pizza Grotto **5**
The Green Flash **10**
High Tide Cafe **8**

The Mission **12**
Qwiig's **17**
Sushi Ota **1**
Thee Bungalow **16**

1404 Vacation Rd. (off Ingraham St.), San Diego, CA 92109. ☎ **800/344-2626** or
858/274-4630. Fax 858/581-5924. www.paradisepoint.com. 457 units. $279–$479
double; from $499 suite. Extra person $20. Children 17 and under stay free in parent's room. AE, DC, DISC, MC, V. Parking $14. Follow I-8 west to Mission Bay Dr. exit;
take Ingraham St. north to Vacation Rd. Bus: 9. **Amenities:** 3 restaurants; bar;
pool bar; 6 outdoor pools; 18-hole putting course; tennis courts; fitness center; full-
service spa; Jacuzzi; bike rental; shuttle to Fashion Valley; limited room service
(6am–midnight); laundry service; dry cleaning. *In room:* A/C, TV w/pay movies, dataport, fridge, coffeemaker, hair dryer, iron.

EXPENSIVE

Catamaran Resort Hotel 🅡🅡 *(Kids)*   Ideally situated right on Mission Bay, the Catamaran has its own bay and ocean beaches, complete
with watersports facilities. Built in the 1950s, the hotel has been fully
renovated to modern standards without losing its trademark Polynesian theme; the atrium lobby holds a 15-foot waterfall and full-size
dugout canoe, and koi-filled lagoons meander through the property.
After dark, torches blaze throughout the grounds, with numerous
varieties of bamboo and palm sprouting; during the day, the resident
tropical birds chirp away. Guest rooms—in a 13-story building or one
of the six two-story buildings—have subdued South Pacific decor,
and each has a balcony or patio. High floors of tower rooms have
commanding views of the bay, the San Diego skyline, La Jolla, and
Point Loma. Studios and suites have the added convenience of kitchenettes. The Catamaran is within walking distance of Pacific Beach's
restaurant and nightlife. It's also steps away from the bay's exceptional
jogging and biking path; runners with tots-in-tow can rent jogging
strollers at the hotel. The resort's Mississippi-style sternwheeler, the
Bahia Belle cruises the bay Friday and Saturday evenings (nightly in
summer) and is free to hotel guests.

3999 Mission Blvd. (4 blocks south of Grand Ave.), San Diego, CA 92109. ☎ **800/
422-8386** or 858/488-1081. Fax 858/488-1387. www.catamaranresort.com. 313
units. $209–$349 double; from $299 suite. Children under 12 stay free in parent's
room. AE, DC, DISC, MC, V. Valet parking $10, self-parking $8. Take Grand/Garnet
exit off I-5 and go west on Grand Ave., then south on Mission Blvd. Bus: 27 or 34.
Amenities: Restaurant; 2 bars; outdoor pool; fitness room; Jacuzzi; watersports
equipment rental; bike rental; children's programs; concierge; limited room service
(5am–11pm); in-room massage; laundry service; dry cleaning. *In room:* A/C, TV
w/pay movies, dataport, fridge in most units, coffeemaker, hair dryer, iron.

Crystal Pier Hotel 🅡🅡 *(Finds)*   When historic charm is higher on
your wish list than hotel-style service, head to this utterly unique
cluster of cottages sitting literally over the surf on the vintage Crystal Pier at Pacific Beach. Like renting your own self-contained hideaway, you'll get a separate living room and bedroom, fully equipped

kitchen, and private patio with breathtaking ocean views—all within the whitewashed walls of sweet, blue-shuttered cottages that date from 1936 but have been meticulously renovated. Each of the Cape Cod–style cottages has a deck—the more expensive units farthest out have more privacy. There are six units not actually on the pier, but still offering sunset-facing sea views; these accommodations are cheaper. The sound of waves is soothing, yet the boardwalk action is only a few steps (and worlds) away, and the pier is a great place for watching sunsets and surfers. Guests drive right out and park beside their cottages, a real boon on crowded weekends. But this operation is strictly BYOBT (beach towels), and the office is only open from 8am to 8pm. The accommodations book up fast, especially with long-term repeat guests, so reserve for summer and holiday weekends a couple months in advance.

4500 Ocean Blvd. (at Garnet Ave.), San Diego, CA 92109. © **800/748-5894** or 858/483-6983. Fax 858/483-6811. www.crystalpier.com. 29 units. $195–$320 double; $270–$400 for larger units sleeping 4 to 6. 3-night minimum in summer. DISC, MC, V. Free parking. Take I-5 to Grand/Garnet exit; follow Garnet to the pier. Bus: 27, 30, or 34. **Amenities:** Beach equipment rental. *In room:* TV, kitchen.

Ocean Park Inn ⭑ This modern oceanfront motor hotel offers attractive, spacious rooms with well-coordinated contemporary furnishings. Although the inn has a level of sophistication uncommon in this casual, surfer-populated area, you won't find much solitude and quiet. The cool marble lobby and plushly carpeted hallways will help you feel a little insulated from the boisterous scene outside, though. You can't beat the location (directly on the beach) and the view (ditto). Rates vary according to view, but most rooms have at least a partial ocean view; all have a private balcony or patio. Units in front are most desirable, but it can get noisy directly above the boardwalk; try for the second or third floor, or pick one of the three junior suites, which have huge bathrooms and pool views. The Ocean Park Inn doesn't have its own restaurant, but the casual High Tide Cafe (p. 88) is outside the front door.

710 Grand Ave., San Diego, CA 92109. © **800/231-7735** or 858/483-5858. Fax 858/274-0823. www.oceanparkinn.com. 73 units. $199–$249 double; $239–$269 suite. Rates include continental breakfast. AE, DC, DISC, MC, V. Free indoor parking. Take Grand/Garnet exit off I-5; follow Grand Ave. to ocean. Bus: 34 or 34A/B. **Amenities:** Outdoor pool; Jacuzzi; laundry service; dry cleaning. *In room:* A/C, TV, dataport, fridge, coffeemaker, hair dryer.

MODERATE

Dana Inn and Marina The closest lodging to SeaWorld, with a complimentary shuttle to and from the park, this friendly, low-tech hotel features several low-rise buildings next to Mission Bay. Some overlook bobbing sailboats in the recreational marina, others face onto the sunny kidney-shaped pool whose surrounding Tiki torch–lit gardens offer shuffleboard and Ping-Pong. You'll pay a little extra for bay and marina views; if the view doesn't matter, save your money—every room is the same size, with plain but well-maintained furnishings. Beaches or SeaWorld are a 15-minute walk away. Meals and room service (including poolside food and cocktail ministrations) are available through the casual Red Hen Country Kitchen next door. An expansion is planned that will add rooms to the west of the current accommodations.

1710 W. Mission Bay Dr., San Diego, CA 92109. © 800/345-9995 or 619/222-6440. Fax 619/222-5916. www.danainn.com. 196 units. $133–$191 double (sleeps up to 4). AE, DC, DISC, MC, V. Free parking. Follow I-8 west to Mission Bay Dr. exit; take W. Mission Bay Dr. Bus: 27 or 34. **Amenities:** Outdoor heated pool and Jacuzzi; tennis court; bike rental; watersports equipment rental; limited room service (7am–8:30pm); coin-op laundry and laundry service; dry cleaning. *In room:* A/C, TV, dataport, fridge, coffeemaker, hair dryer, iron.

INEXPENSIVE

The Beach Cottages   This family-owned operation has been around since 1948 and offers a variety of guest quarters, most of them geared to the long-term visitor. It's the 17 cute little detached cottages just steps from the sand that give it real appeal, though some of them lack a view (of anything!); each has a patio with tables and chairs. Adjoining apartments are perfectly adequate, especially for budget-minded families who want to log major hours on the beach—all cottages and apartments sleep four or more and have full kitchens. There are also standard motel rooms that are worn but cheap (most of these sleep two). The property is within walking distance of shops and restaurants—look both ways for speeding cyclists before crossing the boardwalk—and offers shared barbecue grills, shuffleboard courts, and table tennis. The cottages themselves aren't pristine, but have a rustic charm that makes them popular with young honeymooners and those nostalgic for the golden age of laid-back California beach culture. Reserve the beachfront cottages well in advance.

4255 Ocean Blvd. (1 block south of Grand Ave.), San Diego, CA 92109-3995. © 858/483-7440. Fax 858/273-9365. www.beachcottages.com. 61 units, 17 cottages. $110–$200 double; $210–$240 cottages for 4 to 6. Monthly rates available mid-Sept to Apr. AE, DC, DISC, MC, V. Free parking. Take I-5 to Grand/Garnet exit, go west on Grand Ave. and left on Mission Blvd. Bus: 27, 30, or 34. **Amenities:** Coin-op laundry. *In room:* TV, fridge, microwave, coffeemaker.

Beach Haven Inn   A great spot for beach lovers who can't quite afford to be on the beach, this motel lies 1 block from the sand. Rooms face an inner courtyard, where guests enjoy a secluded ambience for relaxing by the pool. On the street side it looks kind of marginal, but once on the property you'll find all quarters well maintained and sporting clean, up-to-date furnishings; nearly all units have eat-in kitchens. The friendly staff provides free coffee in the lobby and rents VCRs and movies.

4740 Mission Blvd. (at Missouri St.), San Diego, CA 92109. ✆ 800/831-6323 or 858/272-3812. Fax 858/272-3532. www.beachhaveninn.com. 23 units. $120–$170 double; 2-night minimum on weekends. Extra person $5. Children under 12 stay free in parent's room. Rates include continental breakfast. AE, DC, DISC, MC, V. Free parking. Take I-5 to Grand/Garnet exit, follow Grand Ave. to Mission Blvd. and turn right. Bus: 30 or 34. **Amenities:** Outdoor pool; Jacuzzi. *In room:* A/C, TV, kitchenette in most units.

Elsbree House ⍟   Katie and Phil Elsbree have turned this modern Cape Cod–style building into an immaculate, exceedingly comfortable B&B, half a block from the water's edge in Ocean Beach. One condo unit with a private entrance rents only by the week; the Elsbrees occupy another. Each of the six guest rooms has a patio or balcony. Guests share the cozy living room (with a fireplace and TV), breakfast room, and kitchen. Although other buildings on this tightly packed street block the ocean view, sounds of the surf and fresh sea breezes waft in open windows, and a charming garden—complete with trickling fountain—runs the length of the house. This Ocean Beach neighborhood is eclectic, occupied by ocean-loving couples, dedicated surf bums, and the occasional contingent of punk skater kids who congregate near the pier. Its strengths are proximity to the beach, a limited but pleasing selection of eateries that attract mostly locals, and San Diego's best antiquing (along Newport Ave.).

5054 Narragansett Ave., San Diego, CA 92107. ✆ 800/607-4133 or 619/226-4133. www.bbinob.com. 7 units. $110–$135 double; $1,600 per week 3-bedroom condo (lower rates if only 1 or 2 rooms used). Room rates include continental breakfast. MC, V. From airport, take Harbor Dr. west to Nimitz Blvd. to Lowell St., which becomes Narragansett Ave. Bus: 23 or 35. *In room:* Hair dryer, iron, no phone.

5 La Jolla

You'll have a hard time finding bargain accommodations in upscale, conservative La Jolla, which often translates from the Spanish as "the jewel." But remember, most hotels—even those in the "Very Expensive" category—have occupancy-driven rates, meaning you can score surprising discounts during the off season or when the beds go begging.

Most of my choices are in the "Village," with two below the bluffs right on the beach. Chain hotels farther afield include the **Hyatt Regency,** 3777 La Jolla Village Dr. (📞 **800/233-1234** or 858/552-1234). It's a glitzy, business-oriented place with several acclaimed restaurants next door. The **Marriott Residence Inn,** 8901 Gilman Dr. (📞 **800/331-3131** or 858/587-1770), is a good choice for those who want a fully equipped kitchen and more space. Both are near the University of California, San Diego.

VERY EXPENSIVE

Hotel Parisi ★★★ *Finds*   Nestled within the "Village's" fashionable clothing boutiques, and across the street from the vaunted pink lady, La Valencia, the sleek boutique Hotel Parisi caters to the traveler seeking inner peace for both entertainment and relaxation. The hotel is on the second floor overlooking one of La Jolla's main intersections (street-facing rooms are well insulated from the modest din). Parisi's nurturing, wellness-inspired intimacy first becomes evident in the lobby, where elements of earth, wind, fire, water, and metal are blended according to classic feng shui principles. The Italy-meets-Zen composition is carried into the 20 rooms, where custom furnishings are modern yet comfy. Parisi calls the spacious rooms "suites," (some are more like junior suites) and each has an ergonomic desk, dimmable lighting, goose-down superluxe bedding, and creamy neutral decor to further that calming effect—10-foot ceilings and original art throughout allow your head to wander. Each darkly cool marble bathroom boasts a shower (some with dual shower heads), separate tub with contoured backrest, and smoothly sculpted fixtures. Less expensive rooms are smaller and have little or no view. Though primped and elegant, Parisi is not stuffy, yet the personal service stops at nothing—there's a menu of 24-hour in-room holistic health services (from individual yoga to Thai massage, psychotherapy, and obscure Asian treatments). If the W Hotel downtown is too swinging, but chic design is your style, the Parisi may be just right.

1111 Prospect St. (at Herschel Ave.), La Jolla, CA 92037. 📞 **877-4-PARISI** or 858/454-1511. Fax 858/454-1531. www.hotelparisi.com. 20 units. $295–$475 double. Rates include continental breakfast. AE, DC, DISC, MC, V. Free covered parking. Take Torrey Pines Rd. to Prospect Place and turn right; Prospect Place becomes Prospect St., turn left on Herschel. Bus: 30 or 34. **Amenities:** 24-hr. in-room spa treatments; limited room service (11:30am–2:30pm and 5:30–10pm) from Tapenade Restaurant; laundry service; dry cleaning. *In room:* A/C, TV w/VCR, dataport, minibar w/complimentary beverages, coffeemaker, hair dryer, iron, safe.

La Jolla Accommodations & Dining

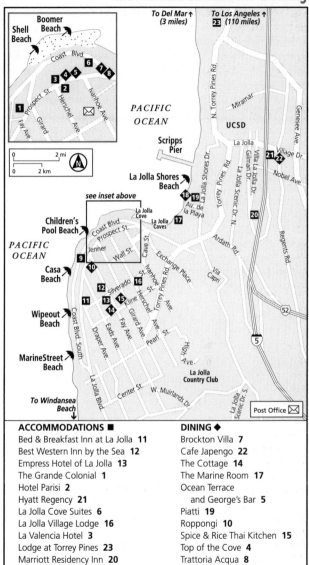

ACCOMMODATIONS ■

Bed & Breakfast Inn at La Jolla **11**
Best Western Inn by the Sea **12**
Empress Hotel of La Jolla **13**
The Grande Colonial **1**
Hotel Parisi **2**
Hyatt Regency **21**
La Jolla Cove Suites **6**
La Jolla Village Lodge **16**
La Valencia Hotel **3**
Lodge at Torrey Pines **23**
Marriott Residency Inn **20**
Scripps Inn **9**
The Sea Lodge **18**

DINING ◆

Brockton Villa **7**
Cafe Japengo **22**
The Cottage **14**
The Marine Room **17**
Ocean Terrace
   and George's Bar **5**
Piatti **19**
Roppongi **10**
Spice & Rice Thai Kitchen **15**
Top of the Cove **4**
Trattoria Acqua **8**

La Valencia Hotel 🐦🐦🐦   Within its bougainvillea-draped walls and wrought-iron garden gates, this gracious bastion of gentility does a fine job of resurrecting golden-age elegance, when celebrities like Greta Garbo and Charlie Chaplin vacationed here alongside the world's moneyed elite. The blufftop hotel, which looks much like a Mediterranean villa, has been the centerpiece of La Jolla since opening in 1926, and a $10-million renovation in 2000 refined some of the details and added 15 villas and an enlarged pool, without breaking with its historical glamour. Brides still pose in front of the lobby's picture window (against a backdrop of the Cove and Pacific Ocean), well-coiffed ladies lunch in the dappled shade of the garden patio, and neighborhood cronies quaff libations in the clubby Whaling Bar (La Jolla's version of the power lunch). The latter was once a western Algonquin for literary inebriates as well as a watering hole for Hollywood royalty. One chooses La Valencia for its history and unbeatably scenic location, but you won't be disappointed by the old-world standards of service and style.

All rooms are comfortably and traditionally furnished, each boasting lavish appointments, and all-marble bathrooms with signature toiletries. Because rates vary wildly according to view (from sweeping to *nada*), my advice is to get a cheaper room and enjoy the scene from one of the many lounges, serene garden terraces, or the amazing pool, which fronts the Pacific and nearby Scripps Park. Room decor, layouts, and size (starting at a relatively snug 246 sq. ft.) are all over the map, too—a few extra minutes spent with the reservationist will ensure a custom match for you. If you've got the bucks, spring for one of the newer villas, which feature fireplaces and butler service. The hotel's 12-table Sky Room is one of the city's most celebrated dining rooms.

1132 Prospect St. (at Herschel Ave.), La Jolla, CA 92037. ℂ **800/451-0772** or 858/454-0771. Fax 858/456-3921. www.lavalencia.com. 117 units. $300–$550 double; from $775 suites and villas. 2-night minimum summer weekends. AE, DC, DISC, MC, V. Valet parking $15. Take Torrey Pines Rd. to Prospect Place and turn right. Prospect Place becomes Prospect St. Bus: 30 or 34. **Amenities:** 3 restaurants; bar; outdoor pool; exercise room w/spa treatments; Jacuzzi; sauna; concierge; secretarial services; 24-hr. room service; babysitting; laundry service; dry cleaning. *In room:* A/C, TV w/VCR, dataport, minibar, coffeemaker, hair dryer, iron, safe.

The Lodge at Torrey Pines 🐦🐦🐦   Located 10 minutes north of La Jolla proper, this triumphant *trompe l'oeil* creation at the edge of the Torrey Pines Golf Course is the fantasy of a local hotelier who took his appreciation for Craftsman-style homes and amplified it into a 175-room upscale hotel. Patterned largely after the 1908

Gamble House of Pasadena, the Lodge brims with perfectly assembled nuances of the era: clinker-brick masonry, art glass windows and doors, Stickley furniture, and exquisite pottery. Most guest rooms fall into two categories. The least expensive rooms are an unstinting 520 square feet and lavished with Tiffany-style lamps, period wallpaper, framed Hiroshige prints, and lots of wood accents; views face a courtyard carefully landscaped to mimic the rare coastal environment that exists just beyond the hotel grounds. More expensive rooms overlook the golf course and the sea in the distance; most of these have balconies, fireplaces, and giant bathrooms with separate tub and shower. Sumptuous suites are also available.

The 9,500-square-foot spa specializes in treatments utilizing coastal sage and other local plants. An excellent restaurant named after painter A.R. Valentien features superb seasonal vegetables served with most entrees; Valentien's wildflower watercolors line the walls and his personal effects and medals are found in glass bookcases.

11480 N. Torrey Pines Rd., La Jolla, CA 92037. ℂ **800/656-0087** or 858/453-4420. Fax 858/453-7464. www.lodgetorreypines.com. 175 units. $450–$625 double; suites $900 and up. Children under 18 stay free in parent's room. AE, DC, DISC, MC, V. $14 self-parking, $17 valet parking. From I-8 take La Jolla Village Dr. West, bear right (north) onto N. Torrey Pines Rd. Bus: 301. **Amenities:** 2 restaurants; outdoor pool; Jacuzzi; fitness center; spa; preferential tee times at the golf course; concierge; 24-hr. room service; laundry service; dry cleaning. *In room:* A/C, TV, dataport in many units, minibar, coffeemaker, hair dryer, safe.

EXPENSIVE

The Grande Colonial 🏆🏆 *Finds*   Possessed of an old-world European flair that's more London or Georgetown than seaside La Jolla, the Grande Colonial earned accolades for the complete restoration in 2001 of its polished mahogany paneling, brass fittings, and genteel library and lounge. During the original heyday of the La Jolla Playhouse, it was the temporary home for everyone from Groucho Marx to Jane Wyatt. Today, a large spray of fresh flowers is the focal point in the lounge, where guests gather in front of the fireplace for drinks—often before enjoying dinner at the hotel's superb **Nine-Ten** restaurant. Guest rooms are quiet and elegantly appointed, with beautiful draperies and traditional furnishings. The hotel is 1 block from the ocean, but many of the rooms have sea views. The guest rooms have modern air-conditioning and thoughtful amenities; terry robes are available on request. Relics from the early days include oversize closets, meticulously tiled bathrooms, and heavy fireproof doors suspended in the corridors.

910 Prospect St. (between Fay and Girard), La Jolla, CA 92037. © 800/826-1278 or 858/454-2181. Fax 858/454-5679. www.thegrandecolonial.com. 75 units. $249–$379 double.; from $319 suite. AE, DC, DISC, MC, V. Valet parking $14. Take Torrey Pines Rd. to Prospect Place and turn right. Prospect Place becomes Prospect St. Bus: 30 or 34. **Amenities:** Restaurant; outdoor pool; access to nearby health club; limited room service (6:30am–10:30pm); laundry service; dry cleaning. *In room:* A/C, TV w/pay movies, dataport, hair dryer, iron, safe.

Scripps Inn 🏆🏆   This meticulously maintained inn is tucked away behind the Museum of Contemporary Art, and you'll be rewarded with seclusion even though the attractions of La Jolla are just a short walk away. Only a small, grassy park comes between the inn and the beach, cliffs, and tide pools; the view from the second-story deck can hypnotize guests, who gaze out to sea indefinitely. Rates vary depending on the ocean view (all have one, but some are better than others); rooms have a pleasant pale cream/sand palette, and are furnished in "Early American comfortable." All rooms have sofa beds; two have wood-burning fireplaces, and four have kitchenettes. The inn supplies beach towels, firewood, and French pastries each morning. Repeat guests keep their favorite rooms for up to a month each year, so book ahead for the best choice.

555 Coast Blvd. S. (at Cuvier), La Jolla, CA 92037. © 858/454-3391. Fax 858/456-0389. 14 units. $225–$255 double; from $295 suite. Extra person $10. Children under 5 stay free in parent's room. Rates include continental breakfast. AE, DC, DISC, MC, V. Free parking. Take Torrey Pines Rd., turn right on Prospect Place; past the museum, turn right onto Cuvier. Bus: 30 or 34. *In room:* TV, fridge, coffeemaker, hair dryer, iron, safe.

The Sea Lodge 🏆 🅺🅸🅳🆂   This three-story 1960s hotel in a mainly residential enclave is under the same management as the La Jolla Beach & Tennis Club next door. It has an identical on-the-sand location, minus the country club ambience—there are no reciprocal privileges. About half the rooms have some view of the ocean, and the rest look out on the pool or a tiled courtyard. The rooms are pretty basic, with perfunctory, outdated furnishings, priced by view and size. Bathrooms feature separate dressing areas with large closets; balconies or patios are standard, and some rooms have fully equipped kitchenettes. From the Sea Lodge's beach you can gaze toward the top of the cliffs, where La Jolla's Village hums with activity (and relentless traffic). Like the "B&T," the Sea Lodge is popular with families but also attracts business travelers looking to balance meetings with time on the beach or the tennis court.

8110 Camino del Oro (at Avenida de la Playa), La Jolla, CA 92037. © 800/237-5211 or 858/459-8271. Fax 858/456-9346. 128 units. $249–$559 double; $739 suite.

Extra person $20. Children under 12 stay free in parent's room. AE, DC, DISC, MC, V. Free covered parking. Take La Jolla Shores Dr., turn left onto Avenida de la Playa, turn right on Camino del Oro. Bus: 34. **Amenities:** Restaurant; 2 pools (including a wading pool for kids); 2 tennis courts; fitness room; Jacuzzi; babysitting; laundry service; dry cleaning. *In room:* A/C, TV, dataport, fridge, coffeemaker, hair dryer, iron.

MODERATE

The Bed & Breakfast Inn at La Jolla 🐾🐾   A 1913 Cubist house designed by San Diego's first important architect Irving Gill—and occupied in the 1920s by John Philip Sousa and his family—is the setting for this cultured and elegant B&B. Reconfigured as lodging, the house has lost none of its charm, and its appropriately unfrilly period furnishings add to the sense of history. The inn also features lovely enclosed gardens and a cozy library and sitting room. Sherry and fresh-cut flowers await in every room, some of which feature a fireplace or ocean view. Each room has a private bathroom, most of which are fairly compact . The furnishings are tasteful and cottage-style, with plenty of historic photos of La Jolla. Gourmet breakfast is served wherever you desire—dining room, patio, sun deck, or in your room. Picnic baskets (extra charge) are available with a day's notice. The gardens surrounding the inn were originally planned by Kate Sessions, who went on to create much of the landscaping for Balboa Park.

7753 Draper Ave. (near Prospect), La Jolla, CA 92037. © **800/582-2466** or 858/456-2066. Fax 858/456-1510. www.InnLaJolla.com. 15 units. $179–$359 double; $399 suite. 2-night minimum on weekends. Rates include full breakfast and after-noon wine and cheese. AE, DISC, MC, V. Take Torrey Pines Rd. to Prospect Place and turn right. Prospect Place becomes Prospect St.; proceed to Draper Ave. and turn left. Bus: 30 or 34. *In room:* A/C, hair dryer, iron.

Best Western Inn by the Sea 🐾   Occupying an enviable location at the heart of La Jolla's charming Village, this independently managed property puts guests just a short walk from the cliffs and beach. The low-rise tops out at five stories, with the upper floors enjoying ocean views (and the highest room rates). The Best Western (and the more formal Empress, a block away), offers a terrific alternative to pricier digs nearby. Rooms here are Best Western standard issue—freshly maintained, but nothing special. All rooms do have balconies, though, and refrigerators are available at no extra charge; the hotel offers plenty of welcome amenities.

7830 Fay Ave. (between Prospect and Silverado sts.), La Jolla, CA 92037. © **800/526-4545** or 858/459-4461. Fax 858/456-2578. www.bestwestern.com/innbythe sea. 132 units. $139–$209 double; from $399 suite. Rates include continental breakfast. AE, DC, DISC, MC, V. Parking $9. Take Torrey Pines Rd. to Prospect Place and turn right. Prospect Place becomes Prospect St.; proceed to Fay Ave. and turn left. Bus 30 or 34. **Amenities:** Outdoor heated pool; car-rental desk; limited room service from adjacent IHOP (7am–10pm); coin-op laundry and laundry service; dry cleaning. *In room:* A/C, TV w/pay movies, dataport, coffeemaker, hair dryer, iron.

Empress Hotel of La Jolla ☞

The Empress Hotel offers spacious quarters with traditional furnishings a block or two from La Jolla's main drag and the ocean. It's quieter here than at the premium cliff-top properties, and you'll sacrifice little other than direct ocean views (many rooms on the top floors afford a partial view). If you're planning to explore La Jolla on foot, the Empress is a good base, and it exudes a classiness many comparably priced chains lack, with warm service to boot. Rooms are tastefully decorated (and regularly renovated), and well equipped. Bathrooms are of average size but well appointed, and four "Empress" rooms have sitting areas with full-size sleeper sofas. Breakfast is set up next to a serene sun deck.

7766 Fay Ave. (at Silverado), La Jolla, CA 92037. © **888/369-9900** or 858/454-3001. Fax 858/454-6387. www.empress-hotel.com. 73 units. $179–$189 double; $299 suite. Rates include continental breakfast. AE, DC, DISC, MC, V. Valet parking $8. Take Torrey Pines Rd. to Girard Ave., turn right, then left on Silverado St. Bus: 30 or 34. **Amenities:** Fitness room and spa; limited room service (lunch and dinner hours). *In room:* A/C, TV, dataport, fridge, coffeemaker, hair dryer, iron.

La Jolla Cove Suites *(Value)*

Tucked in beside prime oceanview condos across from Ellen Browning Scripps Park, this family-run 1950s-era catbird seat actually sits closer to the ocean than its pricey uphill neighbor La Valencia. The to-die-for ocean view is completely unobstructed, and La Jolla Cove—one of California's prettiest swimming spots—is steps away from the hotel. The six-story property is peaceful at night, but Village dining and shopping are only a short walk away. You'll pay more depending on the quality of your view; about 80% of guest quarters gaze upon the ocean. On the plus side, most rooms are wonderfully spacious, each featuring a fully equipped kitchen, plus private balcony or patio. On the minus side, their functional but almost institutional furnishings could use a touch of Martha Stewart. An oceanview rooftop deck offers lounge chairs and cafe tables; breakfast is served up here each morning, indoors or outdoors depending on the weather.

1155 Coast Blvd. (across from the cove), La Jolla, CA 92037. © **888/LA-JOLLA** or 858/459-2621. Fax 858/551-3405. www.lajollacove.com. 90 units. $164–$269 double; from $324 suite. Rates include continental breakfast. AE, DC, DISC, MC, V. Parking $8. Take Torrey Pines Rd. to Prospect Place and turn right. When the road forks, veer right (downhill) onto Coast Blvd. Bus: 30 or 34. **Amenities:** Outdoor (nonview) pool; Jacuzzi; car-rental desk; coin-op laundry. *In room:* TV, kitchen, safe.

INEXPENSIVE

Wealthy, image-conscious La Jolla is *really* not the best place for deep bargains, but if you're determined to stay here as cheaply as possible, you won't do better than the **La Jolla Village Lodge,** 1141 Silverado St., at Herschel Avenue (© **858/551-2001;** www.lajolla villagelodge.com), a 30-room motel arranged around a small parking lot with cinder-block construction and small, basic rooms. Rates reach $110 in July and August, including breakfast, but are under $100 the rest of the year.

6 Coronado

The "island" (really a peninsula) of Coronado is a great escape. It offers quiet, architecturally rich streets, a small-town, navy-oriented atmosphere, and laid-back vacationing on one of the state's most beautiful and welcoming beaches. Coronado's resorts are especially popular with Southern California and Arizona families for weekend escapes. Although downtown San Diego is just a 10-minute drive or 20-minute ferry ride away, you may feel pleasantly isolated in Coronado, so it isn't your best choice if you're planning to spend lots of time in more central parts of the city.

VERY EXPENSIVE

Hotel del Coronado 🌟🌟🌟   Opened in 1888 and designated a National Historic Landmark in 1977, the "Hotel Del," as it's affectionately known, is the last of California's grand old seaside hotels. This monument to Victorian grandeur boasts tall cupolas, red turrets, and gingerbread trim, all spread out over 31 acres. Rooms— almost no two alike—run the gamut from compact to extravagant, and all are packed with antique charm; most have custom-made furnishings. There are nine cottages lining the sand that are more private (Marilyn Monroe stayed in the first one during the filming of *Some Like It Hot*). Note that almost half the hotel's rooms are in the seven-story contemporary tower and offer more living space, but none of the historical ambience; personally, I can't imagine staying here in anything but the Victorian structure, but you pay a premium for the privilege (especially for an ocean view), and 2-night minimums often apply.

In 2001, the hotel completed a painstaking, $55-million, 3-year restoration. Purists will rejoice to hear that historical accuracy was paramount, resulting in this priceless grande dame being returned to its turn-of-the-20th-century splendor.

1500 Orange Ave., Coronado, CA 92118. © 800/468-3533 or 619/435-6611. Fax 619/522-8238. www.hoteldel.com. 688 rooms. $260–$800 double; from $625 cottages and suites. Children under 18 stay free in parent's room. Additional person $25. Minimum stay requirements apply most weekends. AE, DC, DISC, MC, V. Valet parking $20, self-parking $15. From Coronado Bridge, turn left onto Orange Ave. Bus: 901 or 902. **Amenities:** 5 restaurants; 4 bars; 2 outdoor pools; 3 tennis courts; health club and spa; 2 Jacuzzis; bike rental; children's activities; concierge; shopping arcade; 24-hr. room service; babysitting; laundry service; dry cleaning. *In room:* A/C, TV w/pay movies, dataport, minibar, hair dryer, iron, safe.

Loews Coronado Bay Resort 🐾🐾 *(Kids)*   This luxury resort on the Silver Strand opened in 1991, situated on a secluded 15-acre peninsula, well removed from San Diego and even downtown Coronado, 5 miles away. It's perfect for those who prefer a self-contained resort in a get-away-from-it-all location, and is surprisingly successful in appealing to business travelers, convention groups, vacationing families, and couples. Rooms offer terraces that look either onto the hotel's private 80-slip marina, or the San Diego–Coronado Bridge and San Diego Bay. A private pedestrian underpass leads to nearby Silver Strand Beach. Rooms boast generous, well-appointed marble bathrooms with deep tubs; VCRs come standard in suites, and are available free upon request to any room (video rentals are also available). A highlight here is the Gondola Company (© 619/429-6317), which offers romantic and fun gondola cruises through the canals of tony Coronado Cays. The seasonal Commodore Kids Club, for children ages 4 to 12, offers supervised half-day, full-day, and evening programs with meals, and pets are encouraged, at no additional charge.

4000 Coronado Bay Rd., Coronado, CA 92118. © 800/81-LOEWS or 619/424-4000. Fax 619/424-4400. www.loewshotels.com. 438 units. $295–$345 double; from $525 suite. Children under 18 stay free in parent's room. AE, DC, DISC, MC, V. Valet parking $18, covered self-parking $13. From Coronado Bridge, go left onto Orange Ave., continue 6 miles down Silver Strand Hwy. Turn left at Coronado Bay Rd. Bus: 904. Pets welcomed. **Amenities:** 3 restaurants (including acclaimed Azzura Point); bar; 3 outdoor pools; tennis courts; fitness center; spa; Jacuzzi; watersports equipment rental; bike and skate rental; children's programs; concierge; car-rental desk; business center; salon; 24-hr. room service; babysitting; laundry service; dry cleaning. *In room:* A/C, TV, dataport, minibar, coffeemaker, hair dryer, iron.

EXPENSIVE

Marriott Coronado Island Resort 🐾🐾   Once expected to give competitor Loews a run for its money in the leisure market, this high-end Marriott seems content with the substantial group business it gets from the convention center across the bay. Elegance and luxury here are understated. Although the physical property is

Coronado Accommodations & Dining

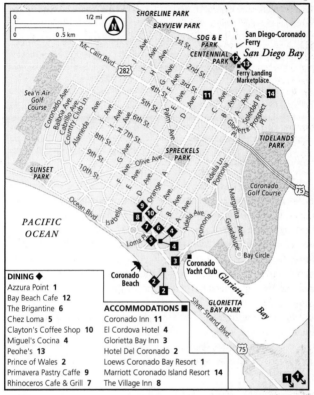

SHORELINE PARK
BAYVIEW PARK

SDG & E PARK

CENTENNIAL PARK

San Diego-Coronado Ferry

San Diego Bay

Ferry Landing Marketplace

Mc Cain Blvd.

(282)

PACIFIC OCEAN

SPRECKELS PARK

SUNSET PARK

TIDELANDS PARK

Coronado Golf Course

(75)

Bay Circle

Coronado Yacht Club

Coronado Beach

Glorietta Bay

GLORIETTA BAY PARK

Silver Strand Blvd.

(75)

DINING ◆
Azzura Point **1**
Bay Beach Cafe **12**
The Brigantine **6**
Chez Loma **5**
Clayton's Coffee Shop **10**
Miguel's Cocina **4**
Peohe's **13**
Prince of Wales **2**
Primavera Pastry Caffe **9**
Rhinoceros Cafe & Grill **7**

ACCOMMODATIONS ■
Coronado Inn **11**
El Cordova Hotel **4**
Glorietta Bay Inn **3**
Hotel Del Coronado **2**
Loews Coronado Bay Resort **1**
Marriott Coronado Island Resort **14**
The Village Inn **8**

generic, with impersonal architecture, the staff goes out of its way to provide upbeat attention: Guests just seem to get whatever they need, be it a lift downtown (by water taxi from the private dock), a tee time at the neighboring golf course, or a prime appointment at the spa.

Despite its mostly business clientele, this hotel offers many enticements for the leisure traveler: a prime waterfront setting offering a sweeping view of the San Diego skyline; a location within a mile of Coronado shopping and dining, and walking distance from the ferry landing; casual, airy architecture; lushly planted grounds filled with preening exotic birds; and a wealth of sporting and recreational activities. Guest rooms are generously sized and attractively furnished—actually decorated—in colorful French country style, and all feature balconies or patios. The superbly designed bathrooms hold an array of fine toiletries. In terms of room size and amenities, your dollar goes a lot farther here than at the Hotel Del.

2000 Second St. (at Glorietta Blvd.), Coronado, CA 92118. ℭ **800/228-9290** or 619/ 435-3000. Fax 619/435-3032. http://marriotthotels.com/sanci. 300 units. $209–$399 double; from $449 suites and villas. Children under 12 stay free in parent's room. AE, DC, MC, V. Valet parking $20, self-parking $15. From Coronado Bridge, turn right onto Glorietta Blvd., take 1st right to hotel. Bus: 901 or 902. Ferry: From Broadway Pier. **Amenities:** 2 restaurants; bar; 3 outdoor pools; 6 night-lit tennis courts; fitness center; spa; 2 Jacuzzis; watersports equipment rental; bike rental; concierge; courtesy shuttle to Horton Plaza; water taxi to convention center $5; business center; salon; 24-hr. room service; babysitting; laundry service; dry cleaning. *In room:* A/C, TV w/pay movies, dataport, minibar, coffeemaker, hair dryer, iron, safe.

MODERATE

Coronado Inn 🐾 Well located and terrifically priced, this renovated 1940s courtyard motel has such a friendly ambience, it's like staying with old friends. Iced tea, lemonade, and fresh fruit are even provided poolside on summer days. It's still a motel, though—albeit with fresh paint and a tropical floral decor—so rooms are pretty basic. The six rooms with bathtubs also have small kitchens; microwaves are available for the rest, along with hair dryers and irons (just ask upfront). Rooms close to the street are noisiest, so ask for one toward the back. The Coronado shuttle stops a block away; it serves the shopping areas and Hotel Del.

266 Orange Ave. (corner of 3rd St.), Coronado, CA 92118. ℭ **800/598-6624** or 619/435-4121. www.coronadoinn.com. 30 units (most with shower only). $125–$195 double (sleeps up to 4). Rates include continental breakfast. AE, DISC, MC, V. Free parking. From Coronado Bridge, stay on 3rd St. Bus: 901 or 902. Pets accepted with $10 nightly fee. **Amenities:** Outdoor pool; coin-op laundry. *In room:* A/C, TV, fridge.

Glorietta Bay Inn 🐾🐾 Only 11 rooms are in the historic John D. Spreckels mansion (1908), which boasts original fixtures, a grand staircase, and old-fashioned wicker furniture; the guest rooms are also decked out in antiques, and have a romantic and nostalgic ambience.

Rooms and suites in the 1950s annexes are much less expensive but were upgraded from motel-plain to better match the main house's classy ambience (though lacking the mansion's superluxe featherbeds); some have kitchenettes and marina views. The least expensive units are small and have parking-lot views. Wherever your room is, you'll enjoy the inn's trademark personalized service, including extra-helpful staffers who remember your name and happily offer dining and sightseeing recommendations or arrange tee times; special attention to return guests and families with toddlers; and a friendly continental breakfast. In addition to offering bikes and boat rentals on Glorietta Bay across the street, the hotel is within easy walking distance of the beach, golf, tennis, watersports, shopping, and dining. Rooms in the mansion get booked early, but are worth the extra effort and expense.

1630 Glorietta Blvd. (near Orange Ave.), Coronado, CA 92118. ℂ **800/283-9383** or 619/435-3101. Fax 619/435-6182. www.gloriettabayinn.com. 100 units. Double $150–$215 annex; $275–$415 mansion; suites from $275 annex; penthouse suite $650 mansion. Extra person $10. Children under 18 stay free in parent's room. Rates include continental breakfast and afternoon refreshment. AE, DC, DISC, MC, V. Self-parking $7. From Coronado Bridge, turn left on Orange Ave. After 2 miles, turn left onto Glorietta Blvd.; the inn is across the street from the Hotel del Coronado. Bus: 901 or 902. **Amenities:** Outdoor pool; Jacuzzi; in-room massage; babysitting; coin-op laundry and laundry service; dry cleaning. *In room:* A/C, TV w/pay movies, dataport, fridge, coffeemaker, hair dryer.

INEXPENSIVE

El Cordova Hotel ⓡ This Spanish hacienda across the street from the Hotel del Coronado began life as a private mansion in 1902. By the 1930s it had become a hotel, the original building augmented by a series of attachments housing retail shops along the ground-floor arcade. Shaped like a baseball diamond and surrounding a courtyard with meandering tiled pathways, flowering shrubs, a swimming pool, and patio seating for Miguel's Cocina Mexican restaurant, El Cordova hums pleasantly with activity.

Each room is a little different from the next—some sport a Mexican colonial ambience, while others evoke a comfy beach cottage. All feature ceiling fans and brightly tiled bathrooms, but lack the frills that would command exorbitant rates. El Cordova has a particularly inviting aura, and its prime location makes it a popular option; reserving several months in advance is advised for summer months. Facilities include a barbecue area with picnic table.

1351 Orange Ave. (at Adella Ave.), Coronado, CA 92118. ℂ **800/229-2032** or 619/435-4131. Fax 619/435-0632. www.elcordovahotel.com. 40 units. $119–$189 double; from $229 suite. Children under 12 stay free in parent's room. Weekly and monthly rates available in winter. AE, DC, DISC, MC, V. Parking in neighboring structure $6 per day. From Coronado Bridge, turn left onto Orange Ave. Bus: 901 or 902. **Amenities:** Restaurant; outdoor pool; shopping arcade; coin-op laundry. *In room:* A/C, TV.

The Village Inn *Value* Its location a block or two from Coronado's main sights—the Hotel Del, the beach, shopping, and cafes—is this inn's most appealing feature. Historic charm runs a close second; a plaque outside identifies the three-story brick-and-stucco hotel as the once-chic Blue Lantern Inn, built in 1928. The charming vintage lobby sets the mood in this European-style hostelry; each simple but well-maintained room holds antique dressers and armoires, plus lovely Battenberg lace bedcovers and shams. Front rooms enjoy the best view, and coffee and tea are available all day in the kitchen where breakfast is served. The appealing inn's only Achilles' heel is tiny, tiny bathrooms, so cramped that you almost have to stand on the toilet to use the small-scale sinks. Surprisingly, some bathrooms have been updated with Jacuzzi tubs.

1017 Park Place (at Orange Ave.), Coronado, CA 92118. ✆ 619/435-9318. www. coronadovillageinn.com. 15 units. Summer $85–$95 double; winter and weekly rates available. Rates include continental breakfast. AE, MC, V. Parking available on the street. From Coronado Bridge, turn left onto Orange Ave., then right on Park Place. Bus: 901 or 902.

7 Near the Airport

The accommodations reviewed in the downtown, Hillcrest, and Old Town/Mission Valley sections are only 5 to 10 minutes from the airport, but for those who wish to stay even closer, there are two good airport hotels: the 1,045-room **Sheraton San Diego Hotel & Marina,** 1380 Harbor Island Dr. (✆ 800/325-3535 or 619/291-2900), offers rooms from $369; and the 208-room **Hilton San Diego Airport/Harbor Island,** 1960 Harbor Island Dr. (✆ 800/774-1500 or 619/291-6700), has rooms starting from $249. Both hotels offer a marina view, a pool, and proximity to downtown San Diego—as always, hefty discounts are usually available. I also recommend the nearby **Bay Club Hotel,** 2131 Shelter Island Dr. (✆ 800/672-0800 or 619/224-8888; www.bayclubhotel.com), a pretty marina-front low-rise offering a vacation ambience even for business travelers; rates start at $145, including breakfast.

5

Where to Dine

San Diego's dining scene, once a culinary backwater, has come into its own during the past decade. The spark for this new spirit of experimentation and style has been an explosion in the transplant population and cultural diversification. But other factors are at play. A bustling economy helps, motivating folks to step out and exercise their palates. These new foodies have been taught to respect the seasonality of vegetables, allowing chefs to revel in the bounteous agriculture of San Diego County by focusing on vegetables when flavors are at their peak at specialized North County growers like Chino Farms and Be Wise Ranch.

Top young cooks are increasingly lured by San Diego's agreeable lifestyle and the chance to make a fast impression in the region's dining scene. How many chefs have been seduced by the idea that you can surf in the ocean each morning, then hand-select fresh produce at the farm where it was grown for preparation that afternoon? And although we import chefs from around the world, we've even started exporting them—Marine Room wizard Bernard Guillas represents America at illustrious events like the Masters of Food and Wine.

As you can imagine, San Diego offers terrific seafood: Whether at unembellished market-style restaurants that let the fresh catch take center stage or at upscale restaurants that feature extravagant presentations, the ocean's bounty is everywhere. Those traditional mainstays, American and Continental cuisine, still carry their share of the weight in San Diego. But, with increasing regularity, they're mating with lighter, more contemporary, often ethnic styles. The movement is akin to the eclectic fusion cuisine that burst onto the scene in the early 1990s. That's not to say traditionalists will be disappointed: San Diego still has plenty of clubby steak-and-potatoes stalwarts, and we're loaded with the chain restaurants you'll probably recognize from home.

Number one on most every visitor's list of priorities is Mexican food—a logical choice given the city's history and location. You'll find lots of highly Americanized interpretations of Mexican fare along with a few hidden gems, like El Agave and Berta's, that serve true south-of-the-border cuisine. The most authentic Mexican import may be the humble fish taco, perhaps the city's favorite fast food.

If you love Italian food, you're also in luck. Not only does San Diego boast a strong contingent of old-fashioned Sicilian-style choices, but you almost can't turn a corner without running into a trattoria. The Gaslamp Quarter corners the market with upscale northern Italian bistros on virtually every block. Hillcrest, La Jolla, and other neighborhoods also boast their fair share. They cater mostly to locals (usually a good thing) and their menus almost always include gourmet pizzas baked in wood-fired ovens, a trend that shows no signs of slowing down.

San Diego's multicultural fabric ensures that ethnic foods are a good option when you want something more exotic than Mexican or Italian fare. While Chinese restaurants have long had a place at the table, Asian cuisine today also means Japanese, Thai, Vietnamese, and Cambodian restaurants. A drive through the heart of Kearny Mesa reveals a panoply of Asian eateries at all prices, along with vast grocery stores brimming with quirky delicacies. But also note that many intrepid "mainstream" chefs fuse Asian ingredients and preparations with more familiar Mediterranean or French menus.

For diners on a budget, the more expensive San Diego restaurants are usually accommodating if you want to order a few appetizers instead of a main course, and many offer more reasonably priced lunch menus. Worthwhile discount coupons are found in the *San Diego Weekly Reader,* available free on Thursdays (and known as *The Weekly* in an edited version distributed at local hotels). In keeping with our beach culture, even in the more pricey places, dress tends to be casual; some notable exceptions are downtown and La Jolla's more expensive restaurants and the hotels on Coronado, where jeans are a no-no and gentlemen will feel most comfortable in a dinner jacket.

A note on parking: Unless a listing specifies otherwise, drivers can expect to park within 2 or 3 blocks of the restaurants listed here. If you can't find a free or metered space on the street, you can seek out a garage or lot; most Gaslamp Quarter and La Jolla venues offer valet parking.

1 Downtown & Little Italy

Downtown dining tends to be more formal than elsewhere, because of the business clientele and evening theater- and opera-goers. Once the domain of a few high-priced and highfalutin Continental and

American restaurants, downtown was turned on its ear when swank spots began moving in to the Gaslamp Quarter's restored Victorian buildings in the late 1980s. If you stroll down Fifth Avenue between E and Market streets, you'll find a month's worth of restaurants, all packed with a hip local crowd. The Embarcadero, a stretch of waterfront along the bay, is also home to several great eating spots, all of which capitalize on their bay views. And Little Italy—home to stalwart **Filippi's Pizza Grotto**—has benefited from the arrival of **Indigo Grill,** where the fusion of cuisines seems to include almost everything *but* Italian. There are several excellent restaurants just north of the "border" created by the I-5—these are described in the Hillcrest/Uptown section that follows.

Note: To locate these restaurants, please see the "Downtown San Diego Accommodations & Dining" map on p. 37.

VERY EXPENSIVE

Star of the Sea 𝔊𝔊𝔊 SEAFOOD A millennium makeover banished Star of the Sea's stuffy, outmoded aura to the past; gone is that dated dress code and off-putting formality, replaced by a comfortable ambience and modern decor matched to the still-glorious harbor view.

The focus here is on the fine dining, though: Executive chef Paul McCabe imbues the menu with sophisticated nuances that show he's in touch with today's gourmands. The menu is market driven (and changes nightly); representative dishes include grilled baquetta (sea bass) with wild mushrooms and white truffle risotto, and New Zealand John Dory with fennel pollen, lemon caper brown butter, and parsnip purée. There are always a few offerings for carnivores like a Black Angus rib-eye or boneless beef short ribs, but otherwise, smart diners stick to the always-fresh seafood delights. There's a reasonably priced wine list and a welcoming bar with its own abbreviated menu.

1360 N. Harbor Dr. (at Ash St.). © **619/232-7408.** www.starofthesea.com. Reservations recommended. Main courses $26–$29. AE, DC, DISC, MC, V. Daily 5:30–10:30pm. Valet parking $4. Bus: All Harbor Dr. routes. Trolley: America Plaza.

EXPENSIVE

Chive 𝔊𝔊𝔊 AMERICAN/ECLECTIC This big city–style Gaslamp venue introduced San Diego to the sleek and chic dining rooms of the East Coast, and to daring kitchen inventions. Start with a fashionable cocktail, of course: The local martini is embellished with Gorgonzola-stuffed olives, and Chive's twist on the *mojito* adds a gingery splash to the Cuban trademark.

Chef A. J. Voytko's menu changes every 6 to 8 weeks, but popular dishes found more often than not include spice-crusted lamb loin, a roasted baby beet salad, a nightly "noodle" (pasta) of the chef's whim, and salads that balance crispy greens with pungent, creamy cheeses and sweet fruit accents. But don't be surprised to encounter culinary curiosities like foie gras with banana bread and caramelized bananas—diners who take a chance on such eccentricities are usually richly rewarded. An international wine list offers many intriguing selections by "cork" or "stem," and includes post-meal sipping tequilas, ports, and Scotch. Chive balances its angular, wide space with cozy lighting, warm fabrics, and a pervasive sense of relaxed fun. One lament: In pursuit of elegant modernity, the cement floors and other hard surfaces amplify the noise level.

558 Fourth Ave. (at Market St.). ☎ 619/232-4483. www.chiverestaurant.com. Reservations recommended. Main courses $17–$28. AE, DC, DISC, MC, V. Daily 5–11pm. Live jazz Sat. Valet parking $7. Bus: 1, 3, 4, 5, 16, or 25. Trolley: Convention Center.

Croce's ✿✿ AMERICAN/ECLECTIC   Ingrid Croce, widow of singer-songwriter Jim, was instrumental in the resurgence of the once-decayed Gaslamp Quarter, and her establishment has expanded to fill every corner of this 1890 Romanesque building. Croce's features a menu that fuses Southern soul and Southwestern spice with Asian flavors and Italian pastas. The food is good, not terribly memorable, service can be clunky, and the dinner tab can be breathtaking. But add the adjacent, raucous Top Hat Bar & Grille and the intimate Jazz Bar, and the complex is a hot ticket among conventioneers, with crowds lining up for dinner tables and nightclub shows. An evening in the Gaslamp Quarter isn't complete without at least strolling by the Croce's corner; expect a festive good time any night of the week. Those who dine in either of the restaurant's side-by-side seating areas can enter the two nightspots (see chapter 8 for a full listing) without paying the cover charge.

802 Fifth Ave. (at F St.). ☎ 619/233-4355. www.croces.com. Reservations not accepted; call for same-day "priority seating" (before walk-ins). Main courses $19–$32. AE, DC, DISC, MC, V. Daily 5pm–midnight. Valet parking $7. Bus: 1, 3, 5, 16, or 25. Trolley: Gaslamp Quarter.

Dakota Grill & Spirits ✿✿ AMERICAN/SOUTHWESTERN   This downtown business lunch favorite is always busy and noisy; the Southwestern cowboy kitsch matches the cuisine in a beautiful room on the ground floor of San Diego's first high-rise. An open, copper-accented kitchen bustles smoothly, and is most easily enjoyed from the second-level terrace that circles the room. Among the most popular items are the spit-roasted chicken with orange chipotle glaze or Dakota barbecue sauce, the mixed grill served with roasted garlic and grilled red potatoes, and the pan-seared halibut accompanied by tequila cream potatoes and roasted pepper-chipotle coulis. There's also a short list of New Mexican–style pasta and pizzas (made with chipotle-spiced dough) that can keep the dinner bill at a moderate level. When the kitchen is on, Dakota's innovation makes it one of the Gaslamp's best, and the atmosphere is the right mix of informal and smooth to fit the lively cuisine. A pianist plays Wednesday through Saturday nights.

901 Fifth Ave. (at E St.). ✆ 619/234-5554. Reservations recommended. Main courses $9–$12 lunch, $11–$27 dinner. AE, DC, DISC, MC, V. Mon–Fri 11:30am–2:30pm; Mon–Thurs 5–10pm; Fri–Sat 5–11pm; Sun 5–9pm. Valet parking (after 5pm) $7–$9. Bus: 1, 3, 5, 16, or 25. Trolley: Gaslamp Quarter.

Indigo Grill 🟢🟢 AMERICAN/ECLECTIC/VEGETARIAN Bracing "aboriginal" cuisine of the Pacific coast—from Mexico to Alaska—is showcased at Chef Deborah Scott's Little Italy venture. This dance of diverse cooking ingredients and styles is as perilous as a tango, but memorable for its quantity of shrewd moves. Root veggies, game, and fruit are integral to the menu, and unusual spices are used liberally. Start with the Oaxaca Fire, a tequila-based cocktail with a salt-and-pepper rim (lotsa kick there), and move on to a lush salad of spinach, spaghetti squash, and strawberries. The alderwood plank salmon, served with a tangle of squid-ink pasta spotted with smoky Oaxacan cheese, is a wonderful entree, or go for the rack of lamb, lacquered in wild blueberries—both are extravagantly garnished.

The room is filled with native iconography, rippling water, and glass dividers that mimic sheets of ice; sharp angles, masks, and varied textures of wood, stone, metal, and leather invoke elements of the geographical territory encompassed by the menu. If you enjoy Indigo Grill, it's worth checking out Scott's other venture, Kemo Sabe (where Pacific Rim meets Southwestern), at 3958 Fifth Ave., between University Avenue and Washington Street, Hillcrest (✆ 619/220-6802).

1536 India St. (at Cedar St.). ✆ 619/234-6802. Reservations recommended. Main courses $9–$13 lunch, $18–$28 dinner. AE, DC, DISC, MC, V. Mon–Fri 11:30am–2pm; Sun–Wed 5–9pm; Thurs 5–10pm; Fri–Sat 5–11pm. Bus: 5 or 16. Trolley: Little Italy.

MODERATE

Fat City 🅥𝒂𝒍𝒖𝒆 AMERICAN   If you need a steak but don't want to get caught up with the Gaslamp's roster of pricey chophouses and also don't want to settle for one of those chain eateries, Fat City is your place. Overlook the vaguely scary name (the owner's name is Tom Fat) and the overly vivid hot-pink paint job (the building is vintage Art Deco), and settle in to one of the cushy booths, with Tiffany lamps hovering overhead. You can skip the skimpy list of appetizers since the entrees come with a potato side, and specials on the blackboard throw in a salad for a couple bucks more. The steaks are USDA Choice, aged 21 days and grilled to order over mesquite charcoal. Better yet, aim for the USDA Prime top sirloin: A hunky 12-oz. cut is just $14, and miles ahead in flavor of what you get at a Black Angus–type joint. For those who haven't signed on to the Atkins regimen, you'll also find teriyaki salmon, brandy-marinated chicken, and a couple pasta dishes. I haven't tried those—I come here for the economical steaks and haven't found a reason to look farther down the menu.

2137 Pacific Hwy. (at Hawthorn). ☎ **619/232-9303**. Main courses $10–$19. AE, MC, V. Daily 5–10pm. Free parking. Bus: 34.

The Fish Market ✸ SEAFOOD Ask any San Diegan where to go for the biggest selection of the freshest fish, and they'll probably send you to the bustling Fish Market on the end of the G Street Pier on the Embarcadero. Chalkboards announce the day's catches—be it Mississippi catfish, Maine lobster, Canadian salmon, or Mexican yellowtail—which are sold by the pound or available in a number of classic, simple preparations in the casual, always-packed restaurant. Upstairs, the fancy offshoot **Top of the Market** offers sea fare with souped-up presentations (and jacked-up prices). Either way, the fish comes from the same trough, so I recommend having a cocktail in Top's posh, clubby atmosphere to enjoy the stupendous panoramic bay views, and then head downstairs for solid affordable fare or treats from the sushi and oyster bars.

750 N. Harbor Dr. ☎ **619/232-FISH**. www.thefishmarket.com. Reservations not accepted. Main courses $12–$27 (Top of the Market main courses $17–$43). AE, DC, DISC, MC, V. Daily 11am–10pm. Valet parking $5. Bus: 7 or 7B. Trolley: Seaport Village.

Karl Strauss Brewery & Grill ✸ AMERICAN Brew master Karl Strauss put San Diego on the microbrewery map with this unpretentious factory setting, now all but engulfed by the W Hotel. The smell of hops and malt wafts throughout, and the stainless steel tanks are visible from the bar. Brews, all on tap, range from pale ale to amber lager. Five-ounce samplers are $1 each; if you like what you taste, 12-ounce glasses, pints, and hefty schooners stand chilled and ready. There's also non-alcoholic beer and wine by the glass. It used to be that the Cajun fries, hamburgers, German sausage (sans sauerkraut), and other greasy bar foods were secondary to the stylin' suds, but they've dressed up the lunch and dinner menu with items like Southwestern salmon linguini and filet mignon. Beer-related memorabilia and brewery tours are available.

There's another location in La Jolla at 1044 Wall St. (© **858/551-2739**).

1157 Columbia St. (at B St.). © **619/234-BREW.** Main courses $8–$15 lunch, $8–$23 dinner. AE, MC, V. Mon–Fri open 11am, Sat–Sun 11:30am; Sun–Thurs kitchen serves till 10pm (bar serves till 11pm); Fri kitchen till 11pm (bar till midnight); Sat kitchen till midnight (bar till 1am). Bus: 5 or 16. Trolley: America Plaza.

INEXPENSIVE

Café Lulu BREAKFAST/COFFEE & TEA Smack-dab in the heart of the Gaslamp Quarter, Café Lulu aims for a hip, bohemian mood despite little clues to the contrary (like the *Wall Street Journal* hanging on racks for browsing). Ostensibly a coffee bar, the cafe also makes a good choice for casual dining; if the stylishly dark interior is too harsh for you, watch the street action from a sidewalk table. The food is health conscious, largely prepared with organic ingredients. Soups, salads, cheese melts, and veggie lasagna are on the list; breads come from the incomparable Bread & Cie. uptown (p. 79). Eggs, granola, and waffles are served in the morning, but anytime is the right time to try one of the inventive coffee drinks, like cafe Bohème (mocha with almond syrup) or cafe L'amour (iced latte with a hazelnut tinge). Beer and wine are also served, and if you're staying downtown they offer free delivery in the Gaslamp Quarter.

419 F St. (near Fourth Ave.). © **619/238-0114.** Main courses $6–$9. No credit cards. Sun–Thurs 10am–1am; Fri–Sat 10am–3am. Bus: 1, 3, 5, 16, or 25. Trolley: Convention Center.

Filippi's Pizza Grotto (Kids) (Value) ITALIAN For longtime locals, when we think "Little Italy," Filippi's comes to mind—it was a childhood fixture for many of us. To get to the dining area, decorated with Chianti bottles and red-checked tablecloths, you walk through a "cash and carry" Italian grocery store and deli strewn with cheeses, pastas, wines, bottles of olive oil, and salamis. You might even end up eating behind shelves of canned olives, but don't feel bad—this has been a tradition since 1950. The intoxicating smell of pizza wafts into the street; Filippi's has more than 15 varieties (including vegetarian), plus old-world spaghetti, lasagna, and other pasta. Children's portions are available, and kids will feel right at home under the sweeping mural of the Bay of Naples. The Friday- and Saturday-night lines to get in can look intimidating, but they move quickly.

The original of a dozen branches throughout the county, this Filippi's has free parking. Other locations include 962 Garnet Ave. in Pacific Beach (© **858/483-6222**).

1747 India St. (between Date and Fir sts.), Little Italy. © **619/232-5095**. Reservations not accepted on weekends. Main courses $5–$13. AE, DC, DISC, MC, V. Sun–Mon 9am–10pm; Tues–Thurs 9am–10:30pm; Fri–Sat 9am–11:30pm. Free parking. Bus: 5. Trolley: Little Italy.

Kansas City Barbecue AMERICAN   Kansas City Barbecue's honky-tonk mystique was fueled by its appearance as the fly-boy hangout in the movie *Top Gun* ("one of our better business decisions," reflects the understated owner). Posters from the film share wall space with county-fair memorabilia, old Kansas car tags, and a photograph of official "bar wench" Carry Nation. This homey dive is right next to the railroad tracks and across from the tony Hyatt Regency. The spicy barbecue ribs, chicken, and hot links are slow-cooked over an open fire and served with sliced white bread and your choice of coleslaw, beans, fries, onion rings, potato salad, or corn on the cob. The food is just okay, but the cheerfully rough-and-tumble atmosphere is the real draw.

610 W. Market St. © **619/231-9680**. Reservations not accepted. Main courses $7–$12. MC, V. Daily 11am–1am. Trolley: Seaport Village.

2 Hillcrest & Uptown

Hillcrest and the other gentrified uptown neighborhoods to its west and east are jam-packed with great food for any palate (and any wallet). Some are old standbys filled nightly with loyal regulars; others are cutting-edge experiments that might be gone next year. Whether it's ethnic food, French food, health-conscious bistro fare, retro comfort food, specialty cafes and bakeries, or California cuisine, they're often mastered with the innovative panache you'd expect in the most nonconformist part of town.

Hash House a Go Go, 3628 Fifth Ave. (© **619/298-4646**), serves three meals a day, including mountainous breakfast dishes; and the popular **Whole Foods** supermarket, 711 University Ave. (© **619/294-2800**), has a mouthwatering deli and a robust salad bar.

EXPENSIVE

California Cuisine 🍴🍴 CALIFORNIAN   Justin Hoehn took over the kitchen in early 2003 and reworked and slimmed down the menu to bring back the qualities that put this restaurant on the map when it originally opened in 1982. The spare, understated dining room and delightfully romantic patio set the stage as a smoothly professional and respectful staff proffers fine dining at fair prices to a casual crowd.

The menu changes daily but often contains mouthwatering appetizers like sesame-seared ahi with hot-and-sour raspberry sauce and a jicama papaya slaw. Main courses include maple-glazed pork loin with yam spaetzle and grilled radicchio; a spinach-asparagus risotto; or chanterelle-dusted lamb loin, topped with whole grain mustard-sherry sauce and accompanied by crispy polenta. And don't miss desserts by pastry chef Laurel Hufnagle, who tries inventive twists on old standards, like the jasmine and green tea crème brûlée. Allow time to find parking, which can be scarce along this busy stretch of University Avenue.

1027 University Ave. (east of 10th St.). ✆ 619/543-0790. www.californiacuisine.cc. Reservations recommended for dinner. Main courses $7–$16 lunch, $17–$27 dinner. AE, DISC, MC, V. Tues–Fri 11am–10pm; Sat–Sun 5–10pm. Bus: 908.

Parallel 33 ⟨𝒦𝒦 (Finds ECLECTIC/INTERNATIONAL Inspired by a theory that all locales along the 33rd parallel (San Diego's latitude) of the globe might share the rich culinary traditions of the Tigris-Euphrates Valley (birthplace of civilization), chef Amiko Gubbins presents a cuisine that beautifully combines flavors from Morocco, Lebanon, India, China, and Japan. Even if the globe-girdling concept doesn't quite make sense, sit back and savor the creativity displayed in a menu that leaps enthusiastically from fragrant Moroccan chicken *b'stilla* to soft shell crab crusted with *panko* (wispy Japanese bread crumbs) and black sesame seeds; from scallops pan-seared in garam masala and served over couscous to oven-roasted *za'atar* chicken with basmati rice, English peas, and harissa. The *ahi poke* (raw tuna) appetizer fuses a Hawaiian mainstay with Asian pear and mango and Japanese wasabi—it's a winner! The restaurant is nice but not fancy, just an upscale neighborhood joint that's easily overlooked by visitors.

741 W. Washington St. (at Falcon), Mission Hills. ✆ 619/260-0033. Reservations recommended. Main courses $18–$27. AE, DISC, MC, V. Mon–Thurs 5:30–10pm; Fri–Sat 5:30–11pm. Bus: 3, 16, or 908.

MODERATE

Café W 𝒦 FUSION It's hard not to be seduced by the chic modern ambience and cooler-than-thou crowd at Café W. But if the surroundings don't wow you, the food surely will. Wittily divided into "raw bar," "field," "ocean," and "farm," this is fusion cooking at its very best. Scallop tempura skewers with a dark soy-tangerine-ginger dipping sauce and baked stuffed artichoke with rock crab, shiitake, baby bok choy, and fortine cheese fondue may sound precious, but one bite will have you convinced. One of San Diego's most adventurous kitchens, Café W never fails to wow. (But don't be misled by the prices—plates are relatively small, and designed to mix and match.)

3680 Sixth Ave. (near Washington). © 619/291-0200. Main courses $8–$13. AE, MC, V. Wed–Mon 6–10:30pm. Closed Tues.

Extraordinary Desserts ✿✿ DESSERTS If you're a lover of sweets—heck, if you've ever eaten a dessert at all—you owe it to yourself to visit this unique café. Chef and proprietor Karen Krasne's talent surpasses the promise of her impressive pedigree, which includes a *Certificat de Patisserie* from Le Cordon Bleu in Paris. Dozens of divine creations are available daily, and many are garnished with edible gold or flowers. Among them: a passion fruit ricotta torte bursting with kiwis, strawberries, and bananas; a *gianduia* of chocolate cake lathered with hazelnut butter cream, chocolate mousse, and boysenberry preserves, and sprinkled with shards of praline; or the bête noir, which is a dark chocolate cake layered with vanilla crème brûlée, chocolate mousse, and chocolate truffle cream. Originally educated in Hawaii, Krasne likes to incorporate island touches like macadamia nuts, fresh coconut, fruit, and pure Kona coffee, but her Parisian experience is present; the shop sells tea and accouterments from the fine salon Mariage Frères, plus candles and bath products and boutique Asian items. There is a second location at 1430 Union St. (© **619/294-7001**) in Little Italy.

2929 Fifth Ave. (between Palm and Quince sts.) © **619/294-7001**. www. extraordinarydesserts.com. Desserts $2–$9. MC, V. Open Mon–Fri 8:30am, Sat–Sun 11am; closes Sun–Thurs 11pm, Fri–Sat midnight. Street parking usually available. Bus: 1, 3, or 25.

Fifth & Hawthorn ✿ (Value) AMERICAN You won't find a sign in front of this neighborhood hideaway—just look for the street sign marking the intersection of Fifth and Hawthorn, a few blocks north of downtown, and aim for the red neon "open" sign. Inhabited by a slew of regulars, the comfortable room is somewhat dark, vaguely romantic—just enough, anyway, to take your mind off the planes coming in for a landing overhead. The menu has pretty much stayed the same for 16 years: You won't find anything daring, but you will find lots of well-executed basics, like a filet mignon in green

California Wood-Fired Pizza

This is not the marinara-and-pepperoni variety found in other pizza meccas like New York and Chicago—for a whole generation of Californians, pizza will always mean barbecued chicken, tomato-basil, or goat cheese and sun-dried tomato.

Always tops in San Diego polls is **Sammy's Woodfired Pizza** at 770 Fourth Ave., at F Street, in the Gaslamp Quarter (© **619/230-8888**); 1620 Camino de la Reina in Mission Valley (© **619/298-8222**); 702 Pearl St., at Draper Street, La Jolla (© **858/456-5222**); and 12925 El Camino Real, at Del Mar Heights Road, Del Mar (© **858/259-6600**). Sammy's serves creations like duck sausage, potato garlic, or Jamaican jerk shrimp atop 10-inch rounds. It also excels at enormous salads, making it easy to share a meal and save a bundle.

A similar menu is available at **Pizza Nova**, a similarly stylish minichain with a vibrant atmosphere, 3955 Fifth Ave., north of University Avenue in Hillcrest (© **619/296-6682**); and 5120 N. Harbor Dr., west of Nimitz Boulevard in Point Loma (© **619/226-0268**).

peppercorn sauce and linguini with clams, white wine, and garlic. There are a few dishes Fifth & Hawthorn excels at: The mustard-crusted catfish is simple and delicious, and the calamari, sautéed "abalone style," are rendered tender and sweet. The restaurant also offers a terrific four-course meal: appetizer, soup or salad, one of six entrees, and dessert for $50 per couple, *including* a bottle of wine to share.

515 Hawthorn St. (at Fifth Ave.). © **619/544-0940**. Main courses $15–$25. AE, MC, V. Mon–Thurs 5–9pm; Fri–Sat 5–10:15pm; Sun 4:30–8:30pm. Street parking usually available. Bus: 1, 3, or 25.

INEXPENSIVE

Bread & Cie. BREAKFAST/LIGHT FARE/MEDITER-RANEAN Delicious aromas permeate this cavernous Hillcrest bakery, where the city's most treasured breads are baked before your eyes all day long. The traditions of European artisan bread-making and attention to the fine points of texture and crust quickly catapulted Bread & Cie. to local stardom—they now supply bread to more than 75 local restaurants. Among my favorites available daily are anise and fig, black olive, jalapeño and cheese—even the relatively plain sourdough *batard* is tart, chewy perfection. Others are available just 1 or 2 days a week, like the *panella dell'uva* (grape bread; weekends), or the hunky walnut and scallion (Wed and Sat). Ask for a free sample, or order one of the many Mediterranean-inspired sandwiches. Try tuna niçoise with walnuts and capers; the mozzarella, roasted peppers, and olive tapenade on focaccia; or, roast turkey with hot pepper cheese on rosemary/olive oil bread. Specialty coffee drinks delivered in bowl-like mugs are a perfect accompaniment to a light breakfast of fresh scones, muffins, and homemade granola with yogurt. Seating is at bistro-style tables in full view of the busy ovens and tattoo-embraced staff.

350 University Ave. (between Third and Fourth sts.). ⓒ 619/683-9322. Sandwiches and light meals $4–$8. MC, V. Mon–Fri 7am–7pm; Sat 7am–6pm; Sun 8am–6pm. Bus: 1, 3, 16, 25, or 908.

Corvette Diner (Kids) AMERICAN   Travel back in time to the rockin' 1950s at this theme diner, where the jukebox is loud, the gum-snapping waitresses slide into your booth to take your order, and the decor is neon and vintage Corvette to the highest power. Equal parts *Happy Days* hangout and Jackrabbit Slim's (as in *Pulp Fiction*), the Corvette Diner is a comfy, family-friendly time warp in the midst of Hillcrest, and the diner-esque eats ain't bad for the price, either. Burgers, sandwiches, appetizer munchies, blue-plate specials, and salads share the menu with a *very* full page of fountain favorites. Beer and wine are served, and there's a large bar in the center of the cavernous dining room. The party jumps a notch at night, with a DJ providing more entertainment (on top of the already captivating atmosphere)—the decibel level is always high. A reliable favorite for preteen birthdays.

3946 Fifth Ave. (between Washington St. and University Ave.). ⓒ 619/542-1001. Reservations not accepted. Main courses $5–$11. AE, DC, DISC, MC, V. Sun–Thurs 11am–10pm; Fri–Sat 11am–midnight. Valet parking $4. Bus: 1, 3, 16, 25, or 908.

Crest Cafe AMERICAN/BREAKFAST   This long-popular Hillcrest diner is a great refuge from sleek designer food and swank settings. The cheery pink interior announces 1940s style, and the room bubbles with upbeat waiters and comfort food doled out on Fiestaware. The church pew–like booths are comfortable enough, but the small stucco room doesn't do much to mask the near constant clang of plates. No matter: Burger-lovers will fall in love with the spicy, rich "butter burger"—a dollop of herb butter is buried in the patty before cooking (it's even better than it sounds). And the East Texas fried chicken breast crusted with hunks of jalapeño peppers is none too subtle, either, but it's tasty. A variety of sandwiches and salads, the popular steamed vegetable basket, and broiled chicken dishes are healthier options. During the early evening, the joint brims with neighborhood bohemians in search of a cholesterol fix, while later the club contingent swoops in; the breakfast of omelets or hot cakes is a happy eye-opener.

425 Robinson Ave. (between Fourth and Fifth aves.). © 619/295-2510. www. crestcafe.com. Reservations not accepted. Main courses $5–$12. AE, MC, V. Daily 7am–midnight. Bus: 1, 3, 25, or 908.

3 Old Town & Mission Valley

Visitors usually have at least one meal in Old Town, and although this area showcases San Diego at its most touristy, I can't argue with the appeal of dining in California's charming and oldest settlement. Mexican food and bathtub-size margaritas are the big draws, as are mariachi music and colorful decor.

Old Town is also the gateway to the decidedly less historic Mission Valley. Here you'll find plenty of chain eateries, both good and bad, and not discussed in depth below.

EXPENSIVE

Cafe Pacifica ☆☆ CALIFORNIAN/SEAFOOD   You can't tell a book by its cover: Inside this cozy Old Town casita, the decor is cleanly contemporary (but still romantic) and the food anything but Mexican. Established in 1980, Cafe Pacifica serves upscale, imaginative seafood at decent prices and produces kitchen alumni who go on to enjoy local fame. Among the temptations are crab-stuffed portobello mushrooms topped with grilled asparagus, anise-scented bouillabaisse, and daily fresh fish selections served grilled with your choice of five sauces. Signature items include Hawaiian ahi with shiitake mushrooms and ginger butter, griddled mustard catfish, and the "Pomerita," a pomegranate margarita. To avoid the crush, arrive before 6:30pm—you'll also get to take advantage of the early-bird special, entree with soup or salad for $21. On Tuesdays the corkage fee is waived for bottles you bring in yourself (though the wine list is hardly a slouch).

2414 San Diego Ave. © 619/291-6666. www.cafepacifica.com. Reservations recommended. Main courses $17–$28. AE, DC, DISC, MC, V. Daily 5–10pm. Valet parking $4. Bus: 5 or 5A. Trolley: Old Town.

Baja Fish Tacos

San Diego is conscious of its Hispanic roots, but it's hard to find anything other than gringo-ized combo plates in most local Mexican restaurants. Perhaps the most authentic recipes are those found at **Rubio's Baja Grill,** which serves batter-dipped, deep-fried fish fillets folded in corn tortillas and garnished with shredded cabbage, salsa, and tangy *crema* sauce. Many of the two-dozen-or-so newer locations have a homogenous fast-food look to them, so it's fun to stop by the original stand, at 4504 E. Mission Bay Dr., at Bunker Hill Street (© **858/272-2801**), if you're in the neighborhood.

El Agave Tequileria 𝆑𝆑 MEXICAN   Don't be misled by this restaurant's less than impressive location above a liquor store on the outskirts of Old Town. This warm, bustling eatery continues to draw local gourmands for the regional Mexican cuisine and rustic elegance that leave the touristy fajitas-and-cerveza joints of Old Town far behind. El Agave is named for the agave plant from which tequilas are derived, and they boast more than 850 boutique and artisan tequilas from throughout the Latin world—bottles of every size, shape, and jewel-like hue fill shelves and cases throughout the dining room. But even teetotalers will enjoy the restaurant's authentically flavored *mole* sauces (from Chiapas, rich with peanuts; tangy tomatillo from Oaxaca; and the more familiar dark mole flavored with chocolate and sesame), along with giant shrimp and sea bass prepared in a dozen variations, or El Agave's signature beef filet with goat cheese and dark tequila sauce. On the other hand, I could almost make a meal out of the warm watercress salad dressed with onions and bacon, folded into tortillas. Lunches are simpler affairs without the exotic sauces, and inexpensive.

2304 San Diego Ave. © **619/220-0692.** www.elagave.com. Reservations recommended. Main courses $7–$10 lunch, $16–$32 dinner. AE, MC, V. Daily 11am–10pm. Street parking. Bus: 5. Trolley: Old Town.

MODERATE

Berta's Latin American Restaurant 𝆑 *Finds* LATIN AMERICAN Berta's is a welcome change from the nacho-and-fajita joints that dominate Old Town dining, though the small room can attract as large a crowd on weekends. Housed in a charming, basic cottage tucked away on a side street, Berta's faithfully re-creates the sunny flavors of Central and South America, where slow cooking mellows the heat of chiles and other spices. Try the Salvadoran *pupusas* (at lunch only)—dense corn-mash turnovers with melted cheese and black beans, their texture perfectly offset with crunchy cabbage salad and one of Berta's special salsas. Or opt for a table full of Spanish-style tapas, grazing alternately on crispy *empanadas* (filled turnovers), strong Spanish olives, or *Pincho Moruno,* skewered lamb and onion redolent of spices and red saffron.

3928 Twiggs St. (at Congress St.). © **619/295-2343.** www.bertasinoldtown.com. Main courses $6–$9 lunch, $11–$16 dinner. AE, MC, V. Tues–Sun 11am–10pm (lunch menu till 3pm). Free parking. Bus: 5 or 5A. Trolley: Old Town.

Casa Guadalajara (Kids) MEXICAN   The best of the minichain of restaurants operated by Bazaar del Mundo, Casa Guadalajara is actually located a block away from the shops, which provides another advantage: It's often less crowded than its counterparts (though waits of 30 min. or more are not unusual here Fri and Sat). Mariachi tunes played by strolling musicians enliven the room nightly, and you can also dine alfresco, in a picturesque courtyard occupied by a 200-year-old pepper tree. Birdbath-size margaritas start most meals, while dining ranges from gourmet Mexican to simpler south-of-the-border fare. My favorite is the *tacos de cochinita*—two soft corn tacos bulging with achiote-seasoned pork and marinated red onions—but the extensive menu features all the fajita and combo plates most people expect. This place (like the Bazaar) is touristy, but it's where

(Kids) Family-Friendly Restaurants

Casa Guadalajara (see above)   With the ambient noise of fountains and mariachis, fidgety children won't feel like they have to be on their best behavior at this pleasant Mexican eatery—there's also plenty for them to see.

Corvette Diner (p. 80)   Resembling a 1950s diner, this place appeals to teens and preteens. Parents will have fun reminiscing, and kids will enjoy the burgers and fries or other short-order fare, served in sock-hop surroundings.

Filippi's Pizza Grotto (p. 75)   Children's portions are available, and kids will feel right at home at this red-checked-vinyl-tablecloth joint. The pizzas are among the best in town.

I bring out-of-towners for old California ambience and reliable Mexican food.

4105 Taylor St. (at Juan St. in Old Town). ℂ 619/295-5111. www.casaguadalajara. com. Reservations recommended. Main courses $8–$16. AE, DC, DISC, MC, V. Sun–Thurs 11am–10pm; Fri–Sat 11am–11pm. Free parking. Bus: 5 or 5A. Trolley: Old Town.

INEXPENSIVE

Living Room Coffeehouse COFFEE & TEA/LIGHT FARE
You're liable to hear the whir of laptops from college students who use this spot as a sort of off-campus study hall. Grab a sidewalk table and enjoy some splendid people-watching any time of day; indoors you'll find faux antiques, appropriately weathered for a lived-in feel. I think the pastries and coffee fall a bit short, but this local minichain is also known for surprisingly good light meals that make it a good choice for early risers and insomniacs alike. Breakfast includes omelets and waffles, while the rest of the day's fare is posted on a chalkboard menu; try the turkey lasagna, chicken Dijon, tuna melt, or one of several hearty entree salads. Plus you'll find exotic iced and hot coffee drinks, like the Emerald Isle (espresso, white chocolate, and mint). Other locations are in La Jolla at 1010 Prospect St. (ℂ **858/ 459-1187**), in Hillcrest at 1417 University Ave. (ℂ **619/295-7911**), the Sports Arena area at 1018 Rosecrans (ℂ **619/222-6852**), and in the College area near San Diego State University, at 5900 El Cajon Blvd. (ℂ **619/286-8434**).

2541 San Diego Ave. ℂ 619/523-4445. www.livingroomcafe.com. Menu items $3–$8. AE, MC, V. Sun–Thurs 7am–10pm; Fri–Sat 7am–midnight. Bus: 5. Trolley: Old Town.

Old Town Mexican Cafe *(Overrated)* MEXICAN This place is so popular that it's become an Old Town tourist attraction in its own right. You, on the other hand, might proceed with caution. The original structure is wonderfully funky and frayed, but the restaurant long ago expanded into additional, less appealing dining rooms and outdoor patios—still, the wait for a table is often 30 to 60 minutes. You can pass the time by gazing in from the sidewalk as tortillas are hand-patted the old-fashioned way, soon to be a hot-off-the-grill treat accompanying every meal, or by watching the chickens spinning around the barbecue. But the place is loud and crowded, and the food usually fails to impress. When I come here it's for one of three things: the margarita, served neat, in a shaker for two; the delicious rotisserie chicken accompanied by tortillas, guacamole, sour cream, beans, and rice; or the cheap breakfasts, when the place is pleasantly sleepy and throng-free. Otherwise, the fried *carnitas*—reputedly a specialty—remind me of mystery meat that's been pitched into the deep-fat fryer.

2489 San Diego Ave. ℂ **619/297-4330**. Reservations accepted only for parties of 10 or more. Main courses $6–$9 breakfast, $9–$15 lunch and dinner. AE, DISC, MC, V. Sun–Thurs 7am–11pm; Fri–Sat 7am–midnight (bar till 2am). Bus: 5. Trolley: Old Town.

4 Mission Bay & the Beaches

Generally speaking, restaurants at the beach exist primarily to pro-vide an excuse for sitting and gazing at the water. Because this activ-ity is most commonly accompanied by steady drinking, it stands to reason that the food isn't often remarkable. I've tried to balance the most scenic of these typical hangouts with places actually known for above-average food—with a little effort, they can be found.

VERY EXPENSIVE

Baleen 𝒜𝒜𝒜 SEAFOOD/CALIFORNIAN   This fine water-front eatery at the Paradise Point Resort in the middle of Mission Bay is exactly the touch of class the hotel owners hoped for when they lured celebrity restaurateur Robbin Haas (creator of two Baleens in Florida).

Start with chilled lobster in a martini glass (avoid sticker shock by asking the price first), a warm salad of roasted mushrooms and asparagus, or fresh oysters delivered in a small cart and shucked table side. Then savor a selection of seafood simply grilled, wood-roasted, or sautéed with hummus crust, honey wasabi glaze, or ginger sauce. Wood-roasted meats include Roquefort-crusted filet mignon and Sonoma Farms chicken with goat cheese dumplings and forest mushroom sauté. Should you have an appetite—and credit—left over, indulge in an intricately rich dessert like chocolate fondue, or the quartet of fruit-infused custards.

1404 Vacation Rd., Mission Bay (Paradise Point Resort). ℂ **858/490-6363**. www.paradisepoint.com. Reservations recommended. Main courses $19–$35. AE, DC, DISC, MC, V. Sun–Thurs 5–9pm; Fri–Sat 5–10pm. Free parking. Bus: 9.

EXPENSIVE

Qwiig's 𝒜 CALIFORNIAN   Large and welcoming, Qwiig's hums pleasantly with conversation and serves food that's better than any other view-oriented oceanfront spot in this area. The fresh-fish specials are most popular; choices often include rare ahi with braised spinach and soy-sesame sauce, and fettuccine with seafood. Meat and poultry dishes include a popular prime rib, an outstanding half-pound burger, and nightly specials that always shine. The dessert list stars a boysenberry-peach cobbler made by the on-site pastry chef. Wines are well matched to the cuisine, and there are imaginative, special cocktails each night. The restaurant got its strange name from a group of Ocean Beach surfers nicknamed "qwiigs."

5083 Santa Monica Ave. (at Abbott St.), Ocean Beach. ℂ 619/222-1101. Reservations recommended. Main courses $6–$14 lunch, $14–$25 dinner. AE, MC, V. Lunch Sun–Fri 11:30am–2pm; dinner daily 5:30–9pm. Bus: 35 or 923.

Thee Bungalow ★★ FRENCH/CONTINENTAL By far the fanciest restaurant in laid-back Ocean Beach, Thee Bungalow endears itself to the local crowd with daily early-bird specials ($14–$16), but oenophiles will revel in a wine list that doesn't suffer snobs yet features a multitude of classy older wines at surprisingly reasonable prices. The house specialty is crispy roast duck, served with your choice of sauce (the best is black cherry), ideally followed by one of the decadent, made-to-order dessert soufflés for two (chocolate or Grand Marnier). Another menu standout is *osso buco*-style lamb shank adorned with shallot–red wine purée. Equally appealing first courses include brie and asparagus baked in puff pastry, and warm chicken salad (stuffed with sun-dried tomatoes and basil, and then presented with feta cheese and fruit, it also doubles as a light meal). There's always a sampler plate featuring house-made pâtés with Dijon, cornichons, capers, and little toasts.

Regular special events and noteworthy wine-tasting dinners are listed on the website.

4996 W. Point Loma Blvd. (at Bacon St.), Ocean Beach. ℂ 619/224-2884. www.theebungalow.com. Reservations recommended. Main courses $19–$29; early-bird specials $14–$16. AE, MC, V. Mon–Thurs 5:30–9:30pm; Fri–Sat 5–10pm; Sun 5–9pm. Free parking. Bus: 35 or 923.

MODERATE

Caffe Bella Italia ★★ ITALIAN Although located well away from the surf, it's lovely inside, and the food can knock your socks off. It's the best spot in the area for shellfish-laden pasta, wood-fired pizzas, and management that welcomes guests like family. Romantic lighting, sheer draperies, and warmly earthy walls create a vaguely North African ambience, assisted by the lilting Milan accents of the staff (when the din of a few dozen happy diners doesn't drown them out, that is). Every item on the menu bears the unmistakable flavor of freshness and homemade care—even the simplest curled-edge ravioli stuffed with ricotta, spinach, and pine nuts is elevated to culinary perfection, while salmon is dealt with unusually firmly, endowed with olives, capers, and thick hunks of tomato in wine and garlic. You may leave wishing you could be adopted by this gracious family.

1525 Garnet Ave. (between Ingraham and Haines), Pacific Beach. ☎ **858/273-1224.** www.caffebellaitalia.com. Reservations suggested for dinner. Main courses $7–$15 lunch, $9–$27 dinner. AE, MC, V. Tues–Thurs 11:30am–2:30pm and 5:30–10:30pm; Fri–Sat 11am–2:30pm and 5:30–11pm; Sun 5–10:30pm. Free (small) parking lot. Bus: 9 or 27.

The Green Flash AMERICAN   Known throughout Pacific Beach for its location and hip, local clientele, the Green Flash serves adequate (and typically beachy) food at decent prices. The menu includes plenty of grilled and deep-fried seafood, straightforward steaks, and giant main-course salads. You'll also find appetizer platters of shellfish (oysters, clams, shrimp) and jalapeño "poppers" (cheese-stuffed fried peppers). The glassed-in patio is probably P.B.'s best place for people-watching, and locals congregate at sunset to catch a glimpse of the optical phenomenon for which this boardwalk hangout is named. It has something to do with the color spectrum at the moment the sun disappears below the horizon, but the scientific explanation becomes less important—and the decibel level rises—with every round of drinks.

701 Thomas Ave. (at Mission Blvd.), Pacific Beach. ☎ **858/270-7715.** Reservations not accepted. Main courses $4–$8 breakfast, $8–$13 lunch, $10–$35 dinner. AE, DC, DISC, MC, V. Daily 8am–10pm (bar till 2am). Bus: 27 or 34.

Sushi Ota ★★ JAPANESE   Masterful chef-owner Yukito Ota creates San Diego's finest sushi. This sophisticated, traditional restaurant (no Asian fusion here) is a minimalist bento box with stark white walls and black furniture, softened by indirect lighting. The sushi menu is short, because discerning regulars look first to the daily specials posted behind the counter. The city's most experienced chefs, armed with nimble fingers and very sharp knives, turn the day's fresh catch into artful little bundles accented with mounds of wasabi and ginger. The rest of the varied menu features seafood, teriyaki-glazed meats, feather-light tempura, and a variety of small appetizers perfect to accompany a large sushi order.

This restaurant is difficult to find, mainly because it's hard to believe that such outstanding dining would hide behind a laundromat and convenience store in the rear of a minimall that's perpendicular to the street. It's also in a nondescript part of Pacific Beach, a stone's throw from I-5, but none of that should discourage you from seeking it out.

4529 Mission Bay Dr. (at Bunker Hill), Pacific Beach. ℂ **858/270-5670.** Reservations strongly recommended on weekends. Main courses $6–$9 lunch, $8–$16 dinner; sushi $4–$10. AE, MC, V. Tues–Fri 11:30am–2pm; daily 5:30–10:30pm. Free parking (additional lot behind the mall). Bus: 27.

INEXPENSIVE

High Tide Cafe AMERICAN   This cheerful, comfortably crowded place offers pleasant rooftop dining with an ocean view if you're lucky enough to snag a seat. Just off the Pacific Beach boardwalk, the cafe sees a lot of foot traffic and socializing locals. Those in the know go for great breakfasts—till 2pm on weekends, when there's a make-your-own Bloody Mary bar. Choices include skillets of *huevos rancheros* (eggs Mexican style) and breakfast burritos, French toast, and omelets. During happy hour (Mon–Sat 4–7pm), you'll find bargain prices on drinks and finger-lickin' appetizers. The rest of the menu is adequate, running the gamut from fish tacos to tequila fajita chicken pasta to all-American burgers.

722 Grand Ave., Pacific Beach. ℂ **858/272-1999.** www.hightidecafe.com. Reservations recommended on weekends. Main courses $4–$10 breakfast, $6–$15 lunch and dinner. MC, V. Mon–Fri 9am–midnight; Sat–Sun 8am–1am. Limited free parking. Bus: 27 or 34.

The Mission *Value* BREAKFAST/COFFEE & TEA   Located alongside the funky surf shops, bikini boutiques, and alternative galleries of bohemian Mission Beach, the Mission is the neighborhood's central meeting place. But it's good enough to attract more than just locals, and now has an upscale sister location east of Hillcrest—at either spot expect waits of half an hour or more on weekends. The menu features all-day breakfasts (from traditional pancakes to nouvelle egg dishes to Latin-flavored burritos and quesadillas), plus light lunch sandwiches and salads. Standouts include tamales and eggs with tomatillo sauce, chicken-apple sausage with eggs and a mound of rosemary potatoes, and cinnamon French toast with blackberry purée. Seating is casual, comfy, and conducive to lingering (tons of students, writers, and diarists hang out here), if only with a soup bowl–size latte. The other location is at 2801 University Ave. in North Park (ℂ **619/220-8992**); it has a similar menu and hours.

3795 Mission Blvd. (at San Jose), Mission Beach. ℂ **858/488-9060.** Menu items $6–$10. AE, MC, V. Daily 7am–3pm. Bus: 27 or 34.

5 La Jolla

As befits an upscale community with time (and money) on its hands, La Jolla seems to have more than its fair share of good restaurants.

Happily, they're not all expensive and are more ethnically diverse than you might expect in a community that still supports a haberdashery called The Ascot Shop. While many restaurants are clustered in the village, on Prospect Street and the few blocks directly east, you can also cruise down La Jolla Boulevard or up by the La Jolla Beach & Tennis Club for additional choices.

VERY EXPENSIVE

George's at the Cove ✿✿✿ CALIFORNIAN   George Hauer greets loyal regulars by name, and his confidence assures newcomers that they'll leave impressed with this beloved La Jolla institution. George's wins consistent praise for impeccable service, gorgeous views of the cove, and outstanding California cuisine.

The menu, in typical San Diego fashion, presents many inventive seafood options, filtered through the myriad influences of chef Trey Foshee, selected as one of America's top 10 chefs by *Food & Wine*. Foshee starts each day with a trek up to Chino Farms to select the evening's produce, which work its way into exquisite starters like the Jerusalem artichoke and leek soup. Main courses combine divergent flavors with practiced artistry, ranging from the Neiman Ranch pork tasting (three variations of naturally raised pork) to roasted lamb loin and braised lamb shoulder with a spicy medjool date couscous and baby spinach. George's signature smoked chicken, broccoli, and black-bean soup is still a mainstay at lunch; they'll even give out the recipe for this local legend. The tasting menu offers a seasonally composed five-course sampling for $52 per person. The informal Ocean Terrace (p. 92) is upstairs.

1250 Prospect St. ✆ 858/454-4244. www.georgesatthecove.com. Reservations strongly recommended for dinner. Main courses $13–$17 lunch; $25–$36 dinner. AE, DC, DISC, MC, V. Daily 11:30am–2:30pm; Sun–Thurs 5:30–10:30pm Fri–Sat 5–11pm. Valet parking $6. Bus: 34.

The Marine Room ✿✿✿ (Moments) FRENCH/CALIFORNIA For more than 6 decades, San Diego's most celebrated dining room has been this shorefront institution, perched within kissing distance of the waves that snuggle up to La Jolla shores. But it wasn't until the 1994 arrival of Executive Chef Bernard Guillas of Brittany that the food finally lived up to its glass-fronted room with a view. A 2001 spruce-up did away with most of the dated decor, and today the Marine Room is the city's top "special occasion" destination. Guillas and Chef de Cuisine Ron Oliver work with local produce, but never hesitate to pursue unusual flavors from other corners of the globe. So, a favored entree includes barramundi, a delicate white fish from Australia, encrusted with a hazelnut fennel pollen, garnished with flowering chive and a lacy crisp of fried lotus root. The vigilant service is charmingly deferential, yet never condescending.

The Marine Room ranks as one of San Diego's most expensive venues, but usually is filled to the gills on weekends; weekdays it's much easier to score a table, and the four-course tasting menu available Monday through Wednesday for $49 ($65 paired with wines) is an excellent value.

2000 Spindrift Dr. ℰ 858/459-7222. www.marineroom.com. Reservations recommended, especially weekends. Main courses $15–$20 lunch, $26–$39 dinner. AE, DC, DISC, MC, V. Tues–Sat 11:30am–2pm; Sun brunch 11am–2pm; Sun–Thurs 5:30–9pm; Fri–Sat 5:30–10pm. Complementary valet parking. Bus: 34.

Top of the Cove ⭐⭐⭐ CONTINENTAL   Always vying with George's and the Marine Room for "most romantic" in local diner surveys, Top of the Cove is a mainstay for special occasions—first dates, marriage proposals, anniversaries.

The menu is peppered with French names and classic preparations with just a few welcome contemporary accents. Standouts include bacon-wrapped filet mignon in a syrah sauce, duck breast dressed with a balsamic-orange reduction, and a molasses-seared elk with Swiss chard, grilled boniato, and a blackberry shallot compote. Sorbet is served between courses. The dessert specialty is a bittersweet-chocolate box filled with cream and fruit in a raspberry sauce—try it with a liqueur-laced house coffee. Aficionados will thrill to the epic wine list, but its steep markup threatens to spoil the mood. Lunch is lighter—salads, sandwiches, and pastas, along with a few cuts of meat and fish.

1216 Prospect St. ℰ 858/454-7779. www.topofthecove.com. Reservations recommended. Jackets suggested for men at dinner. Main courses $8–$22 lunch, $24–$38 dinner. AE, MC, V. Daily 11:30am–11:30pm. Valet parking $6. Bus: 34.

EXPENSIVE

Cafe Japengo ⭐⭐ JAPANESE/SUSHI/PACIFIC RIM/ASIAN FUSION   Despite being contrived and self-conscious, Cafe Japengo is worth a trip for the food alone. The beautiful people know they look even more so among the warm woods and leafy shadows here, so there's lots of posing and people-watching, and it's always packed.

Appetizers like duck pot stickers in coriander pesto, or the lemongrass-marinated swordfish, are superb; others, like the seared ahi "napoleon," suffer from extra ingredients that just make the dish fussy. Sushi here is the same way; Japengo features the finest and freshest fish, but churns out enormously popular specialty rolls (combinations wrapped in even more ingredients, often drenched in sauce and garnished even further). The dramatic, colorfully presented inventions are enormously popular, but sushi purists will be happiest sticking to the basics.

8960 University Center Lane (opposite the Hyatt Regency La Jolla). © **858/450-3355**. www.cafejapengo.com. Reservations recommended. Main courses $12–$16 lunch, $16–$30 dinner. AE, DC, DISC, MC, V. Mon–Fri 11:30am–2:30pm; Sun–Wed 5:30–10pm; Thurs–Sat 6–11pm. Valet parking $4, validated self-parking free. Bus: 41.

Roppongi ✿ PACIFIC RIM/ASIAN FUSION/ECLECTIC   At Roppongi, the cuisines of Japan, Thailand, China, Vietnam, Korea, and India collide, sometimes gracefully, in a vibrant explosion of flavors. You might not get past the first menu page, a long list of small tapas dishes designed for sharing—each table is even preset with a tall stack of plates that quietly encourage a communal meal of successive appetizers.

Highlights include the Polynesian crab stack, and the seared scallops on potato pancakes floating in a silky puddle of Thai basil hollandaise. Traditionally sized main courses feature seafood, meat, and game, all colorfully prepared, and the weekend brunch menu is also a real eye-opener. If your sweet tooth hasn't been sated, indulge in dessert—the caramelized Tahitian banana, framed by dollops of ice cream and a "lid" of candy glass, is scrumptious. Although the restaurant claims to utilize the Chinese discipline of feng shui to enhance contentment among diners, the bamboo-and-booth atmosphere feels a little like Denny's-meets-upscale Bangkok; the outdoor patio is always preferable, anchored by a leaping fire pit and accented with ponds and torches.

875 Prospect St. (at Fay Ave.). © **858/551-5252**. www.roppongiusa.com. Reservations recommended. Main courses $16–$30; tapas $8–$24. AE, DISC, MC, V. Sun–Thurs 11:30am–10pm; Fri–Sat 11:30am–11pm.

Trattoria Acqua ✿✿ ITALIAN/MEDITERRANEAN   Nestled on tiled terraces close enough to catch ocean breezes, this excellent northern Italian spot has a more relaxed ambience than similarly sophisticated Gaslamp Quarter trattorias. Rustic walls and outdoor seating shaded by flowering vines evoke a romantic Tuscan villa. A mixed crowd of suits and well-heeled couples gather to enjoy expertly prepared seasonal dishes; every table starts with bread served with an indescribably pungent Mediterranean spread. Acqua's pastas (all available as appetizers or main courses) are as good as it gets—rich, heady flavor combinations like spinach, chard, and four-cheese gnocchi, or veal-and-mortadella tortellini in fennel cream sauce. Other specialties include *osso buco alla pugliese* (veal shank braised with tomatoes, olives, capers, and garlic and served over pappardelle pasta), *quaglie a beccafico* (roasted Sonoma quails with Italian bacon, spinach, raisins, and pinenuts), and *salmone con lenticchie* (grilled Atlantic salmon served over Beluga lentils with a lemon-coriander vinaigrette). The well-chosen wine list has received *Wine Spectator* accolades several years in a row.

1298 Prospect St. (on Coast Walk). © 858/454-0709. www.trattoriaacqua.com. Reservations recommended. Main courses $9–$19 lunch, $14–$30 dinner. AE, MC, V. Daily 11:30am–2:30pm; Sun–Thurs 5–9:30pm; Fri–Sat 5–10:30pm. Validated self-parking. Bus: 34.

MODERATE

Brockton Villa ★★ *Finds* BREAKFAST/CALIFORNIAN/ COFFEE & TEA   In a restored 1894 beach bungalow, this charming cafe has a history as intriguing as its varied, eclectic menu. Named for an early resident's hometown (Brockton, Massachusetts), the cottage is imbued with the spirit of artistic souls drawn to this breathtaking perch overlooking La Jolla Cove. Rescued by the trailblazing Pannikin Coffee Company in the 1960s, the restaurant is now independently run by a Pannikin alum.

The biggest buzz is at breakfast, when you can enjoy inventive dishes such as soufflélike "Coast Toast" (the house take on French toast) and Greek "steamers" (eggs scrambled with an espresso steamer, then mixed with feta cheese, tomato, and basil). The dozens of coffee drinks include the "Keith Richards"—four shots of espresso topped with Mexican hot chocolate (Mother's Little Helper indeed!). The expanding supper menu includes Moroccan halibut with a spicy tomato relish, and villa paella (seafood and shellfish tumbled with artichoke hearts and a warm caper vinaigrette), plus pastas, stews, and grilled meats. Steep stairs from the street limit access for wheelchair users.

1235 Coast Blvd. (across from La Jolla Cove). © 858/454-7393. www.brockton villa.com. Reservations recommended (call by Thurs for Sat–Sun brunch). Main courses $5–$9 breakfast, $7–$11 lunch, $15–$25 dinner. AE, DISC, MC, V. Mon 8am–3pm; Tues–Sun 8am–9pm.

Ocean Terrace and George's Bar ★★ *Value* CALIFORNIAN The legendary main dining room at George's at the Cove has won numerous awards for its haute cuisine. But George's also accommodates those seeking good food and a spectacular setting with a more reasonable price tag: The upstairs Ocean Terrace and George's Bar prepare similar dishes as well as new creations in the same kitchen as the high-priced fare. The two areas offer indoor and spectacular outdoor seating overlooking La Jolla Cove, and the same great service as the main dining room. For dinner, you can choose from several seafood or pasta dishes, or have something out of the ordinary like George's meatloaf served with mushroom-and-corn mashed potatoes. The award-winning smoked chicken, broccoli, and black-bean soup appears on both menus.

1250 Prospect St. ℂ 858/454-4244. www.georgesatthecove.com. Reservations recommended. Main courses $9–$12 lunch, $12–$20 dinner. AE, DC, DISC, MC, V. Daily 11am–10pm (Fri–Sat till 10:30pm). Valet parking $6. Bus: 34.

Piatti ℱ ITALIAN/MEDITERRANEAN   La Jolla's version of the reliable neighborhood hangout is this pasta-centric trattoria, a couple blocks inland from La Jolla Shores. Come here on busy Friday or Saturday evenings—well, any night, really—and you're likely to be surrounded by a crew of regulars that pops in once or twice a week and knows all the staff by name. You won't feel left out, however, and the food is well priced. Lemon herb-roasted chicken, peppercorn-crusted *bistecca* (rib-eye), plus the Thursday night special of *osso buco* with risotto lead the short list of entrees, but it's the pastas that parade out to most tables. Try orecchiette bathed in Gorgonzola, grilled chicken and sun-dried tomatoes, or pappardelle "fantasia"—shrimp-crowned ribbons of saffron pasta, primed with garlic, tomato, and white wine. The outdoor patio, beneath the romantic sprawl of an enormous ficus tree, is ideal for dining any night, thanks to the cozy heaters.

2182 Avenida de la Playa. ℂ 858/454-1589. Reservations recommended. Main courses $9–$21; Sat–Sun brunch $7–$12. AE, DC, MC, V. Sun–Thurs 11am–10pm; Fri–Sat 11am–11pm. Street parking usually available. Bus: 34.

Spice & Rice Thai Kitchen ℱ THAI   This attractive Thai restaurant is a couple of blocks from the village's tourist crush—far enough to ensure effortless parking. The lunch crowd consists of shoppers and curious tourists, while dinner is quieter; all the local businesses have shut down. The food is excellent, with polished presentations and expert renditions of the classics like pad Thai, satay, curry, and glazed duck. The starters often sound as good as the entrees: Consider making a grazing meal of house specialties like "gold bags" (minced pork, vegetables, glass noodles, and herbs wrapped in crispy rice paper and served with earthy plum sauce) or prawns with yellow curry lobster sauce; crispy calamari is flavored with tamarind sauce and chili sauce. The romantically lit covered front patio has a secluded garden feel, and inside tables also have

Moments   **To See, Perchance to Eat**

Incredible ocean views, a sweeping skyline, and sailboats fluttering along the shore—it's the classic backdrop for a memorable meal. So where can you find the best views?

Downtown, the **Fish Market** and its pricier cousin **Top of the Market** overlook San Diego Bay, and the management even provides binoculars for getting a good look at aircraft carriers and other vessels. Not far is **Star of the Sea,** where an intimate room faces the elegant *Star of India* ship. Across the harbor in Coronado, the **Bay Beach Cafe** and **Peohe's,** 1201 1st St. (© 619/437-4474), offer panoramic views of the San Diego skyline, and the tony **Azzura Point** at Loews Coronado Bay Resort looks out across the bay.

In Ocean Beach, **Qwiig's** sits on a second-floor perch across the street from the sand, while in Pacific Beach, the **Green Flash** is just 5 feet from the sand (although the year-round parade of bodies may prove a distraction from the ocean). Nearby, the **Atoll** (© 619/539-8635), in the Catamaran Resort Hotel, has a romantic patio facing tranquil Mission Bay. In La Jolla, **George's at the Cove** and **Top of the Cove** are near the water (and offer panoramic elevated views), but **Brockton Villa** actually offers the La Jolla Cove outlook as advertised on every postcard stand in town.

My two favorite vistas to feast on give you a choice of city or sea view. **Bertrand at Mr. A's** (© 619/239-1377) sits on the 12th floor at Fifth and Laurel; the panorama here encompasses Balboa Park to the east, downtown to the south, and the San Diego Harbor to the west, and it's punctuated every few minutes by aircraft on their final approach. If you want to get up close and personal with the marine scene, grab your gold card and head to **The Marine Room,** where Sea-World technology (yes, SeaWorld) helped build the windows that withstand the crashing tide each day.

indirect lighting. Despite the passage of time, this all-around satisfier remains something of an insider's secret.

7734 Girard Ave. © 858/456-0466. Reservations recommended. Main courses $8–$13. AE, MC, V. Mon–Thurs 11am–3pm and 5–10pm; Fri–Sat 11am–3pm and 5–11pm; Sun 5–10pm. Bus: 34.

INEXPENSIVE

The Cottage ⟨R⟩ BREAKFAST/CALIFORNIAN   La Jolla's best—and friendliest—breakfast is served at this turn-of-the-20th-century bungalow on a sunny village corner. The cottage is light and airy, but most diners opt for tables outside, where a charming white picket fence encloses the trellis-shaded brick patio. Omelets and egg dishes feature Mediterranean, Asian, or classic American touches; my favorite has creamy mashed potatoes, bacon, and melted cheese folded inside. The Cottage bakes its own muffins, breakfast breads, and—you can quote me on this—the best brownies in San Diego. While breakfast dishes are served all day, toward lunch the kitchen begins turning out freshly made, healthful soups, light meals, and sandwiches. Summer dinners (never heavy, always tasty) are a delight, particularly when you're seated before dark on a balmy seaside night.

7702 Fay Ave. (at Kline St.). ⟨C⟩ 858/454-8409. www.cottagelajolla.com. Reservations accepted for dinner only. Main courses $6–$9 breakfast, $7–$11 lunch, $9–$15 dinner. AE, DISC, MC, V. Daily 7:30am–3pm; dinner (June–Sept only) Tues–Sat 5–9:30pm. Bus: 34.

6 Coronado

Rather like the conservative, old-school navy aura that pervades the entire "island," Coronado's dining options are reliable and often quite good, but the restaurants aren't breaking new culinary ground.

Some notable exceptions are the resort dining rooms, which seem to be waging a little rivalry over who can attract the most prestigious, multiple-award-winning executive chef. If you're in the mood for a special-occasion meal that'll knock your socks off, consider **Azzura Point** ⟨RR⟩ (⟨C⟩ 619/424-4000), in Loews Coronado Bay Resort (p. 64). With its plushly upholstered, gilded, and view-endowed setting, this stylish dining room wins continual raves from deep-pocketed San Diego foodies willing to cross the bay for inventive and artistic California-Mediterranean creations. The Hotel Del's fancy **Prince of Wales** ⟨RR⟩ (⟨C⟩ 619/522-8496) is equally scenic, gazing at the beach across the hotel's regal Windsor Lawn; the eclectic California menu always showcases the best of seasonally fresh ingredients.

But if you seek ethnic or funky food, better head back across the bridge. Mexican fare (gringo-style, but well practiced) is served on the island at popular **Miguel's Cocina,** inside El Cordova Hotel (⟨C⟩ 619/437-4237).

EXPENSIVE

The Brigantine ✿ SEAFOOD   The Brigantine is best known for its oyster-bar happy hour from 3 to 6pm and 10 to 11pm Monday through Saturday (4:30pm–close on Sun). Beer, margaritas, and food are heavily discounted, and you can expect standing room only. Early bird "sundowner" specials include a seafood, steak, or chicken entree served with soup or salad, a side of veggies, and bread for $16. The food is good, not great, but the congenial atmosphere is the certifiable draw. Inside, the decor is upscale and resolutely nautical; outside, there's a pleasant patio with heaters to take the chill off the night air. At lunch, you can get everything from crab cakes or fish and chips to fresh fish or pasta. Lunch specials come with sourdough bread and two side dishes. The bar and oyster bar are open nightly until at least 11pm.

1333 Orange Ave. ✆ **619/435-4166.** www.brigantine.com. Reservations recommended on weekends. Main courses $7–$11 lunch, $16–$26 dinner. AE, DC, MC, V. Lunch daily 11am–2:30pm (Sun opens at 10am); dinner Mon–Thurs 5–10pm; Fri–Sat 5–10:30pm; Sun 4:30–9:30pm. Bus: 901, 902, or 904.

Chez Loma ✿✿ FRENCH   You'd be hard-pressed to find a more romantic dining spot than this intimate Victorian cottage filled with antiques and subdued candlelight. The house dates from 1889, the French-Continental restaurant from 1975. Tables are scattered throughout the house and on the enclosed garden terrace; an upstairs wine salon, reminiscent of a Victorian parlor, is a cozy spot for coffee or conversation.

   Among the creative entrees are salmon with smoked-tomato vinaigrette, and roast duckling with lingonberry, port, and burnt orange sauce. All main courses are served with soup or salad, rice or potatoes, and fresh vegetables. California wines and American microbrews are available. Follow dinner with a silky crème caramel or Kahlúa crème brûlée. Chez Loma's service is attentive, the herb rolls are addictive, and early birds enjoy specially priced meals.

1132 Loma (off Orange Ave.). ✆ **619/435-0661.** www.chezloma.com. Reservations recommended. Main courses $20–$30. AE, DC, MC, V. Daily 5–10pm; Sun brunch 10am–2pm. Bus: 901, 902, or 904.

MODERATE

Bay Beach Cafe AMERICAN   This loud, friendly gathering place isn't on a real beach, but enjoys a prime perch on San Diego Bay. Seated indoors or on a glassed-in patio, diners gaze endlessly at the city skyline, which is dramatic by day and breathtaking at night. The cafe is quite popular at happy hour, when the setting sun glimmers on downtown's mirrored high-rises. The ferry docks at a wooden pier a few steps away, discharging passengers into the complex of gift shops and restaurants with a New England fishing-village theme. Admittedly, the food takes a back seat to the view, but the lunchtime menu of burgers, sandwiches, salads, and appetizers is modestly priced and satisfying; dinner entrees—chops and pastas—aren't quite good enough for the price.

1201 First St. (Ferry Landing Marketplace). (C) **619/435-4900.** Reservations recommended for dinner on weekends. Main courses $9–$11 lunch, $14–$19 dinner. DISC, MC, V. Mon–Fri 11am–9pm; Sat–Sun 8am–9pm. Free parking. Bus: 901, 903, or 904.

Rhinoceros Cafe & Grill 𝕮 AMERICAN   With its quirky name and something-for-everyone menu, this light, bright bistro is a welcome addition to the Coronado dining scene. It's more casual than it looks from the street and offers large portions, though the kitchen can be a little heavy-handed with sauces and spices. At lunch, every other patron seems to be enjoying the popular penne à la vodka in creamy tomato sauce; favorite dinner specials are Italian cioppino, Southwestern-style meatloaf, and simple herb-roasted chicken. Plenty of crispy fresh salads balance out the menu. There's a good wine list, or you might decide to try Rhino Chaser's American Ale.

1166 Orange Ave. (C) **619/435-2121.** Main courses $10–$22. AE, DISC, MC, V. Daily 11am–2:45pm, Sun–Thurs 5–9pm; Fri–Sat 5–10pm. Street parking usually available. Bus: 901, 902, or 904.

INEXPENSIVE

Clayton's Coffee Shop AMERICAN/BREAKFAST   The Hotel Del isn't the only relic of a bygone era in Coronado—just wait until you see this humble neighborhood favorite. Clayton's has occupied this corner spot seemingly forever, at least since a time when *everyone's* menus were full of plain American good eatin' in the $1-to-$5 range. Now their horseshoe counter, chrome barstools, and well-worn pleather-lined booths are "retro," but the burgers, fries, and chicken noodle soup are just as good—plus you can still play three oldies for a quarter on the table-side jukebox. Behind the restaurant, Clayton's Mexican takeout kitchen does a brisk business in homemade tamales.

959 Orange Ave. (C) **619/437-8811.** Menu items under $10. No credit cards. Mon–Sat 6am–8pm; Sun 6am–2pm. Bus: 901, 902, or 904.

Primavera Pastry Caffe 𝕮 *Value* BREAKFAST/LIGHT FARE   If the name sounds familiar, it's because this fantastic little cafe—the best of its kind on the island—is part of the family that includes

Primavera Ristorante, up the street. In addition to fresh-roasted coffee and espresso drinks, it serves omelets and other breakfast treats (until 1:30pm), burgers and deli sandwiches on the delicious house bread, and a daily fresh soup. It's the kind of spot where half the customers are greeted by name. Locals rave about the "Yacht Club" sandwich, a croissant filled with yellowfin tuna, and the breakfast croissant, topped with scrambled ham and eggs and cheddar cheese. I can't resist Primavera's fat, gooey cinnamon buns.

956 Orange Ave. ℭ 619/435-4191. Main courses $4–$7. MC, V. Daily 6:30am–5pm (closes at 6pm in summer). Bus: 901, 902, or 904.

7 Off the Beaten Path

Don't limit your dining experience in San Diego to the main tourist zones outlined above. Five minutes north of Mission Valley is the mostly business neighborhood of Kearny Mesa, home to San Diego's best Asian venues, including **Emerald Restaurant** ⋦⋦, 3709 Convoy St. (ℭ 858/565-6888). Its kitchen exhibits finesse with southern Chinese delicacies and always has excellent (sometimes pricey) live fish specials. Nearby is **Jasmine** ⋦, 4609 Convoy St. (ℭ 858/268-0888), which at lunch showcases Hong Kong–style dumplings that are wheeled around the room on carts.

Just east of Hillcrest (south and parallel to Mission Valley) is Adams Avenue, where you'll find the **Kensington Grill** ⋦⋦, 4055 Adams Ave. next to the Ken Cinema (ℭ 619/281-4014), owned by the same crew in charge of the Gaslamp's hip Chive restaurant and featuring contemporary American cuisine in a chic setting. In nearby Normal Heights, **Jyoti Bihanga,** 3351 Adams Ave. (ℭ 619/282-4116), delivers a cheap vegetarian menu of Indian-influenced salads, wraps, and curries; the "neatloaf" is a winner.

6

Exploring San Diego

You won't run out of things to see and do, especially if outdoor activities are high on the agenda. The San Diego Zoo, SeaWorld, and the Wild Animal Park are the city's three top attractions, but leave room in the schedule for Balboa Park's museums, downtown's Gaslamp Quarter, the beaches, shopping in Old Town, and perhaps a performance at one of our prized live theaters.

1 The Three Major Animal Parks

San Diego Zoo ★★★ *Kids*   More than 4,000 creatures reside at this celebrated, influential zoo, run by the Zoological Society of San Diego. Started in 1916, in the early days the zoo's founder, Dr. Harry Wegeforth, traveled around the world and bartered native Southwestern animals such as rattlesnakes and sea lions for more exotic species. The zoo is also an accredited botanical garden, lavished with more than 700,000 plants; "Dr. Harry" brought home plants from every location where he acquired animals, ensuring what would become the zoo's naturalistic and mature environment.

The zoo is one of only four in the U.S. with giant pandas, and many other rare species live here, including Buerger's tree kangaroos of New Guinea, long-billed kiwis from New Zealand, wild Przewalski's horses from Mongolia, lowland gorillas from Africa, and giant tortoises from the Galapagos. The Zoological Society is involved with animal preservation efforts around the world and has engineered many "firsts" in breeding. The zoo was also a forerunner in creating barless, moated enclosures that allow animals to roam in sophisticated environments resembling their natural ones.

The **Monkey Trails and Forest Tales** is the largest, most elaborate habitat in the zoo's history, recreating a wooded forest full of endangered species such as the mandrill monkey, clouded leopard, and pygmy hippopotamus. An elevated trail through the treetops allows for close observation of the primate, bird, and plant life that thrives in the forest canopy. **Absolutely Apes** showcases orangutans and siamangs of Indonesia; while next door is **Gorilla Tropics,** where two troops of Western lowland gorillas roam an 8,000-square-foot habitat. Despite the hype, I find the **Giant Panda Research Center** *not* worth the hassle when a long line is in place (lines are shortest first thing in the morning or toward the end of the day). More noteworthy is **Ituri Forest,** which simulates a central African rainforest with forest buffalos, otters, okapis, and hippos, which are viewed underwater from a glassed-in enclosure; and the **Polar Bear Plunge,** where you'll find a 2¼-acre summer tundra habitat populated by Siberian reindeer, yellow-throated martens, and diving ducks, as well as polar bears. The **Children's Zoo** features a nursery with baby animals and a petting area where kids can cuddle up to sheep, goats, and the like. There's also a **sea lion show** at the 3,000-seat amphitheater (easy to skip if you're headed to SeaWorld).

If a lot of walking—some of it on steep hills—isn't your passion, a 40-minute **Guided Bus Tour** provides a narrated overview and covers about 75% of the facility. It costs $10 for adults, $5.50 for children 3 to 11; it's included in the so-called "Best Value" admission package. Since you get only brief glimpses of the enclosures, and animals won't always be visible, you'll want to revisit some areas. Included in the bus ticket is access to the un-narrated **Express Bus,** which allows you to get on and off at one of five different stops along the same route. You can also get an aerial perspective from the **Skyfari,** which costs $3 per person each way, though you won't see many creatures. Ideally, take the complete bus tour first thing in the morning, when the animals are more active (waits for the bus tour can top an hour by midday). After the bus tour, take the Skyfari to the far side of the park and wend your way back on foot or by Express Bus to revisit animals you missed.

In addition to several fast-food options, the restaurant **Albert's** is a beautiful oasis at the lip of a canyon and a lovely place in which to break up the day.

2920 Zoo Dr., Balboa Park. ℂ **619/234-3153** (recorded info), or 619/231-1515. www.sandiegozoo.org. Admission $21 adults, $14 children 3–11, free for military in uniform. The "Best Value" package (admission, guided bus tour, round-trip Skyfari aerial tram) $32 adults, $29 seniors, $20 children. AE, DISC, MC, V. Sept to mid-June daily 9am–4pm (grounds close at 5 or 6pm); mid-June to Aug daily 9am–8pm (grounds close at 9pm). Bus: 7, 7A/B. Interstate 5 south to Pershing Dr., follow signs.

San Diego Wild Animal Park 𝑅𝑅𝑅 *(Kids)*   Located 34 miles north of San Diego, outside of Escondido, this terrific "zoo of the future" will transport you to the African plains and other faraway landscapes. Originally started as a breeding facility for the San

San Diego Area Attractions

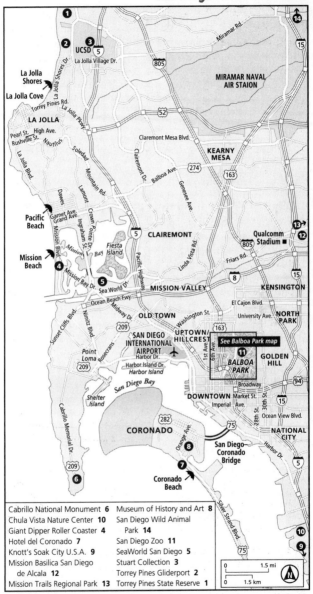

Cabrillo National Monument **6**
Chula Vista Nature Center **10**
Giant Dipper Roller Coaster **4**
Hotel del Coronado **7**
Knott's Soak City U.S.A. **9**
Mission Basilica San Diego
   de Alcala **12**
Mission Trails Regional Park **13**
Museum of History and Art **8**
San Diego Wild Animal
   Park **14**
San Diego Zoo **11**
SeaWorld San Diego **5**
Stuart Collection **3**
Torrey Pines Gliderport **2**
Torrey Pines State Reserve **1**

(Value) Now *That's* a Deal!

San Diego's three main animal attractions have joined forces to offer combo tickets—and big savings. Here's how it works: If you plan to visit both the zoo and Wild Animal Park, a two-park ticket (the "Best Value" zoo package, plus Wild Animal Park admission) is $54 for adults, $34 for children 3 to 11 (for a $61/$37 value). You get one visit to each attraction, to be used within 5 days of purchase. Or throw in SeaWorld within the same 5 days, and the combo works out to $99 for adults, $75 children ages 3 to 9 (a $111/$78 value).

Other value options include the **San Diego Passport** ($79 for adults, $45 for children 3–11), which includes zoo admission, an Old Town Trolley city tour, Hornblower bay cruises, and more; passports are sold at the attractions themselves. **City Pass** (© 707/256-0490, www.citypass.com) covers the zoo, SeaWorld, Disneyland Resorts, and Knott's Berry Farm in Orange County; passes are $185 for adults, and $127 for kids age 3 to 9 (a $266/$184 value), valid for 14 days.

Diego Zoo, the 1,800-acre Wild Animal Park now holds 3,500 animals representing 430 different species. What makes the Park unique is that many of the animals roam freely in vast enclosures, allowing giraffe to interact with antelopes, much as they would in Africa. You'll find the largest crash of rhinos at any zoological facility in the world, an exhibit for the critically endangered California condor, and a mature landscape of exotic vegetation from many corners of the globe. Although the San Diego Zoo may be "world famous," it is the Wild Animal Park that many visitors celebrate as their favorite—to me, both are essential components of the San Diego experience.

The central focus is the 5-mile **Wgasa Bush Line Railway** ⟨★★, a 60-minute monorail ride that's included in the price of admission. Trains leave every 10 minutes or so from the station, and lines build up by late morning—make this your first or last attraction of the day (the animals are more active anyway). The monorail passes through areas designated as East Africa, South Africa, Asian Plains, and the Asian Waterhole, through swaying grasses and along rocky outcrops. Although many of the animals can be hundreds of feet away, the monorail is not meant to give you the up close experience of a traditional zoo, but to experience the open plains and wildlife diversity.

Other exhibits bring you closer to the animals, like the three self-guided **walking tours** ⭐⭐, which visit various habitats. **Nairobi Village** is the commercial hub of the park, but even here are interesting animal exhibits, including the **nursery area,** where irresistible young 'uns can be seen frolicking, being bottle-fed, and sleeping; a **petting station;** the **lowland gorillas** ⭐; and the **South American Aviary** ⭐. There are amphitheaters for a bird show and another featuring elephants, scheduled two or three times daily. Within Nairobi Village are souvenir stores, and several spots for mediocre dining. Visitors should be prepared for sunny, often downright hot weather (it's not unusual for temperatures to be 5 to 10 degrees warmer here than in San Diego).

If you want to get up-close-and-personal with the animals, take one of the park's **Photo Caravans,** which shuttle groups of eight in flatbed trucks out into the open areas that are inaccessible to the general public. Two different itineraries are available, each 1¾ hours long, and you'll want to make reservations ahead of your visit (📞 **619/718-3050**). The price is $90 per person for one caravan (park admission not included), or $130 for both; children must be at least 8 years old, and ages 8 through 17 must be accompanied by an adult. The new **Cheetah Run Safari** allows a limited number of guests (reservations required, 📞 **619/718-3000**) to watch the world's fastest land mammal in action, sprinting after a mechanical lure. Cost is $69 per person, excluding park admission.

15500 San Pasqual Valley Rd., Escondido. 📞 760/747-8702. www.wildanimal park.org. Admission $29 adults, $26 seniors 60 and over, $18 children 3–11, free for children under 3 and military in uniform. AE, DISC, MC, V. Daily 9am–4pm (grounds close at 5pm); extended hours during summer and Festival of Lights (2 weekends in Dec). Parking $8. Take I-15 to Via Rancho Pkwy.; follow signs for about 3 miles.

SeaWorld San Diego ⭐⭐ (Kids)   One of California's most heavily marketed attractions, SeaWorld is a big draw for a number of visitors coming to San Diego. The aquatic theme park celebrated its 40th year of operation in 2004. With each passing year the educational pretext increasingly takes a back seat to slick shows and rides, but the park—owned by the Anheuser-Busch Corporation—is perhaps still the country's premiere showplace for marine life, made politically correct with a nominally informative atmosphere. At its heart, SeaWorld is a shoreside family entertainment center where the performers are dolphins, otters, sea lions, orcas, and seals. The 20-minute shows run several times each throughout the day, with visitors rotating through the various open-air amphitheaters and aquarium features.

Several successive 4-ton black-and-white killer whales have functioned as the park's mascot, and the **Shamu Adventure** ✦✦✦ is SeaWorld's most popular show. Performed in a 5,500-seat stadium, the stage is a 7-million-gallon pool lined with Plexiglas walls that magnify the huge performers. But think twice before you sit in the seats down front—a high point of the act is multiple drenchings of the first 12 or so rows of spectators. Most days, the venue fills before the two or three performances even start, so arrive early to get the seat you want. The slapstick **Fools with Tools** (sea lions and otters), the fast-paced **Dolphin Discovery** ✦, and **Pets Rule!** are other performing animal routines, each in arenas seating more than 2,000. There are also shows focusing on humans: a "4-D" movie; *R.L. Stine's Haunted Lighthouse,* starring a roster of multi-sensory effects; and in summer, **Cirque de la Mer,** which features acrobatic acts.

The collection of rides is led by **Journey to Atlantis** ✦, a 2004 arrival which combines a roller coaster and log flume with Atlantis mythology and a simulated earthquake. **Shipwreck Rapids** ✦ is a splashy adventure on raft-like inner tubes through caverns, waterfalls, and wild rivers; and **Wild Arctic** is a motion simulator helicopter trip to the frozen north. The **Skytower** and **Skyride** each cost an additional $3 to ride.

Guests disembarking Wild Arctic (or those using the ride bypass) find themselves in the midst of one of SeaWorld's real specialties: simulated marine environments. In this case it's an **arctic research station** ✦, surrounded by beautiful beluga whales, walruses, and polar bears. Other animal environments worth seeing are **Manatee Rescue, Shark Encounter,** and the **Penguin Encounter.** Each of these attractions exits into a gift shop selling theme merchandise. The 2-acre hands-on area called **Shamu's Happy Harbor** is designed for kids, and features everything from a pretend pirate ship, with plenty of netted towers, to tube crawls, slides, and chances to get wet.

The **Dolphin Interaction Program** creates an opportunity for people to meet bottlenose dolphins. Although the program stops short of allowing you to swim with the dolphins, it does offer the opportunity to wade waist-deep, and plenty of time to stroke the mammals and to try giving training commands. This 1-hour program includes some classroom time before you wriggle into a wet suit and climb into the water for 20 minutes with the dolphins. It costs $140 per person (not including park admission); participants must be age 6 or older. One step further is the **Trainer for a Day** program, which is a 7-hour work shift with an animal trainer. Food preparation, feeding, a training session with a dolphin, and lunch is included; the price is $395 per person. This program is limited to three participants daily, and the minimum age is 13. Advance reservations are required for both programs (© **877/436-5746**).

Although SeaWorld is best known as the home to pirouetting dolphins and fluke-flinging killer whales, the facility also plays a role in rescuing and rehabilitating beached animals found along the West Coast—including an average of 200 seals, sea lions, marine birds, and dolphins annually, almost 65% of which are rehabilitated and returned to the wild.

500 Sea World Dr., Mission Bay. © **800/380-3203** or 619/226-3901. www.seaworld. com. Admission $51 adults, $41 children 3–9, free for children under 3. AE, DISC, MC, V. Open daily. Hours vary seasonally, but always open 10am–5pm; most weekends and during summer the park opens at 9am and stays open as late as midnight during peak periods. Parking $7. Bus: 9 or 27. From I-5, take SeaWorld Dr. exit; from I-8, take W. Mission Bay Dr. exit to Sea World Dr.

2 San Diego's Beaches

San Diego County is blessed with 70 miles of sandy coastline and more than 30 individual beaches that cater equally to surfers, snorkelers, swimmers, sailors, divers, walkers, volleyballers, and sunbathers. Here's a list of San Diego's most accessible beaches, each with its own personality and devotees. They are listed geographically from south to north.

Note: All beaches are good for swimming except as indicated.

IMPERIAL BEACH
A half-hour south of downtown San Diego by car or trolley, and only a few minutes north of the Mexican border, lies Imperial Beach. The beach boasts 3 miles of surf breaks plus a guarded "swimmers only" stretch. Check with lifeguards before getting wet, though, since sewage runoff from nearby Mexico can sometimes foul the water. I.B. also plays host to the annual **U.S. Open Sandcastle Competition** in late July—the best reason to come here—with world-class sand creations ranging from sea scenes to dragons to dinosaurs.

CORONADO BEACH ☆
Lovely, wide, and sparkling, this beach is conducive to strolling and lingering, especially in the late afternoon. South of the Hotel Del, the beach becomes the beautiful, often deserted **Silver Strand.** The

islands visible from here, Los Coronados, are 18 miles away and belong to Mexico.

OCEAN BEACH

The northern end of Ocean Beach Park is officially known as **Dog Beach,** and is one of only a few in the county where your pooch can roam freely on the sand. Surfers generally congregate around the O.B. Pier, mostly in the water but often at the snack shack on the end. Rip currents can be strong here and discourage most swimmers from venturing beyond waist depth. Facilities at the beach include restrooms, showers, picnic tables, volleyball courts, and plenty of metered parking lots. To reach the beach, take West Point Loma Boulevard all the way to the end.

MISSION BAY PARK

This inland, 4,600-acre aquatic playground contains 27 miles of bayfront, picnic areas, children's playgrounds, and paths for biking, in-line skating, and jogging. The bay lends itself to windsurfing, sailing, water-skiing, and fishing. There are dozens of access points, including the area off I-5 at Clairemont Drive (though this is not my favorite area for swimming); and **Fiesta Island,** where the annual **Over the Line Tournament** is held to raucous enthusiasm in July.

BONITA COVE/MARINER'S POINT & MISSION POINT

Also enclosed in Mission Bay Park (facing the bay, not the ocean), this pretty and protected cove's calm waters, grassy picnic areas, and playground equipment make it perfect for families—or as a paddling destination if you've rented kayaks elsewhere in the bay. The water is cleaner for swimming than in the northeastern reaches of Mission Bay. Get there from Mission Boulevard in south Mission Beach.

MISSION BEACH

While Mission Bay Park is a body of saltwater surrounded by land and bridges, Mission Beach is actually a beach on the Pacific Ocean, anchored by the **Giant Dipper** roller coaster. Always popular, the sands and wide cement "boardwalk" sizzle with activity and great people-watching in summer; at the southern end there's always a volleyball game in play. The long beach and path extend from the jetty north to Belmont Park and Pacific Beach Drive. Parking is often tough, with your best bets being the public lots at Belmont Park or at the south end of West Mission Bay Drive. This busy street is the centerline of a 2-block-wide isthmus which leads a mile north to . . .

San Diego Beaches

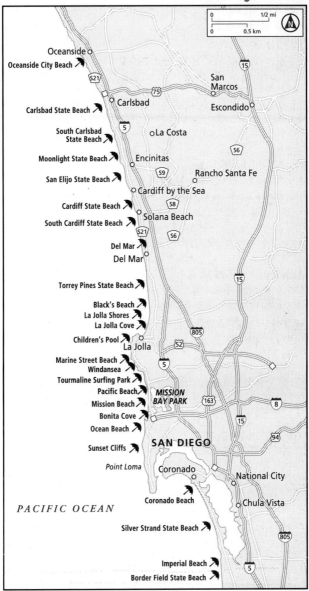

Oceanside

Oceanside City Beach

S21

San Marcos

75 Carlsbad

Escondido

Carlsbad State Beach

5

La Costa

South Carlsbad State Beach

56

Moonlight State Beach

Encinitas

S9

Rancho Santa Fe

San Elijo State Beach

Cardiff by the Sea

Cardiff State Beach

S8

South Cardiff State Beach

Solana Beach

S21

56

Del Mar

Del Mar

15

Torrey Pines State Beach

Black's Beach

La Jolla Shores

La Jolla Cove

805

Children's Pool

La Jolla

52

Marine Street Beach

Windansea

5

Tourmaline Surfing Park

Pacific Beach

MISSION BAY PARK

163

15

8

Mission Beach

Bonita Cove

Ocean Beach

SAN DIEGO

94

Sunset Cliffs

Point Loma

Coronado

National City

Coronado Beach

Chula Vista

PACIFIC OCEAN

Silver Strand State Beach

805

Imperial Beach

5

Border Field State Beach

PACIFIC BEACH

There's always action here, particularly along **Ocean Front Walk,** a paved promenade featuring a human parade akin to that at L.A.'s Venice Beach boardwalk. It runs along Ocean Boulevard (just west of Mission Blvd.) to the pier. Surfing is popular year-round here, in marked sections, and the beach is well staffed with lifeguards. You're on your own to find street parking. Pacific Beach is also the home of **Tourmaline Surfing Park,** a half-mile north of the pier, where the sport's old guard gathers to surf waters where swimmers are prohibited.

WINDANSEA BEACH

The fabled locale of Tom Wolfe's *Pump House Gang,* Windansea is legendary to this day among California's surf elite and remains one of San Diego's prettiest strands. Reached by way of Bonair Street (at Neptune Place), Windansea has no facilities, and street parking is first-come, first-served. Not ideal for swimming, so come to surf, watch surfers, or soak in the camaraderie and party atmosphere.

CHILDREN'S POOL 🦭

A seawall protects this pocket of sand, originally intended as a calm swimming bay for children—many of us first learned to bob in the ocean here. It was also the location of a battle sequence for the movie *The Stuntman.* But since 1994, when a rock outcrop off the shore was designated as a protected mammal reserve, the beach has also been cordoned off for the controversial **harbor seal** population. On an average day you'll spot dozens lolling in the sun. Swimming is now prohibited, as is touching or disturbing the seals, but it's fun to watch them. The beach is at Coast Boulevard and Jenner Street; there's limited free street parking.

LA JOLLA COVE 🦭🦭

The protected, calm waters—celebrated as the clearest along the coast—attract snorkelers and scuba divers, along with a fair share of families. The stunning setting offers a small sandy beach, as well as, on the cliffs above, the **Ellen Browning Scripps Park.** The cove's "look but don't touch" policy protects the colorful garibaldi, California's state fish, plus other marine life, including abalone, octopus, and lobster. The unique Underwater Park stretches from here to the northern end of Torrey Pines State Reserve and incorporates kelp forests, artificial reefs, two deep submarine canyons, and tidal pools.

The Cove is terrific for swimming, cramped for sunbathing, and accessible from Coast Boulevard; parking nearby is free, if sparse.

LA JOLLA SHORES

The wide, flat mile of sand at La Jolla Shores is popular with joggers, swimmers, and beginning body- and board surfers, as well as families. It looks like a picture postcard, with fine sand under blue skies, kissed by gentle waves. In summer, you need to shuffle your feet entering the water so as not to step on occasional (harmless) jellyfish. Weekend crowds can be enormous, though, quickly occupying both the sand and the metered parking spaces in the lot. There are restrooms, showers, and picnic areas here, as well as at the grassy, palm-lined Kellogg Park across the street.

BLACK'S BEACH ⋆

The area's unofficial nude beach, 2-mile-long Black's lies between La Jolla Shores and Torrey Pines State Beach, at the base of steep, 300-foot-high cliffs. The beach is out of the way and not easy to reach, but it draws scores with its secluded beauty and good swimming conditions—the graceful spectacle of hang gliders launching from the cliffs above adds to the show. To get here, take North Torrey Pines Road, park at the Gliderport, and clamber down the makeshift path, staying alert to avoid veering off to one of several false trails. To bypass the cliff descent, you can walk to Black's from beaches north (Torrey Pines) or south (La Jolla Shores). *Note:* There is no permanent lifeguard station, though lifeguards are usually present from spring break to October, and no restroom facilities. Nude sunbathing is *not* legal, and hasn't been since 1977, but citations are rarely issued.

TORREY PINES BEACH ⋆

At the north end of Black's Beach, at the foot of the Torrey Pines State Park, is this fabulous, underused strand, accessed by a pay parking lot at the entrance to the park. In fact, combining a visit to the park with a day at the beach is my concept of the quintessential San Diego insider's experience. It's rarely crowded, though you need to be aware of high tide (when most of the sand gets a bath). In almost any weather, it's a great beach for walking.

DEL MAR BEACH

This long stretch of sand across the city limits in the charming community of Del Mar is backed by grassy cliffs and a playground area.

This area is not heavily trafficked, and you can get a wonderful meal on the beach at Jake's. Del Mar is about 15 miles from downtown San Diego.

3 Attractions in Balboa Park

New York has Central Park, and San Francisco has Golden Gate Park. San Diego's crown jewel is Balboa Park, a 1,174-acre city-owned playground and the largest urban cultural park in the nation. The park was established in 1868 in the heart of the city, bordered by downtown to the southwest and fringed by Hillcrest and Golden Hill to the north and east.

The park's most distinctive features are its mature landscaping, the architectural beauty of the Spanish-Moorish buildings lining **El Prado** (the park's east-west thoroughfare), and the outstanding and diverse museums contained within it. You'll also find eight different gardens, walkways, 4.5 miles of hiking trails in Florida Canyon, historic buildings, several restaurants, an ornate pavilion with the world's largest outdoor organ, a high-spouting fountain, an IMAX domed theater, the acclaimed **Globe Theatres** (p. 132), and the world-famous **San Diego Zoo** (p. 99).

The park is divided by Highway 163 into two distinct sections. The narrow western wing of the park is largely grassy open areas that parallel Sixth Avenue; there are no museums in this section, but it's a good place for picnics, strolling, sunning, and dog walking. The main portion of the park, east of 163, contains the zoo and all of the museums, and is bordered by Park Boulevard; just east is largely undeveloped Florida Canyon. There are two primary entrances to the park. The most distinctive is from Sixth Avenue and Laurel Street: Laurel enters the park via the beautiful **Cabrillo Bridge** across Highway 163 and turns into El Prado. You can also enter via Presidents Way from Park Boulevard, just north of downtown. Major parking areas are at Inspiration Point on the east side of Park Boulevard at Presidents Way, in front of the zoo, and along Presidents Way between the Aerospace Museum and Spreckels Organ Pavilion.

Public **bus routes** 7, 7A, and 7B run along Park Boulevard; for the west side of the park, routes 1, 3, and 25 run along Fourth/Fifth avenues (except for the Marston House, all museums are closer to Park Blvd.). Free **tram** transportation within the park runs daily from 8:30am to 6pm, with extended hours in summer months. The red

Balboa Park

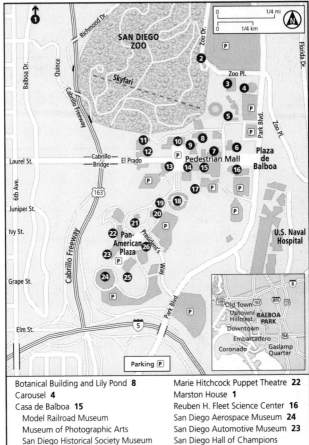

Value **Balboa Park Money-Savers**

If you plan to visit more than three of the park's museums, buy the **Passport to Balboa Park,** a coupon booklet that allows entrance to 13 major museums (the rest are always free) and is valid for 1 week for $30. If you plan to spend a day at the zoo and return for the museums another day, buy the **Best of Balboa Park Combo,** which provides one ticket to the zoo, and 3 days' admission to the 13 museums, for $55. You can purchase the passports at the visitor center and participating museums.

trolley trams originate at the Inspiration Point parking lot to circuit the park, arriving every 8 to 10 minutes and stopping at designated pickup areas. Stop by the **Balboa Park Visitors Center,** located in the House of Hospitality (© **619/239-0512;** www.balboapark.org), to learn about free walking and museum **tours,** or to pick up a brochure about the **gardens** of the park.

Botanical Building and Lily Pond ✿ *Moments*   This is a serene park within the park where ivy, ferns, orchids, impatiens, begonias, and other plants—about 2,100 tropical and flowering varieties, plus rotating exhibits—are sheltered beneath the domed lath house. The striking 250-foot-long building, part of the 1915 Panama-California Exposition, is one of the world's largest wood lath structures, and emerged from a complete renovation in 2002. Kids love the "touch and smell" garden and the smelly bog of carnivorous plants; the lily pond out front attracts sun worshipers, painters, and street entertainers.

1549 El Prado. © **619/235-1100.** Free admission. Fri–Wed 10am–4pm; closed Thurs and major holidays. Bus: 7 or 7A/B.

House of Pacific Relations International Cottages   This cluster of 17 charming one- and two-room cottages disseminates information about the culture, traditions, and history of 28 countries. Light refreshments are served, and outdoor lawn programs are presented on Sundays, March through October. The adjacent **United Nations Building** houses an international gift shop where you can buy jewelry, toys, books, and UNICEF greeting cards (© **619/233-5044**); it's open daily from 10am to 4pm.

Adjacent to Pan American Plaza. © **619/234-0739.** Free admission (donations welcome). Sun noon–4pm; 2nd and 4th Tues of each month 11am–3pm. Bus: 7 or 7A/B.

Japanese Friendship Garden *(Finds)* Of the 11½ acres designated for the garden, only 1 acre—a beautiful, peaceful one—has been developed. The garden's Information Center shows a model of the future installation, San-Kei-En (Three-Scenery Garden). A self-guided tour is available at the main gate. From the gate, a crooked path (to confound evil spirits, who move only in a straight line) threads its way to the information center in a Zen-style house; here you can view the most ancient kind of garden, the *sekitei,* made only of sand and stone.

2125 Park Blvd., adjacent to the Organ Pavilion. ✆ **619/232-2721.** www.niwa. org. Admission $3 adults, $2.50 seniors, $2 students and military, free for children 6 and under. Free 3rd Tues of each month. Tues–Sun 10am–4pm. Bus: 7 or 7A/B.

Marston House ⚘ Noted San Diego architect Irving Gill designed this house in 1905 for George Marston, a local businessman and philanthropist. Listed on the National Register of Historic Places and now managed by the San Diego Historical Society, the house is a classic example of Craftsman-style architecture, reminiscent of the work of Frank Lloyd Wright. Some of its interesting features are wide hallways, brick fireplaces, and redwood paneling. Opened to the public in 1991, it contains few original pieces, but does exhibit Roycroft, Stickley, and Lampert furniture and is slowly being furnished with Craftsman-era pieces or copies as funds become available. Tours take about 45 minutes.

3525 Seventh Ave. (northwest corner of Balboa Park at Balboa Dr. and Upas St.). ✆ **619/298-3142.** Guided tour $5 adults, $4 seniors and students, free for children 5 and under. Fri–Sun 10am–4:30pm (last tour at 3:45pm). Bus: 1, 3, or 25.

Mingei International Museum ⚘⚘ This captivating museum (pronounced *min*-gay, meaning "art of the people" in Japanese) offers changing exhibitions generally describable as folk art. The rotating exhibits—usually four at a time—feature artists from countries across the globe; displays include textiles, costumes, jewelry, toys, pottery, paintings, and sculpture. The small permanent collection includes whimsical contemporary sculptures by the late French artist Niki de Saint Phalle, who made San Diego her home in 1993. Martha Longenecker, a potter and professor emeritus of art at San Diego State University, founded the museum in 1977. It is one of only two major museums in the United States devoted to folk crafts on a worldwide scale (the other is in Santa Fe, New Mexico), and is well worth a look. Allow half an hour to an hour to view the collection.

1439 El Prado, in the House of Charm. ✆ 619/239-0003. www.mingei.org. Admission $6 adults, $3 children 6–17 and students with ID, free for children under 6. AE, MC, V. Free 3rd Tues of each month. Tues–Sun 10am–4pm. Bus: 7 or 7A/B.

Museum of Photographic Arts ★★

If names like Ansel Adams and Edward Weston stimulate your fingers to do the shutterbug, then don't miss a taste of the 7,000-plus collection of images housed by this museum—one of few in the United States devoted exclusively to the photographic arts (which, at MOPA, encompasses cinema, video, and digital photography). A 1999 expansion allowed the museum to display even more of the permanent collection, while leaving room for provocative traveling exhibits that change every few months. Allow 30 to 60 minutes to see the collection. The plush cinema illuminates classic films Friday, Saturday, and some weeknights.

1649 El Prado. ✆ 619/238-7559. www.mopa.org. Admission $6 adults, $4 seniors and students, free for children under 12 with adult; cinema admission $7 adults, $6 seniors and students. Free 2nd Tues of each month. Fri–Wed 10am–5pm; Thurs 10am–9pm. Bus: 7 or 7A/B.

Reuben H. Fleet Science Center ★ Kids

A must-see for kids of any age is this tantalizing collection of interactive exhibits and rides designed to provoke the imagination and teach scientific principles. The Virtual Zone includes SciTours, a motion-simulator ride that lurches you into virtual deep sea, plus two different virtual reality attractions with a scientific bent. The Fleet also houses a 76-foot-high IMAX Dome Theater that shows films so realistic that ocean footage can actually give you motion sickness! And in 2001, the Fleet unveiled a spiffy new planetarium simulator powered by computer graphics.

1875 El Prado. ✆ 619/238-1233. www.rhfleet.org. Fleet Experience admission includes 1 IMAX film and exhibit galleries: $12 adults, $10 seniors 65 and over, $9 children 3–12 (exhibit gallery can be purchased individually). Free 1st Tues of each month (exhibit galleries only). AE, DISC, MC, V. Open daily 9:30am; closing times vary, but always until at least 5pm. Bus: 7 or 7A/B.

San Diego Aerospace Museum ★★ Kids

The other big kid-pleaser of the museums (along with the Fleet Science Center, above), this popular facility provides an overview of the nation's air-and-space history, from the days of hot-air balloons to the space age, with plenty of biplanes and military fighters in between. It emphasizes local aviation history, particularly the construction here of the *Spirit of St. Louis*. Highlights include the only GPS Satellite on display in a museum, and a World War I–era Spad. The museum is housed in a stunning cylindrical hall built by the Ford Motor Company in 1935 (for the park's second international expo), and has an imaginative gift shop with items like old-fashioned leather flight hoods and new-fashioned freeze-dried astronaut ice cream. Allow at least an hour for your visit.

2001 Pan American Plaza. ✆ 619/234-8291. www.aerospacemuseum.org. Admission $9 adults, $7 seniors, $4 juniors 6–17, free for active military with ID and children under 6. Free 4th Tues of each month. Sept–May daily 10am–4:30pm; June–Aug daily 10am–5:30pm. Bus: 7 or 7A/B.

San Diego Automotive Museum ⛟

Even if you don't know a distributor from a dipstick, you're bound to ooh-and-aah over the classic, antique, and exotic cars here. Every one is so pristine you'd swear it just rolled off the line, from an 1886 Benz to a 1931 Rolls Royce Phaeton to the 1981 DeLorean. Most of the time, temporary shows take over the facility, so check ahead to see if it's one you're interested in. Some days you can take a peek at the ongoing restoration program, and the museum sponsors many outdoor car rallies and other events. Allow 30 to 45 minutes for your visit.

2080 Pan American Plaza. ✆ 619/231-2886. www.sdautomuseum.org. Admission $7 adults, $6 seniors and active military, $3 children 6–15, free for children under 6. Free 4th Tues of each month. MC, V. Daily 10am–5pm (last admission 4:30pm). Bus: 7 or 7A/B.

San Diego Hall of Champions Sports Museum

One of the country's few multisport museums, the slick Hall of Champions has been a destination for sports fans since 1961. The museum highlights more than 40 professional and amateur sports. More than 25 exhibits surround a centerpiece statue, the *Discus Thrower.* One particularly interesting exhibit is devoted to athletes with disabilities. You can see it all in under an hour.

2131 Pan American Plaza. ✆ 619/234-2544. www.sandiegosports.org. Admission $6 adults, $4 seniors 65 and older and military, $3 children 6–17, free for children under 6. Free 4th Tues of each month. Daily 10am–4:30pm. Bus: 7 or 7A/B.

San Diego Historical Society Museum

A good place to start if you are a newcomer to San Diego, the recently remodeled museum offers permanent and changing exhibits on topics related to the history of the region, from pioneer outposts in the 1800s to the present day. Many of the museum's photographs depict Balboa Park and the growth of the city. Plan to spend about 30 to 45 minutes here. Docent tours are available; call ✆ 619/232-6203, ext. 117, for information and reservations. Books about San Diego's history are available in the gift shop.

1649 El Prado, in Casa del Balboa. ℂ **619/232-6203.** www.sandiegohistory.org. Admission $6 adults, $4 students, seniors, and military with ID, $2 children 6–12, free for children 5 and under. Free 2nd Tues of each month. Tues–Sun 10am–4:30pm. Bus: 7 or 7A/B.

San Diego Model Railroad Museum ⚡ *Kids*

Okay, so it's not high culture as we know it, but this museum is cool and pleasing, and worth 30 to 60 minutes of your time, especially if you have kids in tow. Six permanent, scale-model railroads depict Southern California's transportation history and terrain with an astounding attention to miniature details—the exhibits occupy a 24,000-square-foot space. Children will enjoy the hands-on Lionel trains, and train buffs of all ages will appreciate the interactive multimedia displays. Allow a half-hour to an hour for your visit.

1649 El Prado (Casa de Balboa), under the Museum of Photographic Arts. ℂ **619/ 696-0199.** www.sdmodelrailroadm.com. Admission $5 adults, $4 seniors, $3 student, $2.50 military; free for children under 15. Free 1st Tues of each month. Tues–Fri 11am–4pm; Sat–Sun 11am–5pm. Bus: 7 or 7A/B.

San Diego Museum of Art ⚡

With one of the grandest entrances along El Prado—the rotunda at the head of dramatic stairs features striking Spanish tile work—the museum is known for its outstanding collection of Spanish baroque painting, and possibly the largest horde of Indian paintings outside India. The American collection includes works by Georgia O'Keeffe and Thomas Eakins, and San Diegans like Maurice Braun and Dan Dickey are represented. Over 12,000 pieces are part of the permanent collection, only a small percentage of which is on display at any given time, in favor of varied, often prestigious touring shows. The museum's high-tech touch is an interactive computer-image system that allows visitors to custom design a tour. Plan to spend at least an hour here.

1450 El Prado. ℂ **619/232-7931.** www.sdmart.org. Admission $9 adults 25 and older, $7 seniors, military, and youths 18–24, $4 children 6–17, free for children under 6. Admission to traveling exhibits varies. Free 3rd Tues of each month. Tues–Sun 10am–6pm (Thurs until 9pm). Bus: 7 or 7A/B.

San Diego Museum of Man

Located under the iconic, rococo, tiled **California building and bell tower** ⚡⚡ just inside the park entrance at the Cabrillo Bridge, this museum is devoted to anthropology, with an emphasis on the peoples of North and South America. Favorite exhibits include life-size replicas of a dozen varieties of Homo sapiens, from Cro-Magnon and Neanderthal to Peking Man, and a small room featuring Egyptian mummies and artifacts. Don't overlook the annex across the street, which houses more exhibits, and the lady making fresh tortillas and quesadillas Wednesday through Sunday. Allow at least an hour for your visit.

1350 El Prado. ✆ 619/239-2001. www.museumofman.org. Admission $6 adults, $5 seniors, $3 children 6–17, free for children under 6. Free 3rd Tues of the month. Daily 10am–4:30pm. Bus: 1, 3, 7, 7A/B, or 25.

San Diego Natural History Museum   This museum focuses on the flora, fauna, and mineralogy of Southern and Baja California. Kids marvel at the animals they find here, including live snakes, tarantulas, and turtles. As a binational museum, research is done on both sides of the border and most exhibits are bilingual. You can see them all in about half an hour. Call or check the museum's website for a current schedule of special visiting exhibits. There's a 300-seat large-format movie theater, and two films are included in the price of admission.

1788 El Prado. ✆ 619/232-3821. www.sdnhm.org. Admission $8 adults, $6 seniors and active-duty military, $5 children 3–17, free for children under 3. Free 1st Tues of each month. Daily 9:30am–4:30pm; open till 5:30pm in summer. Bus: 7 or 7A/B.

SDAI Museum of the Living Artist   Around since 1941, the San Diego Art Institute now has a museum to house exhibits of new artwork by local artists. The 10,000-square-foot municipal gallery rotates juried shows in and out every 4 to 6 weeks, ensuring a variety of mediums and styles. It's a good place to see what the local art community is up to. Plan to spend about half an hour here.

1439 El Prado. ✆ 619/236-0011. www.sandiego-art.org. Admission $3 adults, $2 seniors and students, free to children 12 and under. Free 3rd Tues of the month. Tues–Sat 10am–4pm; Sun noon–4pm. Bus: 7 or 7A/B.

Spreckels Organ Pavilion   Given to San Diego citizens in 1914 by brothers John D. and Adolph Spreckels, the ornate, curved pavilion houses a magnificent organ with over 4,500 individual pipes. They range in length from less than a half-inch to more than 32 feet. With only brief interruptions, the organ has been in continuous use in the park, and today visitors can enjoy free hour-long concerts on Sundays at 2pm. There's seating for 2,400.

South of El Prado. ✆ 619/702-8138. Free 1-hr. organ concerts Sun 2pm year-round; free organ concerts July–Aug Mon 7:30pm; free Twilight in the Park concerts Tues–Thurs mid-June to Aug (call ✆ 619/235-1105 for schedule). Bus: 7 or 7A/B.

Timken Museum of Art ✵ *Finds*   This jewel-like repository houses the Putnam Foundation's collection of 19th-century American paintings and works by European old masters, as well as a worthy display of Russian icons. Yes, it's a small horde, but it's free, and the marquee attractions include a Peter Paul Rubens, *Portrait of a Young Man in Armor;* San Diego's only Rembrandt, *St. Bartholomew;* and a masterpiece by Eastman Johnson, *The Cranberry Harvest.* Because you can tour all of the museum in well under an hour, the Timken also makes for an easy introduction to fine art for younger travelers (pick up a copy of the *Children's Gallery Guide* for $2). Docents are available Tuesday from 10am to noon and 1 to 3pm; Wednesday and Thursday from 10 to noon; or by appointment.

1500 El Prado. ℂ **619/239-5548.** www.timkenmuseum.org. Free admission. Tues–Sat 10am–4:30pm; Sun 1:30–4:30pm. Closed Sept. Bus: 7 or 7A/B.

4 More Attractions

DOWNTOWN & BEYOND

In 2004, downtown San Diego completed a huge construction project, the Padres' **PETCO Park** (p. 145) which has extended the rebuilt downtown a few blocks farther east. Real estate developers in the "East Village" are stepping up to the plate in hopes of cashing in on a home run.

In the meantime, you can wander from the turn-of-the-20th-century **Gaslamp Quarter** 𝄞𝄞 to the joyful, modern architecture of the **Horton Plaza** 𝄞 shopping center (p. 148). The Gaslamp consists of 16½ blocks of restored historic buildings. It gets its name from the old-fashioned street lamps that line the sidewalks. You'll find many of San Diego's best restaurants and our most vigorous nightlife scene here.

Cabrillo National Monument 𝄞𝄞   Sweeping views mingle with the early history of San Diego, which began when Juan Rodríguez Cabrillo arrived in 1542. His statue dominates the tip of Point Loma, which is also a vantage point for watching migrating Pacific gray whales en route from the Arctic Ocean to Baja California December through March. A tour of the restored lighthouse (1855) illuminates what life was like here more than a century ago. National Park Service rangers lead walks at the monument, and there are tide pools at the base of the peninsula that beg for exploration. Free 30-minute films on Cabrillo, tide pools, and the whales are shown on the hour daily from 10am to 4pm. The drive from downtown takes about a half-hour.

1800 Cabrillo Memorial Dr., Point Loma. ℂ **619/557-5450.** www.nps.gov/cabr. Admission $5 per vehicle, $3 for walk-ins. Daily 9am–5:15pm. Bus: 26. By car, take I-8 west to Rosecrans St., right on Canon St., left on Catalina and follow signs.

Firehouse Museum *(Kids)*   Appropriately housed in San Diego's oldest firehouse, the museum features shiny fire engines, including hand-drawn and horse-drawn models, a 1903 steam pumper, and memorabilia such as antique alarms, fire hats, and foundry molds for fire hydrants. There's also a small gift shop. Allow about half an hour for your visit.

1572 Columbia St. (at Cedar St.). ✆ **619/232-FIRE.** Admission $2 adults, $1 seniors and military in uniform, $1 youths 13–17, free for children under 13. Thurs–Fri 10am–2pm; Sat–Sun 10am–4pm. Bus: 5 or 16. Trolley: America Plaza.

Maritime Museum *(Kids)*   This unique museum consists of a trio of fine ships: the full-rigged merchant vessel the *Star of India* (1863), whose impressive masts are an integral part of the San Diego cityscape; the gleaming white San Francisco–Oakland steam-powered ferry the *Berkeley* (1898), which worked round-the-clock to carry people to safety following the 1906 San Francisco earthquake; and the sleek *Medea* (1904), one of the world's few remaining large steam yachts. You can board and explore each vessel. Allow 45 minutes to an hour for your visit.

1306 N. Harbor Dr. ✆ **619/234-9153.** www.sdmaritime.com. Admission $10 adults, $8 seniors over 62 and youths 13–17, $7 children 6–12, free for children under 6. Daily 9am–8pm. Bus: 2, 4, 20, 23, or 29. Trolley: America Plaza.

Museum of Contemporary Art San Diego Downtown Opened in 1993, the downtown branch is the second location of the Museum of Contemporary Art (the original branch is in La Jolla). Two large and two smaller galleries present changing exhibitions of nationally and internationally distinguished contemporary artists; plan to spend about half an hour here. Lectures and tours for adults and children are also offered. In 2005, MCA takes over the baggage building of the Santa Fe depot across the street, which will almost triple the exhibition space at this branch, making it the preeminent museum downtown.

1001 Kettner Blvd. (at Broadway). ✆ **619/234-1001.** www.mcasd.org. Free admission. Thurs–Tues 11am–5pm. Parking $2 with validation at America Plaza Complex. Bus: 2, 4, 7, 7A/B, 15, 20, 23, 34, or 115. Trolley: America Plaza.

Villa Montezuma *(Finds)*   This exquisite mansion just southeast of downtown was built in 1887 for internationally acclaimed musician and author Jesse Shepard. Lush with Victoriana, it features more stained glass than most churches are blessed with. The striking ceilings are of Lincrusta Walton—pressed canvas coated with linseed oil, a forerunner of linoleum, which never looked this good.

Shepard lived here with his life companion, Lawrence Tonner, for only 2 years, and died in obscurity in Los Angeles in 1927. The San Diego Historical Society painstakingly restored the house, which is on the National Register of Historic Places, and furnished it with period pieces. The neighborhood is not as fashionable as the building, but it's safe to park your car in the daytime. If you love Victorian houses, don't miss this one for its quirkiness. Join the 45-minute docent-led tour, which begins every hour on the hour (except the last tour, which starts at 3:45pm).

1925 K St. (at 20th St.). © **619/239-2211.** Admission $5 adults, $4 seniors, military, and students, $2 children 6–17, free for children 5 and under. Fri–Sun 10am–4:30pm. Bus: 3, 3A, 5, or 16. By car, follow Market St. east, turn right on 20th St. and follow it to K St.

William Heath Davis House Museum   Shipped by boat to San Diego in 1850 from Portland, Maine, this is the oldest structure in the Gaslamp Quarter. It is a well-preserved example of a prefabricated "saltbox" family home, and has remained structurally unchanged for more than 150 years. A museum, on the first and second floors, is open to the public, as is the small park adjacent to the house. The house is also home to the Gaslamp Quarter Historical Foundation, which sponsors walking tours of the quarter for $8 ($6 for seniors, students, and military), every Saturday at 11am.

410 Island Ave. (at Fourth Ave.). © **619/233-4692.** www.gaslampquarter.org. Suggested donation $3. Tues–Sun 11am–3pm. Bus: 1, 3, 5, 16, or 25. Trolley: Gaslamp Quarter or Convention Center.

OLD TOWN & MISSION VALLEY

The birthplace of San Diego—indeed, of California—Old Town takes you back to the Mexican California, which existed here until the mid-1800s. **Plaza del Pasado** ⋇ (p. 150) is a 1930s-era motel that was turned into a collection of shops selling well-chosen south-of-the-border wares. It's also popular for California-style Mexican meals and margaritas.

Mission Valley, which starts just north of Presidio Park and heads straight east, is decidedly more modern: Until I-8 was built in the 1950s, it was little more than cow pastures with a couple of dirt roads. Shopping malls, motels, a golf course, condos, car dealerships, and a massive sports stadium fill the expanse today, following the San Diego River upstream to the **Mission Basilica San Diego.**

Heritage Park   This 8-acre county park, dedicated to preservation of Victorian architecture of the 1880s, contains seven original 19th-century houses moved here from other places and given new uses. Among them are a bed-and-breakfast, a doll shop, and a gift shop. The small charming synagogue at the entrance, Temple Beth Israel, was built in 1889 in Classic Revival style and was relocated here in 1989. A glorious coral tree crowns the top of the hill.

2450 Heritage Park Row (corner of Juan and Harney sts.). ☎ **858/694-3049.** Free admission. Daily 9:30am–3pm. Bus: 5, 5A, or 6. Trolley: Old Town.

Junípero Serra Museum   Perched on a hill above Old Town, this stately Spanish mission–style **building** ☆☆ built in 1929 overlooks the slopes where, in 1769, the first mission, first presidio, and first non-native settlement on the west coast of the United States and Canada were founded (in 1774 the San Diego Mission was relocated 6 miles up Mission Valley; see below). The museum's exhibits introduce visitors to the Native American, Spanish, and Mexican people who first called this place home. On display are their belongings, from cannons to cookware; a Spanish furniture collection; and one of the first paintings brought to California, which survived being damaged in an Indian attack. The settlement remained San Diego's only European village until the 1820s, when families began to move down the hill into what is now Old Town. Designed by William Templeton Johnson, the 70-foot tower can be seen from miles around. **Presidio Park,** which was established around the museum, has a large cross, made of floor tile from the presidio ruins.

2727 Presidio Dr., Presidio Park. ☎ **619/297-3258.** Admission $5 adults, $4 seniors, students, and military, $2 children 6–17, free for children under 6. Fri–Sun 10am–4:30pm. Bus: 5, 5A, or 6. Trolley: Old Town. Take I-8 to the Taylor St. exit. Turn right on Taylor, then left on Presidio Dr.

Mission Basilica San Diego de Alcala ☆   Established in 1769 above Old Town, this was the first link in a chain of 21 missions founded by Spanish missionary Junípero Serra. In 1774, the mission was moved from Old Town to its present site for agricultural reasons, and to separate Native American converts from the fortress that included the original building. The mission was burned by Indians a year after it was built—Father Serra rebuilt the structure using 5- to 7-foot-thick adobe walls and clay tile roofs, rendering it harder to burn. In the process he inspired a bevy of 20th-century California architects. A few bricks belonging to the original mission can be seen in Presidio Park in Old Town. Mass is said daily in this active Catholic parish.

10818 San Diego Mission Rd., Mission Valley. ☎ **619/281-8449.** Admission $3 adults, $2 seniors and students, $1 children under 13. Free Sun and for daily Masses. Daily 9am–4:45pm; Mass daily 7am and 5:30pm. Bus: 13. Trolley: Mission

San Diego. Take I-8 to Mission Gorge Rd. to Twain Ave., which turns into San Diego Mission Rd.

Old Town State Historic Park 🅚   Dedicated to recreating the early life in the city from 1821 to 1872, this is where San Diego's Mexican heritage shines brightest. The community was briefly Mexico's informal capital of the California territory; the Stars and Stripes were finally raised over Old Town in 1846. Seven of the park's 20 structures are original, including homes made of adobe; the rest are reconstructed. The park's headquarters is at the Robinson-Rose House, 4002 Wallace St., where you can pick up a map and peruse a model of Old Town, as it looked in 1872. Among the park's attractions are La Casa de Estudillo, which depicts the living conditions of a wealthy family in 1872; and Seeley Stables, named after A. L. Seeley, who ran the stagecoach and mail service in these parts from 1867 to 1871. The stables have two floors of wagons, carriages, stagecoaches, and other memorabilia, including washboards, slot machines, and hand-worked saddles. On Wednesday and Saturday, costumed park volunteers re-enact life in the 1800s with cooking and crafts demonstrations, a working blacksmith, and parlor singing. Free 1-hour walking tours leave daily at 11am and 2pm from the Robinson-Rose House.

4002 Wallace St., Old Town. ✆ **619/220-5422.** Free admission (donations welcome). Daily 10am–5pm. Bus: 5, 5A, or 6. Trolley: Old Town.

Whaley House   In 1856, this striking two-story brick house (the first one in these parts) was built for Thomas Whaley and his family. Whaley was a New Yorker who arrived via San Francisco, where he had been lured by the gold rush. It's probably an urban legend that Whaley's house is designated as "one of only two authenticated haunted houses in California," yet 10,000 schoolchildren visit each year to see for themselves. Besides, no one can really explain why photos taken inside the house often develop with foggy apparitions (it's said that 4 spirits haunt the structure). Exhibits include a life mask of Abraham Lincoln, one of only six made; the spinet piano used in the movie *Gone With the Wind;* and the concert piano that accompanied Swedish soprano Jenny Lind on her final U.S. tour in 1852. In back is the cottage that was San Diego's first drug store (dating to 1867)—it now houses a shop selling attractive Native American art and jewelry. And the nice shop in front is run by the Save Our Heritage Organisation, which offers beautiful Arts and Crafts pottery, architecture-themed books, and crafts.

2482 San Diego Ave. ✆ **619/297-7511.** Admission $5 adults, $4 seniors over 60, $3 children 3–12. Wed–Mon 10am–4:30pm. Bus: 5, 5A, or 6. Trolley: Old Town.

MISSION BAY & THE BEACHES

Mission Bay is a man-made, 4,600-acre aquatic playground created in 1945 by dredging tidal mud flats and opening them to sea water. Today, this is a great area for walking, jogging, in-line skating, biking, and boating. The boardwalk connecting Mission Beach and Pacific Beach is almost always bustling and colorful. If you get fogged out by June Gloom, head for **The Plunge,** the 175-foot-long indoor pool at the foot of the Giant Dipper. For **SeaWorld San Diego,** see p. 103.

Giant Dipper Roller Coaster   A local landmark for almost 80 years, the Giant Dipper is one of two surviving fixtures from the original Belmont Amusement Park (the other is the Plunge swimming pool). After sitting dormant for 15 years, the vintage wooden roller coaster, with more than 2,600 feet of track and 13 hills, underwent extensive restoration and reopened in 1991. If you're in the neighborhood (especially with older kids), it's worth a stop, but adults may find the whole experience a bit too spine-rattling—you must be at least 50 inches tall to ride.

3190 Mission Blvd., corner of W. Mission Bay Dr. ✆ **858/488-1549.** www.giant dipper.com. Ride on the Giant Dipper $4. MC, V. Daily 11am–7 or 8pm (weekend and summer hours later). Bus: 34 or 34A. Take I-5 to the SeaWorld exit, and follow W. Mission Bay Dr. to Belmont Park.

LA JOLLA

One of San Diego's most scenic spots—the star of postcards for more than 100 years—is **La Jolla Cove** 🏖🏖 and the **Ellen Browning Scripps Park** 🏖 on the bluff above it. The walk through the park, along Coast Boulevard (start from the north at Prospect St.), offers some of California's most resplendent coastal scenery. Offshore, the park is a boat-free zone, with protected undersea flora and fauna that draw scuba divers and snorkelers, many of them hoping for a glimpse of the state fish, the rare and brilliant orange garibaldi. Swimming, sunning, picnicking, barbecuing, reading, and strolling along the oceanfront walkway are all ongoing activities, and just south is the **Children's Pool** 🏖, a beach where dozens of harbor seals can be spotted lazing in the sun (sorry, no swimming here). The unique 6,000-acre **San Diego–La Jolla Underwater Park** 🏖🏖, established in 1970, stretches for 10 miles from La Jolla Cove to the northern end of **Torrey Pines State Reserve,** and extends from the shoreline to a

(Finds Hidden Attractions

While droves of folks stroll the sidewalks adjacent to the San Diego–La Jolla Underwater Park and La Jolla Cove, only a few know about **Coast Walk.** Starting behind the **Cave Store,** 1325 Coast Blvd. (© **858/459-0746**), it meanders along the wooded cliffs and affords a wonderful view of the beach and beyond. The shop also serves as the entry for **Sunny Jim Cave,** an evocative natural sea cave reached by a precipitous constricted staircase through the rock. The tunnel was hand-carved in 1903—it lets out on a wood-plank observation deck from which you can gaze out at the sea. It's a cool treat, particularly on a hot summer day, and costs $3 per person ($2 for kids 16 and under). Hold the handrail and your little ones' hands tightly.

depth of 900 feet. It can be reached from La Jolla Cove or La Jolla Shores.

Highlights in town include **Mary Star of the Sea,** 7727 Girard (at Kline), a beautiful Roman Catholic church; and the **La Valencia Hotel,** 1132 Prospect St., a fine example of a Spanish colonial structure. The **La Jolla Woman's Club,** 7791 Draper Ave.; the adjacent **Museum of Contemporary Art San Diego;** the **La Jolla Recreation Center;** and **The Bishop's School** are all examples of village buildings designed by architect Irving Gill.

At La Jolla's north end, you'll find the 1,200-acre, 22,000-student **University of California, San Diego (UCSD),** which was established in 1960 and represents the county's largest single employer. The campus features the **Geisel Library** ⟨⟨, a striking and distinguished contemporary structure, as well as the **Stuart Collection** of public sculpture and the **Birch Aquarium at Scripps** (see individual listings, below).

For a fine scenic drive, follow La Jolla Boulevard to Nautilus Street and turn east to get to 800-foot-high **Mount Soledad** ⟨, which offers a 360-degree view of the area. The cross on top, erected in 1954, is 43 feet high and 12 feet wide, and has recently been a subject of debate about its suitability in a public park.

Birch Aquarium at Scripps ⟨⟨   This beautiful facility is both an aquarium and a museum, operated as the interpretive arm of the world-famous Scripps Institution of Oceanography. The aquarium affords close-up views of the Pacific Northwest, the California coast, Mexico's Sea of Cortez, and the tropical seas, all presented in 33 marine-life tanks. The giant kelp forest is particularly impressive; keep an eye out for a tiger shark or an eel swimming through. Be sure to check out the fanciful white anemones and the ethereal moon jellies, which look like parachutes. The sea horse propagation program here has met with excellent results—nine different species of sea horse are on display. The rooftop demonstration tide pool not only shows visitors marine coastal life but also offers an amazing view of Scripps Pier, La Jolla Shores Beach, the village of La Jolla, and the ocean. Free tidepool talks are offered on weekends, and off-site adventures are conducted year-round (call for more details).

2300 Expedition Way. © 858/534-FISH. www.aquarium.ucsd.edu. Admission $9.50 adults, $8 seniors, $6 children 3–17, free for children under 3. AE, MC, V. Daily 9am–5pm. Parking $3. Bus: 34. Take I-5 to La Jolla Village Dr. exit, go west 1 mile, and turn left at Expedition Way.

Museum of Contemporary Art San Diego La Jolla 𝕣𝕣

Focusing on work produced since 1950, this museum is known internationally for its permanent collection and thought-provoking exhibitions. The MCASD's collection of contemporary art comprises more than 3,000 works of painting, sculpture, drawings, prints, photography, video, and multimedia works. The holdings include every major art movement of the past half-century, with a strong representation by California artists. You'll see particularly noteworthy examples of minimalism, light and space work, conceptualism, installation, and site-specific art—the outside sculptures were designed specifically for this site.

More than a dozen exhibitions are presented each year here, and at the smaller downtown branch of MCASD. Guided docent tours are available daily at 2pm, with a second tour Thursdays at 5:30pm. The bookstore is a great place for cutting-edge gifts, and the cafe is a pleasant stop before or after your visit.

700 Prospect St. © 858/454-3541. www.mcasd.org. Admission $6 adults, $2 students, seniors, and military, free for children under 12. Free 1st Sun and 3rd Tues of each month. Fri–Tues 11am–5pm; Thurs 11am–7pm. Bus: 30, 34, or 34A. Take I-5 north to La Jolla Parkway or take I-5 south to La Jolla Village Dr. west. Take Torrey Pines Rd. to Prospect Place and turn right; Prospect Place becomes Prospect St.

Stuart Collection 𝕣

Through a 1982 agreement between the Stuart Foundation and UCSD, this still-growing collection consists of site-related sculptures by leading contemporary artists. Start by picking up a map from the information booth, and wend your way through the 1,200-acre campus to discover the 14 highly diverse art-works. Among them is Niki de Saint-Phalle's *Sun God,* a jubilant 14-foot-high fiberglass bird on a 15-foot concrete base. Nicknamed "Big Bird," it's been made an unofficial mascot by the students, who use it as the centerpiece of their annual celebration, the Sun God Festival. Also in the collection are Alexis Smith's *Snake Path,* a 560-foot-long slate-tile pathway that winds up the hill from the Engineering Mall to the east terrace of the spectacular Geisel Library (breathtaking architecture that's a fabulous sculpture itself); and Terry Allen's *Trees,* three eucalyptus trees encased in lead. One tree emits songs, and another poems and stories, while the third stands silent in a grove of trees the students call "The Enchanted Forest." Allow at least 2 hours to tour the entire collection.

University of California, San Diego. ℂ 858/534-2117. http://stuartcollection.ucsd. edu. Free admission. Bus: 30, 34, 41, or 101. From La Jolla, take Torrey Pines Rd. to La Jolla Village Dr., turn right, go 2 blocks to Gilman Dr. and turn left into the campus; in about a block the information booth will be visible on the right.

✴ **Torrey Pines State Reserve** 🐸🐸 *(Moments)*   The rare torrey pine tree grows only two places in the world: Santa Rosa Island, 175 miles northwest of San Diego, and here, at the north end of La Jolla. Even if the twisted shape of these awkwardly beautiful trees doesn't lure you to this spot, the equally scarce undeveloped coastal scenery should. The 1,750-acre reserve was established in 1921, from a gift by Ellen Browning Scripps. The parcel encompasses the beach below, as well as a lagoon immediately north, but the focus is the 300-foot-high, water-carved limestone bluffs, which provide a precarious footing for the trees. In spring, the wildflower show includes bush poppies, Cleveland sage, agave, and yucca. A half-dozen trails (all under 1.5 miles in length) travel from the road to the cliff edge or down to the beach, and there's a small visitor center, built in the traditional adobe style of the Hopi Indians and featuring a lovely 12-minute video about the park. Watch for migrating gray whales in winter, or dolphins who patrol these shores year-round. *Note:* There are no facilities for food or drinks inside the park—bring a picnic lunch.

Hwy. 101, La Jolla. ℂ 858/755-2063. www.torreypine.org. Admission $4 per car, $3 seniors. Daily 8am–sunset. Bus: 101. From I-5, take Carmel Valley Rd. west; turn left at Hwy. 101.

CORONADO

It's hard to miss one of Coronado's most famous landmarks: the **San Diego–Coronado Bay Bridge** 🐸. Completed in 1969, this five-lane bridge rises 246 feet above the bay, spanning 2 miles and linking San

Diego and the "island" of Coronado. When it opened, it put the delightful commuter ferries out of business; in 1986, passenger-only ferry service restarted, making Coronado a very pleasant day trip from downtown (see "Getting Around: By Water," p. 29). Crossing the bridge to Coronado by car or bus is a thrill because you can see Mexico and the shipyards of National City to the left, the San Diego skyline to the right, and Coronado, the naval station, and Point Loma in front of you (designated drivers have to promise to keep their eyes on the road!). The bridge toll was abolished in 2002, so passage is free. Bus route 901 from downtown will also take you across the bridge.

Hotel del Coronado 𝘈𝘈𝘈   Built in 1888, this turreted Victorian seaside resort remains an enduring, endearing national treasure. Whether you are lucky enough to stay, dine, or dance here, or simply to wander through to tour its grounds and photo gallery, prepare to be enchanted.

1500 Orange Ave., Coronado. © 619/435-6611. Free admission. Parking $4 per hour. Bus: 901. Ferry: Broadway Pier, then half-hour walk, or take a bus or the Coronado trolley, or rent a bike.

Museum of History and Art   This museum's new facility offers archival materials about the development of Coronado, as well as tourist information. Exhibits range from photographs of the Hotel Del in its infancy; the old ferries; Tent City, a seaside campground for middle-income vacationers from 1900 to 1939; and notable residents and visitors. Other memorabilia include army uniforms, old postcards, and even recorded music. You'll also learn about the island's military aviation history during World Wars I and II. Plan to spend up to half an hour here. The museum has a self-guided walking tour of Coronado available.

1100 Orange Ave. © 619/435-7242. www.coronadohistory.org. Suggested donation $4 adults, $3 seniors and military, $2 youths 9–18, free to children 8 and under. Mon-Fri 10am–5pm; Sat 11am–4pm. Bus: 901.

FARTHER AFIELD

Knott's Soak City U.S.A. 𝘒𝘪𝘥𝘴   Themed to replicate San Diego's surfer towns around the 1950s and 1960s, this 32-acre water park is San Diego's only facility of its type. There are 22 slides of all shapes and sizes, a 500,000-gallon wave pool, a ¼-mile lazy river, and assorted snack facilities. The park is located about 25 minutes south of downtown, just north of the border line.

2052 Entertainment Circle, Chula Vista. © 619/661-7373. www.knotts.com. Admission $23 adults, $17 children ages 3–11; reduced admission after 3pm. Late

May to Aug daily 10am–6pm or later; open weekends late April to mid-May and Sept. Parking $6. Take I-5 or I-805 to Main St.; turn right on Entertainment Circle.

LEGOLAND California 𝒦 Kids

The ultimate monument to the world's most famous plastic building blocks, LEGOLAND is the third such theme park, following branches in Denmark and Britain that have proven enormously successful. Located 40 minutes north of downtown San Diego, just off I-5 in Carlsbad, the park offers a full day of entertainment for families. In addition to 5,000 LEGO models, the park is beautifully landscaped with 1,360 bonsai trees and other plants from around the world, and features more than 50 rides, shows, and attractions.

Attractions include hands-on interactive displays; a life-size menagerie of tigers, giraffes, and other animals; and scale models of international landmarks (the Eiffel Tower, Sydney Opera House, and so on), all constructed of LEGO bricks. "MiniLand" is a 1:20 scale representation of American achievement, from a New England Pilgrim village to Mount Rushmore and a new replica of Washington, D.C. There's a DUPLO building area to keep smaller children occupied, and a high-tech ride where older kids can compete in LEGO TECHNIC car races. To give the park a little more appeal for older kids, there are three relatively gentle but fun roller coasters, but most teenagers will find LEGOLAND a bit of a snooze.

1 Legoland Dr. ✆ **877/534-6526** or 760/918-LEGO. www.legoland.com. $2 adults, $5 seniors and children 3–12, free to children under 3. AE, DISC, MC, V. Summer (late June–Aug) daily 10am–8pm; off season Thurs–Mon 10am–5 or 6pm. Closed Tues–Wed Sept–May, but open daily during Christmas and Easter vacation periods. Parking $7. From I-5 take the Cannon Rd. exit east, following signs for Legoland Dr.

Mission Trails Regional Park 𝒦 Finds

Located just 20 minutes east of Mission Valley but well off the beaten track for most tourists, this is one of the nation's largest urban parks, a 5,800-acre spread that includes abundant birdlife, two lakes, a picturesque stretch of the San Diego River, the Old Mission Dam (probably the first irrigation project in the West), and 1,592-foot Cowles Mountain, the summit of which reveals outstanding views over much of the county. There are trails up to 4 miles in length, including a 1.5-mile interpretive trail, and some of which are designated for mountain bike use, and a 46-space campground (✆ **619/668-2748**).

1 Father Junípero Serra Trail, Mission Gorge. ✆ **619/582-7800.** www.mtrp.org. Free admission. Nov–Mar daily until 5pm, Apr–Oct daily until 7pm. Take I-8 to Mission Gorge Rd.; follow for 4 miles to entrance.

5 Free of Charge & Full of Fun

It's easy to get charged up on vacation—$10 here, $5 there, and pretty soon your credit-card balance looks like the national debt. To keep that from happening, here's a summary of free San Diego activities, most of which are described in detail earlier in this chapter.

DOWNTOWN & BEYOND

It doesn't cost a penny to stroll around the **Gaslamp Quarter,** which brims with restaurants, shops, and historic buildings, or along the Embarcadero (waterfront), and around the shops at Seaport Village or Horton Plaza. **Walkabout International** offers free guided walking tours (p. 135), and Centre City Development Corporation's **Downtown Information Center** gives bus tours (p. 133).

If you'd rather drive around, ask for the map of the **52-mile San Diego Scenic Drive** when you're at the International Visitor Information Center.

The downtown branch of the **Museum of Contemporary Art San Diego** is always free to the public. And you can **fish** free of charge from any municipal pier (that is, if you bring your own pole).

BALBOA PARK

All the **museums** in Balboa Park are open to the public without charge 1 day a month. Here's a list of the free days:

> **First Tuesday of each month:** Natural History Museum, Reuben H. Fleet Science Center, Model Railroad Museum.
> **Second Tuesday:** Museum of Photographic Arts, Historical Society Museum.
> **Third Tuesday:** Museum of Art, Museum of Man, Mingei International Museum, Japanese Friendship Garden, Museum of the Living Artist.
> **Fourth Tuesday:** Aerospace Museum, Automotive Museum, Hall of Champions Sports Museum.

These Balboa Park attractions are always free: The Botanical Building and Lily Pond, House of Pacific Relations International Cottages, and Timken Museum of Art.

Free 1-hour Sunday afternoon organ concerts year-round, and free concerts Monday through Thursday evenings in summer are given at the **Spreckels Organ Pavilion.**

There are four free **tours** of the park available, leaving from in front of the visitor center. See page 112 for more information.

OLD TOWN & MISSION VALLEY

Explore **Heritage Park, Presidio Park,** or **Old Town State Historic Park.** A 1-hour walking tour of Old Town is conducted twice daily. There's free entertainment (mariachis and folk dancers) at the **Plaza del Pasado,** 2754 Calhoun, on Saturdays and Sundays.

Mission Trails Regional Park, which offers hiking trails and an interpretive center, is reached by following Highway 8 east to Mission Gorge Road.

MISSION BAY, PACIFIC BEACH & BEYOND

Walk along the **beach** or around the bay—it's free, fun, and holding hands at sunset is a proven aphrodisiac. Bring a picnic lunch to enjoy on the **Ocean Beach Pier** or the **Crystal Pier** in Pacific Beach.

LA JOLLA

Enjoy free outdoor **concerts** at Scripps Park on Sundays from 2 to 4pm, mid-June through mid-September (© **858/525-3160**).

The half-mile **Coast Walk** between the La Jolla Cove and Children's Pool is San Diego at its most beautiful—dabble in the tide pools along the way and enjoy the harbor seal colony at Seal Rock and the Children's Pool.

It's also fun to meander around the campus of the University of California, San Diego, and view the **Stuart Collection** (bring a pocketful of quarters for the hungry parking meters). The main branch of the **Museum of Contemporary Art San Diego** is free the first Sunday and third Tuesday of each month. Watching the hang gliders and paragliders launching from the **Gliderport** near Torrey Pines is a blast.

For a great **vista,** follow the SCENIC DRIVE signs to Mount Soledad and a 360-degree view of the area.

CORONADO

Drive across the toll-free Coronado Bay Bridge and take a self-guided tour of the **Hotel del Coronado's** grounds and photo gallery (free street parking is usually available within a few blocks). A walk on beautiful Coronado **beach** costs nothing—so does a lookie-loo tour of the neighborhood's restored Victorian and Craftsman homes.

6 Especially for Kids

If you didn't know better, you would think that San Diego was designed by parents planning a long summer vacation. Activities abound for toddlers to teens. For up-to-the-minute information about activities for children, pick up a free copy of the monthly *San Diego Family Press;* its calendar of events is geared toward family activities and kids' interests. The **International Visitor Information Center,** at First Avenue and F Street (© **619/236-1212**), is another good resource. The **Children's Museum of San Diego** (downtown on Island St.) is undergoing a construction project and will reopen in 2005.

THE TOP ATTRACTIONS

- **Balboa Park** (p. 110) has street entertainers and clowns that always rate high with kids. They can usually be found around El Prado on weekends. The **Natural History Museum,** the **Model Railroad Museum,** the **Aerospace Museum,** and the **Reuben H. Fleet Science Center**—with its hands-on exhibits and IMAX theater—draw kids like magnets.
- The **San Diego Zoo** (p. 99) appeals to children of all ages, and the double-decker bus tours bring all the animals into easy view of even the smallest visitors. There's a Children's Zoo within the zoo, and kids adore the performing sea lion show.
- **SeaWorld San Diego** (p. 103), on Mission Bay, entertains everyone with killer whales, pet-able dolphins, and plenty of penguins—the park's penguin exhibit is home to more penguins than are in all other zoos combined. Try out the family adventure land, "Shamu's Happy Harbor," where everyone is encouraged to explore, crawl, climb, jump, and get wet in more than 20 interactive areas; or, brave a raging river in Shipwreck Rapids.
- The **San Diego Wild Animal Park** (p. 100) brings geography classes to life when kids find themselves gliding through the wilds of Africa and Asia in a monorail. For visitors age 8 and up, the Roar & Snore camping program—held April through October on weekends—is immensely popular.
- **LEGOLAND California** (p. 128), in Carlsbad, features impressive models built entirely with LEGO blocks. There are also rides, refreshments, and LEGO and DUPLO building contests. The park advertises itself as a "country just for kids"—need I say more?

OTHER ATTRACTIONS

- **Seaport Village** (p. 149) has an old-fashioned carousel for children to enjoy.
- **Old Town State Historic Park** (p. 122) has a one-room schoolhouse that rates high with kids. They'll also enjoy the

freedom of running around the safe, parklike compound to "discover" their own fun.

- **Birch Aquarium at Scripps** (p. 124), in La Jolla, is an aquarium that lets kids explore the realms of the deep and learn about life in the sea.
- **Knott's Soak City U.S.A.** (p. 127) is a water park with slides, raft adventures, and a wave pool.
- **The Gliderport** (p. 142) will entertain kids as they watch aerial acrobats swoop through the skies.

THAT'S ENTERTAINMENT

San Diego Junior Theatre (© 619/239-8355; www.juniortheatre. com) is the oldest continuing children's theater program in the country, operating since 1948. The productions—shows like *Peter Pan* and *Little Women,* and staged at Balboa Park's Casa del Prado Theatre— are acted and managed by kids 8 to 18. Ticket prices are $7 to $10 for adults, $5 to $7 for children and seniors, and performances are held on Friday evenings and Saturday and Sunday afternoons.

Sunday afternoon is a great time for kids in **Balboa Park.** They can visit the outdoor Spreckels Organ Pavilion for a free concert (the mix of music isn't too highbrow for a young audience), or try the **Marie Hitchcock Puppet Theatre,** in Balboa Park's Palisades Building (© 619/685-5990). Individual shows might feature marionettes, hand puppets, or ventriloquism, and the stories range from classic *Grimm's Fairy Tales* and *Aesop's Fables* to more obscure yarns. Performances are Wednesday through Friday at 10 and 11:30am and Saturday and Sunday at 11am, 1, and 2:30pm. The shows cost $3 for adults, $2 for seniors and children over 2; they're free for children under 2.

The Globe Theatres (© 619/239-2255; www.theglobetheatres. org) showcases *Dr. Seuss' How the Grinch Stole Christmas!* each year during the holidays—performances are scheduled mid-November through December.

7 Organized Tours

It's almost impossible to get a handle on the diversity of San Diego in a short visit, but one way to maximize your time is to take an organized tour that introduces you to the city. Many tours are creative, not as touristy as you might fear, and allow you a great deal of versatility in planning your day.

Centre City Development Corporation's **Downtown Information Center,** 225 Broadway, Suite 160 (⌀ **619/235-2222;** www.ccdc.com), offers free downtown bus tours the first and third Saturdays of the month at 10am and noon. Aimed at prospective home buyers in the downtown area, as well as curious locals trying to stay abreast of the developments, the 90-minute tours require reservations. Go inside the information center to see models of the Gaslamp Quarter and the downtown area. The office is open Monday through Saturday from 9am to 5pm.

BAY EXCURSIONS $30 per person

The Gondola Company   This unique business operates from Loews Coronado Bay Resort, plying the calm waters between pleasure-boat docks in gondolas crafted according to centuries-old designs from Venice. It features all the trimmings, right down to the striped-shirt-clad gondolier with ribbons waving from his or her straw hat. Mediterranean music plays while you and up to five friends recline with snuggly blankets, and the company will even provide antipasto appetizers (or chocolate-dipped strawberries) and chilled wineglasses and ice for the beverage of your choice (BYOB).

4000 Coronado Bay Rd., Coronado. ⌀ **619/429-6317.** 1-hr. cruise $60 per couple, $15 for each additional passenger (up to 6 total). Daily 11am–midnight.

Hornblower Cruises   This company has a fleet of seven yachts ranging from 40-passenger to a three-deck, 880-passenger behemoth. On Hornblower's 2-hour narrated harbor tour you'll see the *Star of India,* cruise under the San Diego–Coronado Bridge, visit the Hotel Del and the Submarine Base, and swing by an aircraft carrier or two; a 1-hour itinerary is also available. Guests are welcome to visit the captain's wheelhouse for a photo op, and harbor seals and sea lions on buoys and barges are a regular sighting. Whale-watching trips (mid-Dec through late Mar) are a blast, and Hornblower does special itineraries for most holidays (like a fireworks route for Fourth of July festivities). There's also a 2-hour Sunday (and Sat in summer) brunch cruise at 11am, with unlimited champagne and a plentiful buffet, and nightly dinner cruises (see "Cruises with Entertainment," p. 165).

1066 N. Harbor Dr. ⌀ **800/ON-THE-BAY** or 619/686-8715. www.hornblower.com. Harbor tours $15–$20 adult ($2 off for seniors and military; half price for children 4–12). Brunch cruise $45; whale-watching trips $25 (both $2 off for seniors and military, half price for children 4–12). Bus: 2. Trolley: Embarcadero.

Tips **San Diego by Land & Sea at the Same Time**

If you can't decide between a bus tour of San Diego's most popular neighborhoods and a cruise of the city's prettiest waterways, then opt for an amphibious tour from **Sea and Land Adventures.** Their 2-hour tours depart from Seaport Village hourly every day starting at 10am; each specially built boat holds 50 passengers. After cruising the streets of the Gaslamp Quarter, Old Town, and Coronado—and garnering the curious stares of passersby—you'll take a dip into both San Diego and Mission bays to experience the maritime and military history of San Diego from the right perspective. The trips cost $24 for adults and $12 for kids 4 to 12. For information and tickets, call ℂ **619/298-8687,** or visit www.historictours.com.

San Diego Harbor Excursion   This company also offers daily 1- and 2-hour narrated tours of the bay, using its fleet of seven boats ranging from a 1940s passenger launch to a modern, paddlewheel-style vessel. The 1-hour itinerary covers 12 miles including the *Star of India,* U.S. Navy surface fleet, the San Diego–Coronado Bridge, and shipyards; the 25-mile 2-hour route also visits the Submarine Base and North Island Naval Air Station. In winter, whale-watching excursions feature naturalists from the Birch Aquarium. The 2-hour Sunday brunch cruise aboard a sleek yacht is popular; dinner cruises sail nightly (see "Cruises with Entertainment," p. 165).

1050 N. Harbor Dr. (foot of Broadway). ℂ **800/44-CRUISE** or 619/234-4111. www. sdhe.com. Harbor tours $13 for 1 hr., $18 for 2 hr. ($2 off for seniors and military; half price for children 4–12). Brunch cruise $40 adults, $30 children; whale-watching trips $25 adults, $21 seniors, $15 children. Bus: 2. Trolley: Embarcadero.

BUS TOURS

Family-owned **Contact Tours** (ℂ **800/235-5393** or 619/477-8687; www.contactours.com) offers city sightseeing tours, including a "Grand Tour" that covers San Diego, Tijuana, and a 1-hour harbor cruise. It also runs trips to the San Diego Zoo, SeaWorld, Disneyland, Universal Studios, Tijuana, Rosarito Beach, and Ensenada. Prices range from $26 for the 3½-hour City Tour to $52 for the full-day Grand Tour ($12–$24 for children 3–11), and include admissions. Multiple tours can be combined for discounted rates. Contact picks up passengers at most area hotels.

TROLLEY TOURS

Not to be confused with the public transit trolley, the narrated **Old Town Trolley Tours** (✆ 619/298-TOUR; www.historictours.com) are an easy way to get an overview of the city, especially if you're short on time. But the open-air trolleys are also a good way to tie together visits to several of San Diego's major attractions without driving or resorting to pricey cabs. The trackless trolleys do a 30-mile circular route, and you can hop off at any one of eight stops, explore at leisure, and reboard when you please (the trolleys run every half-hour). Stops include Old Town, the Gaslamp Quarter and downtown area, Coronado, the San Diego Zoo, and Balboa Park. You can begin wherever you want, but you must purchase tickets before boarding (most stops have a ticket kiosk). The tour costs $24 for adults ($12 for kids 4–12, free for children 3 and under) for one complete loop; the route by itself takes about 2 hours. The trolleys operate daily from 9am to 4pm in winter, and from 9am to 5pm in summer.

Old Town Trolley also operates a humor-fueled **Ghosts & Gravestones** tour. The 2-hour excursion is done in conjunction with the Gaslamp Quarter Foundation and the San Diego Historical Society, and visits the Whaley House, Villa Montezuma, the William Heath Davis House, and concludes with a walk through one of the city's oldest cemeteries. The tour departs most evenings from the Horton Grand Hotel in the Gaslamp Quarter; reservations required, and bringing a sweater or jacket is recommended. Ghosts & Gravestones costs $28 and is restricted to ages 8 and up only.

WALKING TOURS

Walkabout International, 4639 30th St., Suite C, San Diego (✆ 619/231-7463; www.walkabout-int.org), sponsors more than 100 free walking tours every month that are led by local volunteers, listed in a monthly newsletter and on the website. Walking tours hit all parts of the county, including the Gaslamp Quarter, La Jolla, and the beaches, and there's a hike in the mountains every Wednesday and Saturday.

The **Gaslamp Quarter Historical Foundation** offers tours of the quarter every Saturday at 11am. Tours depart from the William Heath Davis House Museum, 410 Island Ave., and cost $8. For more information, contact the foundation directly at ✆ 619/233-4692 or www.gaslampquarter.org.

Volunteers from the Canyoneer group of the **San Diego Natural History Museum** (✆ 619/255-0203; www.sdnhm.org/canyoneers)

lead free guided nature walks throughout San Diego County. The walks are held every Saturday and Sunday (except July–Aug), and usually focus on the flora and fauna of a particular area, which might be a city park or as far away as Anza-Borrego Desert. The hikes are great fun.

At the **Cabrillo National Monument** on the tip of Point Loma (p. 118), rangers often lead free walking tours. Docents at **Torrey Pines State Reserve** in La Jolla (p. 126) lead interpretive nature walks at 10am and 2pm on weekends and holidays. And guided walks are often scheduled at **Mission Trails Regional Park** (p. 128).

WHALE-WATCHING

Along the California coast, whale-watching is an eagerly anticipated wintertime activity, particularly in San Diego—the Pacific gray whale passes close by Point Loma on its annual migratory trek. Local whaling in the 1870s greatly reduced their numbers, but federal protection has allowed the species to re-populate and current estimates number about 27,000 grays in the ocean today. When they approach San Diego, the 40- to 50-foot gray whales are more than three-quarters of the way along their nearly 6,000-mile journey from Alaska to breeding lagoons near the southern tip of Baja California, for mating and calving—or just beginning the trip home to the rich Alaskan feeding grounds (with calves in tow). The epic journey for these cetaceans is one of the longest migrations of any mammal. Mid-December through mid-March is the best time to see the whales, and there are several ways to view their parade.

The easiest (and cheapest) is to grab a pair of binoculars and head to a good land-bound vantage point. The best is **Cabrillo National Monument,** at the tip of Point Loma, where you'll find a glassed-in observatory and educational whale exhibits, 400 feet above sea level. When the weather cooperates, you can often spot the whales as they surface for breathing—as many as eight grays per hour at peak commute (mid-Jan). For more information on Cabrillo National Monument, see p. 118.

If you want to get a closer look, head out to sea on one of the excursions that locate and follow gray whales, taking care not to disturb their journey. **Classic Sailing Adventures** (© **800/659-0141** or 619/224-0800; www.classicsailingadventures.com) offers two trips per day (8:30am and 1pm); each lasts 4 hours and carries a maximum of six passengers. Sailboats are less distracting to the whales than cruises, but more expensive; tickets are $60 per person (minimum two passengers), including beverages and snacks.

Companies that offer traditional, engine-driven expeditions include **Hornblower Cruises** and **San Diego Harbor Excursions** (see "Bay Excursions," above). Excursions are 3 or 3½ hours, and fares run $25 for adults, with discounts for kids.

8 Outdoor Pursuits

See section 2 of this chapter for a complete rundown of San Diego's beaches, and section 7 for details on whale-watching excursions.

BALLOONING & SCENIC FLIGHTS

A peaceful dawn or dusk balloon ride reveals sweeping vistas of the Southern California coast, wine country, rambling estates, and golf courses. For a champagne-fueled glimpse of the county at sunrise or sunset, followed by an hors d'oeuvres party, contact **Skysurfer Balloon Company** (© **800/660-6809** or 858/481-6800; www.san diegohotairballoons.com). The rate for a 40- to 60-minute flight is $135 per person weekdays, $145 Saturday and Sunday; sunrise flights leave from Temecula (70 min. north of downtown) and sunset flights are from Del Mar (25 min. from downtown). Or call **California Dreamin'** (© **800/373-3359** or 760/438-3344; www.californiadreamin.com). They charge $138 for a 1-hour sunrise breakfast flight in Temecula, $148 for sunset flights in Del Mar that last up to 1 hour; both include champagne and a personalized flight photo. California Dreamin' also offers a **biplane adventure** over Temecula's wine country starting at $138 for two people.

BIRD-WATCHING

The birding scene is huge: More than 480 species have been observed in San Diego County, more than any other county in the United States. The area is a haven along the Pacific Flyway—the migratory route along the Pacific Coast—and the diverse range of ecosystems also helps to lure a wide range of winged creatures. It's possible for birders to enjoy four distinct bird habitats in a single day.

Among the best places for bird-watching is the **Chula Vista Nature Center** at Sweetwater Marsh National Wildlife Refuge (© **619/409-5900;** www.chulavistanaturecenter.org), where you may spot rare residents like the light-footed clapper rail and the western snowy plover, as well as predatory species like the American peregrine falcon and northern harrier. The nature center also has aquariums for sharks and rays, aviaries featuring raptors and shorebirds, and a garden featuring native plants. Also worth visiting along the coast are the 25-acre **Kendall Frost Marsh** on the east side of

Crown Point, in Mission Bay, which draws skimmers, shorebirds, brant and, in winter, the large-billed savannah sparrow; and the **Torrey Pines State Reserve** (p. 126), north of La Jolla, a protected habitat for swifts, thrashers, woodpeckers, and wren tits. Inland, **Mission Trails Regional Park** (p. 128) is a 5,800-acre urban park that is visited by orange-crowned warblers, swallows, raptors, and numerous riparian species; and the **Anza-Borrego Desert State Park** ⚑, 90 miles east of downtown, makes an excellent day trip from San Diego—268 species of birds have been recorded here.

Birders coming to the area should obtain a copy of the free brochure **"Birding Hot Spots of San Diego,"** available at the Port Administration Building, 3165 Pacific Hwy., and at the San Diego Zoo, Wild Animal Park, San Diego Natural History Museum, and Birch Aquarium. It is also posted online at www.portofsandiego.org/ sandiego_environment/bird_brochure.asp. The **San Diego Audubon Society** is another source of birding information (✆ **619/682-7200;** www.sandiegoaudubon.org.)

BIKING

San Diego is cyclist friendly, and was named one of the top 10 cities in the U.S. to bicycle by *Bicycling* magazine. Most major thoroughfares offer bike lanes. To obtain a detailed map by mail of San Diego County's bike lanes and routes, call **Ride Link Bicycle Information** (✆ **619/231-BIKE** or 800/COMMUTE). You might also want to talk to the **City of San Diego Bicycle Coordinator** (✆ **619/533-3110**) or the **San Diego County Bicycle Coalition** (✆ **858/487-6063**). For more practical information on biking on city streets, turn to "Getting Around: By Bicycle," p. 29. Always remember to wear a helmet; it's the law.

The paths around Mission Bay, in particular, are great for leisurely rides. The oceanfront boardwalk between Pacific Beach and Mission Beach can get very crowded, especially on weekends (but that's half the fun). Coronado has a 16-mile round-trip bike trail that starts at the Ferry Landing Marketplace and follows a well-marked route around Coronado to Imperial Beach, along the Silver Strand. The road out to Point Loma (Catalina Dr.) offers moderate hills and wonderful scenery. Traveling old State Route 101 (aka the Pacific Coast Hwy.) from La Jolla north to Oceanside offers terrific coastal views, along with plenty of places to refuel with coffee, a snack, or a swim. The 13-mile climb up steep switchbacks to the summit of 6,140-foot Mt. Palomar is perhaps the county's most invigorating challenge, and offers its most gleeful descent.

Bikes are allowed on the San Diego–Coronado ferry, the San Diego Trolley, and most city buses, at no charge. *Cycling San Diego* by Nelson Copp and Jerry Schad (Sunbelt Publications) is a good resource for bicyclists and is available at most local bike shops.

RENTALS, ORGANIZED BIKE TOURS & OTHER TWO-WHEEL ADVENTURES

Downtown, call **Bike Tours San Diego,** 509 Fifth Ave. (✆ **619/ 238-2444**), which offers free delivery as far north as Del Mar. Rates for a city/hybrid bike start at $18 for a day, and include helmets, locks, maps, and roadside assistance.

In Mission Bay, there's **Mission Beach Club,** 704 Ventura Place, off Mission Boulevard at Ocean Front Walk (✆ 858/488-8889), for one-speed beach cruisers; **Cheap Rentals,** 3685 and 3221 Mission Blvd. (✆ 858/488-9070), for mountain bikes and more; and **Hilton San Diego Resort,** 1775 E. Mission Bay Dr. (✆ 619/276-4010), for multispeed bikes. In La Jolla, try **California Bicycle,** 7462 La Jolla Blvd. (✆ 858/454-0316), for front-suspended mountain bikes. In Coronado, check out **Bikes and Beyond,** 1201 First St. at the Ferry Landing Marketplace (✆ 619/435-7180), for beach cruisers and mountain bikes; they also offer surrey and skate rentals. Expect to pay $6 and up per hour for bicycles, $30 for 24 hours.

Adventurous cyclists might enjoy the **Rosarito-Ensenada 50-Mile Fun Bicycle Ride,** held every April and September just across the border in Mexico. This event attracts more than 8,000 riders of all ages and abilities. It starts at the Rosarito Beach Hotel and finishes in Ensenada and rides along a paved highway. For information, contact **Bicycling West, Inc.** (✆ **619/424-6084;** www.rosaritoensenada.com).

BOATING

Sailors have a choice of the calm waters of 4,600-acre **Mission Bay,** with its 26 miles of shoreline; the exciting **San Diego Bay,** which is one of the most beautiful natural harbors in the world; or the **Pacific Ocean,** where you can sail south to the Islas los Coronados (that is, the trio of uninhabited islets on the Mexico side of the border). There are more than 55,000 registered watercraft docked at 26 marinas throughout the county.

Seaforth Boat Rental, 1641 Quivira Rd., Mission Bay (✆ **888/ 834-2628** or 619/223-1681; www.seaforthboatrental.com), has a wide variety of boats for bay and ocean. It rents 15- to 240-horsepower powerboats ranging from $55 to $115 an hour, 14- to 25-foot sailboats for $20 to $40 an hour, and ski boats and jet skis starting at $70 an hour. Half- and full-day rates are available. Canoes, kayaks, and pedal boats are also available, as well as fishing boats and equipment. Seaforth has locations downtown at the San Diego Marriott Marina, 333 W. Harbor Dr. (© **619/239-2628**) and in Coronado at 1715 Strand Way (© **619/437-1514**).

Mission Bay Sportcenter, 1010 Santa Clara Place (© **858/488-1004;** www.missionbaysportcenter.com), rents sailboats, catamarans, sailboards, kayaks, jet skis, and motorboats. Prices range from $18 to $95 an hour, with discounts for 4-hour and full-day rentals. Private instruction is available for $30 per hour.

Sail USA (© **619/298-6822**) offers custom-tailored skippered cruises on a 34-foot Catalina sloop. A half-day bay cruise costs $275 for six passengers. Full-day and overnight trips are also available, as are trips to Ensenada and to Catalina.

Based at Shelter Island Marina, **Classic Sailing Adventures** (© **800/659-0141** or 619/224-0800; www.classicsailingadventures. com) offers two 4-hour sailing trips daily aboard *Soul Diversion,* a 38-foot Ericson. The afternoon cruise leaves at 1pm and a Champagne sunset sail departs at 5pm. The yacht carries a maximum of six passengers (minimum two), and the $60-per-person price includes beverages and snacks.

FISHING

In the late 1940s, the waters off San Diego supplied as much as two-thirds of the nation's supply of tuna, so it's no wonder that San Diego offers exhilaration to sportfishers. The sportfishing fleet consists of more than 75 large commercial vessels and several dozen private charter yachts, and a variety of half-, full-, and multi-day trips are available. The saltwater fishing season kicks off each spring with the traditional **Port of San Diego Day at the Docks,** held the last weekend in April or at the beginning of May at Sportfishing Landing, near Shelter Island; for more information, call © **619/234-8791** or see www.sportfishing.org. Anglers of any age can fish free of charge without a license off any municipal pier in California. Public fishing piers are on Shelter Island (where there's a statue dedicated to anglers), Ocean Beach, and Imperial Beach.

Summer and fall are ideal for fishing, when the waters around Point Loma are brimming with bass, bonito, and barracuda; the Islas los Coronados, which belong to Mexico but are only about 18 miles from San Diego, are popular for abalone, yellowtail, yellowfin, and big-eyed tuna. Some outfitters will take you farther into Baja

California waters on multi-day trips. Fishing charters depart from Harbor and Shelter Islands, Point Loma, the Imperial Beach pier, and Quivira Basin in Mission Bay. Participants over 16 need a California fishing license.

Rates for trips on a large boat average $35 for a half-day trip or $70 for a ¾-day trip, or you can spring $90 for a 20-hour overnight trip to the Islas los Coronados—call around and compare prices. Prices are reduced for kids, and discounts are often available for twilight sailings; charters or "limited load" rates are also available. The following outfitters offer short or extended outings with daily departures: **H & M Landing,** 2803 Emerson (✆ **619/222-1144;** www.hmlanding.com); **Lee Palm Sportfishers,** 2801 Emerson (✆ **619/224-3857;** www.redrooster3.com); **Point Loma Sportfishing,** 1403 Scott St. (✆ **619/223-1627;** www.pointlomasportfishing.com); and **Seaforth Sportfishing,** 1717 Quivira Rd. (✆ **619/224-3383;** www.seaforthlanding.com). All of these shops rent tackle.

For information on lake fishing, call the city's **Lakes Line** ✆ 619/465-3474.

GOLF

With 90-plus courses, more than 50 of them open to the public, San Diego County offers golf enthusiasts endless opportunities to play. For a full listing of area courses, visit **www.golfsd.com**, or request the **Golf Guide** from the San Diego Convention and Visitors Bureau (✆ 619/236-1212; www.sandiego.org). **San Diego Golf Reservations** (✆ **800/905-0230;** or 858/964-5980; www.sandiegogolfreservations.com) can arrange tee times for you at San Diego's premiere golf courses. They will consult with you on the courses, charging a $10 per person/per tee time coordination fee.

The city's most famous links are found at the **Torrey Pines Golf Course** ★★, a pair of 18-hole championship courses on the cliffs between La Jolla and Del Mar. Home of the Buick Invitational Tournament, and the setting for the 2008 U.S. Open, the biggest challenge at Torrey Pines is getting a tee time, which are taken starting at 7pm, 7 days in advance, by automated telephone. Greens fees on the south course are $95 Monday through Friday, $115 Saturday and Sunday; the north course is $65 and $70, respectively. Cart rentals are $30, and twilight rates are available. Golf packages double the cost, but give you much better odds of actually getting onto the course. Call ✆ **858/570-1234** for tee times, or 858/452-3226 for the pro shop and packages; www.torreypinesgolfcourse.com.

In addition to Torrey Pines, other acclaimed, newer links include: **Four Seasons Resort Aviara Golf Club** in Carlsbad (© 760/603-6900; www.fourseasons.com), **The Meadows Del Mar** (© 858/792-6200; www.meadowsdelmar.com), **Maderas Golf Club** in Poway (© 858/726-4653; www.maderasgolf.com), **Barona Creek** in Lakeside (© 619/387-7018; www.barona.com), and **The Auld Course** in Chula Vista (© 619/482-4666; www.theauldcourse.com).

More convenient for most visitors is the **Riverwalk Golf Club** (© 619/296-4653), links that wander along the Mission Valley floor. Non-resident greens fees, including cart, are $78 Monday through Thursday, $88 Friday, and $98 Saturday and Sunday; twilight and bargain evening rates are available.

HANG GLIDING & PARAGLIDING

The windy cliffs at the **Torrey Pines Gliderport,** 2800 Torrey Pines Scenic Dr., La Jolla (© 877/359-8326; www.flytorrey.com), create one of the country's top spots for hang gliding and paragliding, sports which aren't for the timid, yet deliver a bigger thrill than your average roller coaster. The difference between the two nonmotorized sports is subtle: Hang gliders are suspended from a fixed wing, while paragliders hang from a parachute. In both instances, watching the pilots control these delicate crafts for hours along the brink of the precipice is awesome. A 20- to 30-minute tandem flight with a qualified instructor costs $150. Even if you don't muster the courage to try a tandem flight, sitting at the cafe here and watching the graceful acrobatics is stirring.

If you already have experience, you can rent or buy equipment from the shop at the Gliderport—note that the conditions here are considered "P3"—or take lessons from the crew of able instructors. A 3- or 4-day beginner's package is $795, or lessons run $150 to $250 per day. Winds in December and January are slightest (that is, least conducive for the activities here), while March through June is best. The Gliderport is open daily from 9:30am to sunset.

HIKING & WALKING

San Diego's mild climate makes it a great place to walk or hike most of the year, and the options are diverse. The best **beaches** for walking are Coronado, Mission Beach, La Jolla Shores, and Torrey Pines, but pretty much any shore is a good choice. You can also walk around most of Mission Bay on a series of connected footpaths. If a four-legged friend is your walking companion, head for Dog Beach in

Ocean Beach or Fiesta Island in Mission Bay—two of the few areas where dogs can legally go unleashed. The **Coast Walk** in La Jolla—along the bluffs near the Cove—offers supreme surf-line views.

The **Sierra Club** sponsors regular hikes in the San Diego area, and nonmembers are welcome to participate. There's always a Wednesday mountain hike, usually in the Cuyamaca Mountains, sometimes in the Lagunas; there are evening and day hikes as well. Most are free of charge. For a recorded message about outings, call ℂ **619/299-1744,** or call the office at ℂ **619/299-1743** weekdays from noon to 5pm or Saturday from 10am to 4pm. Volunteers from the **Natural History Museum** (ℂ **619/232-3821**) also lead nature walks throughout San Diego County.

Other places for scenic hikes listed earlier in this chapter include **Torrey Pines State Reserve** (p. 126), **Cabrillo National Monument** (p. 118), and **Mission Trails Regional Park** (p. 128). Guided walks are also offered at each of these parks.

JOGGING

An invigorating route downtown is along the wide sidewalks of the Embarcadero, stretching around the bay. A locals' favorite place to jog is the sidewalk that follows the east side of Mission Bay. Start at the Visitor Information Center and head south past the Hilton to Fiesta Island. A good spot for a short run is La Jolla Shores Beach, where there's hard-packed sand even when it isn't low tide. The beach at Coronado is also a good place for jogging, as is the shore at Pacific Beach and Mission Beach—just watch your tide chart to make sure you won't be there at high tide.

SCUBA DIVING & SNORKELING

San Diego's underwater scene ranges from the magnificent giant kelp forests of Point Loma to a nautical graveyard off Mission Beach known as Wreck Alley. There is an aquatic Ecological Reserve off the La Jolla Cove; fishing and boating activity has been banned in the 533-acre reserve since 1929, but diving and snorkeling is welcome, and it's a reliable place to spot the rare garibaldi, California's state fish, as well as the rare giant black sea bass. Shore diving here, or at nearby La Jolla Shores, is common, and there are dive shops to help you get set up. But boat dives are the rule. Check out the Islas los Coronados, a trio of uninhabited islets off Mexico (a 90-min. boat ride from San Diego), where seals, sea lions, eels, and more cavort against a landscape of boulders (watch for swift currents); and the

Yukon, a 366-foot Canadian destroyer that was intentionally sunk in 2000, 2 miles off Mission Beach at Wreck Alley, joining four other drowned vessels. Water visibility in San Diego is best in the fall, while in the spring, plankton blooms can reduce visibility to 20 feet.

The **San Diego Oceans Foundation** (© **619/523-1903;** www. sdoceans.org) is a local non-profit organization devoted to the stewardship of local marine waters. The website features good information about the local diving scene. **San Diego Divers Supply,** 4004 Sports Arena Blvd. (© **619/224-3439**) and 5701 La Jolla Blvd. (© **858/ 459-2691**), will set you up with scuba and snorkeling equipment. **Blue Escape Dive and Charter** (© **619/223-3483**) and **Scuba San Diego** (© **800/586-3483** or 619/260-1880; www.scubasandiego. com) are other good outfits.

SKATING

Gliding around San Diego, especially the Mission Bay area, on in-line skates is the quintessential Southern California experience. In Pacific Beach, rent a pair of regular or in-line skates from **Resort Watersports** (© **858/488-2582**), based at the Catamaran Resort, 3981 Mission Blvd.; or **Pacific Beach Sun and Sea,** 4539 Ocean Blvd. (© **858/483-6613**). In Coronado, go to **Bikes and Beyond,** 1201 First St. and at the Ferry Landing (© **619/435-7180**). Be sure to ask for protective gear.

If you'd rather ice skate, try the **Ice Capades Chalet** at University Towne Center, La Jolla Village Drive at Genesee Street (© **858/452-9110**).

SURFING

With its miles of beaches, San Diego is a popular surf destination. Some of the best spots include Windansea, La Jolla Shores, Pacific Beach, Mission Beach, Ocean Beach, and Imperial Beach. In North County, you might consider Carlsbad State Beach and Oceanside. The best waves are in late summer and early fall; surfers visiting in winter or spring will want to bring along a wet suit. For surf reports, check out www.surfingsandiego.com or www.surfline.com.

If you didn't bring your own board, they are available for rent at stands at many popular beaches. Many local surf shops also rent equipment; they include **La Jolla Surf Systems,** 2132 Avenida de la Playa, La Jolla Shores (© **858/456-2777**), and **Emerald City–The Boarding Source,** 1118 Orange Ave., Coronado (© **619/435-6677**).

For surfing lessons, with all equipment provided, check with **Kahuna Bob's Surf School** (© **800/KAHUNAS** or 760/721-7700;

www.kahunabob.com) based in Encinitas (30 min. north of downtown); **San Diego Surfing Academy** (© **800/447-SURF** or 760/230-1474; www.surfsdsa.com), which does lessons at Tourmaline in Pacific Beach and San Elijo State Beach in Cardiff by the Sea; and **Surf Diva** (© **858/454-8273;** www.surfdiva.com), the world's first surfing school for women and girls, based in La Jolla.

TENNIS

There are 1,200 public and private tennis courts in San Diego. Public courts include the **La Jolla Tennis Club,** 7632 Draper, at Prospect Street (© **858/454-4434**), which is free and open daily from dawn until the lights go off at 9pm. At the **Balboa Tennis Club,** 2221 Morley Field Dr., in Balboa Park (© **619/295-9278**), court use is free, but reservations are required. The courts are open Monday through Friday from 8am to 8pm, Saturday and Sunday, 8am to 6pm; for lessons, call © **619/291-5248.** The ultra-modern **Barnes Tennis Center,** 4490 W. Point Loma Blvd., near Ocean Beach and SeaWorld (© **619/221-9000;** www.tennissandiego.com), has 20 lighted hard courts and four clay courts; they're open daily from 8am to 9pm. Court rental is $5 to $10 an hour, instruction an additional $12 to $14 per hour.

9 Spectator Sports

BASEBALL & SOFTBALL

The **San Diego Padres,** led to the National League championship in 1998 by stars Tony Gwynn and Trevor Hoffman, play April through September at downtown's brand-new **PETCO Park,** easily accessed via the San Diego Trolley. For schedules, information, and tickets, call © **877/374-2784** or visit www.padres.com.

The highlight of many San Diegans' summer is the softball event known as the **World Championship Over-the-Line Tournament,** held on Fiesta Island in Mission Bay on the second and third weekends of July. For more information, see the "San Diego Calendar of Events," in chapter 2.

BOATING

The **America's Schooner Cup,** held every March or April (© **619/223-3138**), and the **Annual San Diego Crew Classic,** held on Mission Bay every April (© **619/488-0700**), are the major lures. The Crew Classic rowing competition draws teams from throughout the United States and Canada. The **Wooden Boat Festival** is held on

Shelter Island every May (© **619/574-8020**). Approximately 90 boats participate in the festival, which features nautical displays, food, music, and crafts.

FOOTBALL

Although at press time they were holding the city hostage with the threat of leaving for Los Angeles, for now, San Diego's professional football team, the **Chargers** (© **877/CHARGERS;** www.chargers.com), plays at **Qualcomm Stadium** ("The Q"), 9449 Friars Rd., Mission Valley. The season runs from August to December. The Chargers Express bus (© **619/685-4900** for information) costs $5 round-trip and picks up passengers at several locations throughout the city, beginning 2 hours before the game; the stadium is also easily reached via the San Diego Trolley.

The collegiate **Holiday Bowl,** held at Qualcomm Stadium every December, pits the Western Athletic Conference champion against a team from the Big 10. For information, call © **619/283-5808.**

GOLF

San Diego is the site of some of the country's most important golf tournaments, including the **Buick Invitational,** which takes place in February at Torrey Pines Golf Course in La Jolla (© **800/888-BUICK** or 619/281-4653), and the **Accenture Match Play Championship** put on by World Golf Championships and held at La Costa, also in February (© **760/431-9110**). Now you know why February is celebrated as Golf Month by the Convention and Visitors Bureau. The **U.S. Open** will be held at Torrey Pines in 2008.

HORSE RACING & SHOWS

Live Thoroughbred racing takes place at the **Del Mar Race Track** (© **858/755-1141** for information and racing schedules; www.delmarracing.com) from late July to mid-September. Located 20 minutes north of downtown, post time for the nine-race program is 2pm (except for Fri, when it's 4pm); there is no racing on Tuesdays. Admission to the clubhouse is $8, including program; stretch run seating is $5 with program and includes infield access; and reserved seats are $5. The infield area has a jungle gym where kids can play or watch exhibition shows put on by BMX riders and skateboarders. "Four O'Clock Fridays" is designed to lure the martini crowd, with a 4pm post time and live bands at 7pm.

The **Del Mar National Horse Show** takes place at the Del Mar Fairgrounds from late April to early May. Olympic-caliber and national championship riders participate. For information, call ℭ **858/792-4288** or 858/755-1161, or check www.sdfair.com.

ICE HOCKEY

The **San Diego Gulls** of the West Coast Hockey League skate at the San Diego Sports Arena from late October into March. For schedules, tickets, and information, call ℭ **619/224-4625** or 619/224-4171, or visit www.sandiegogulls.com.

MARATHONS & TRIATHLONS

San Diego is a wonderful place to run or watch a marathon because the weather is usually mild. The **San Diego Marathon** takes place in January. It's actually in Carlsbad, 35 miles north of San Diego, and stretches mostly along the coastline. For more information, call ℭ **858/792-2900,** or visit www.inmotionevents.com.

Drawing about 20,000 runners, the **Suzuki Rock 'n' Roll Marathon** is held in early June and features a route lined with rock bands, usually capped off by a headline act performing at a large venue. For additional information, call ℭ **858/450-6510,** or visit www.eliteracing.com.

Another popular event is the **La Jolla Half Marathon,** held in late April. It begins at the Del Mar Fairgrounds and finishes at La Jolla Cove. For information, call ℭ **858/454-1262,** or see www.lajollahalfmarathon.com.

The **America's Finest City Half Marathon** is held in August every year. The race begins at Cabrillo National Monument, winds through downtown, and ends in Balboa Park. For information, call ℭ **858/792-2900,** or visit www.inmotionevents.com.

The **San Diego International Triathlon,** held in late June, includes an international course comprised of a 1,000m swim, a 30km bike ride, and a 10km run, plus a shorter sprint course. A kids triathlon precedes the event by 1 day. It starts at Spanish Landing on San Diego Bay. For information, call ℭ **858/268-1250** or check www.kozenterprises.com.

SOCCER

The **San Diego Sockers,** members of the Continental Indoor Soccer League, play from September to March at the San Diego Sports Arena, 3500 Sports Arena Blvd. (ℭ **858/836-4625;** www.sockers.com). Tickets range from $10 to $35.

7

Shopping

Whether you're looking for a souvenir, a gift, or a quick replacement for an item inadvertently left at home, you'll find no shortage of stores in San Diego. This is, after all, Southern California, where looking good is a high priority and shopping in sunny outdoor malls is a way of life.

1 The Top Shopping Neighborhoods

DOWNTOWN & THE GASLAMP QUARTER

Space is at a premium in the still-developing Gaslamp Quarter, and rents are rising as the debut of the new ballpark approaches. While only a few intrepid shops—mostly women's boutiques and vintage clothing shops—made the initial commitment to open among the area's multitudinous eateries, in the past few years a number of wonderfully individualistic stores have opened on lower Fourth and Fifth avenues. As the number of condos in the downtown area multiplies, watch for shopping to diversify. Otherwise, downtown shopping is primarily concentrated in two destination malls.

Horton Plaza 𝄫 *Kids*   The Disneyland of shopping malls, Horton Plaza is the heart of the revitalized city center, bounded by Broadway, First and Fourth avenues, and G Street. Covering 6½ city blocks, the multilevel shopping center has more than 130 specialty shops, including art galleries, clothing and shoe stores, several fun shops for kids, and bookstores. There's a 14-screen cinema, three major department stores, and a variety of restaurants and short-order eateries. It's almost as much an attraction as the San Diego Zoo. Parking is free with validation for the first 3 hours, $1 per half-hour thereafter. The parking levels are confusing, and temporarily losing your car is part of the Horton Plaza experience. Open Monday to Friday 10am to 9pm, Saturdays 10am to 8pm, and Sundays 11am to 7pm. 324 Horton Plaza. ✆ **619/238-1596.** www.hortonplaza.shoppingtown.com. Bus: 2, 7, 9, 29, 34, or 35. Trolley: City Center.

Beth Ann!

Seaport Village   This ersatz 14-acre village snuggled alongside San Diego Bay was built to resemble a small Cape Cod community, but the 75 shops are very much the Southern California cutesy variety. The atmosphere is pleasant, and there are a few gems; favorites include the **Tile Shop,** featuring hand-painted tiles from Mexico and beyond; the **San Diego City Store,** with all your local signage needs; **Island Hoppers,** for resort wear; and the **Upstart Crow** bookshop and coffeehouse, with the Crow's Nest children's bookstore inside. Be sure to see the 1890 carousel imported from Coney Island, New York. Two hours free parking with purchase. 849 W. Harbor Dr. (at Kettner Blvd.). ✆ **619/235-4014,** or 619/235-4013 for event information. www.seaportvillage.com. Sept–May daily 10am–9pm; June–Aug daily 10am–10pm. Bus: 7. Trolley: Seaport Village.

Hillcrest/Uptown

Compact Hillcrest is an ideal shopping destination. As the hub of San Diego's gay and lesbian community, swank inspiration and chic housewares rule. There are plenty of establishments selling cool trinkets, used books, vintage clothing, and memorabilia; a couple chain stores (including **Gap**); and of course, bakeries and cafes.

There's no defined zone in which shops are found, so you may as well start at the neighborhood's axis, at the overrun intersection of University and Fifth avenues. From this corner the greatest concentration of boutiques spreads for 1 or 2 blocks in each direction, but farther east on University—between 10th Avenue and Vermont Street—you'll find good options (like the fun **Ace Hardware** store) along the south side of the street, and on the north side a small shopping complex with several choice bets. Metered street parking is available, so be armed with plenty of change. You can also park in a lot—rates vary, but you'll come out ahead if you're planning to stroll for several hours.

If you're looking for postcards or provocative gifts, step into wacky **Babette Schwartz,** 421 University Ave. (✆ **619/220-7048**), a pop-culture emporium named for a local drag queen, and located under the can't-miss "Hillcrest" street sign. You'll find books, clothing, and accessories that follow current kitsch trends. A couple of doors away, **Cathedral,** 435 University Ave. (✆ **619/296-4046**), is dark and heady, filled with candles of all scents and shapes, plus unusual holders.

Around the corner, **Circa a.d.,** 3867 Fourth Ave. (✆ **619/293-3328**), is a floral design shop with splendid gift items; at holiday time it has the most extravagant Christmas ornaments in the area. Head gear from straw hats to knit caps to classy fedoras fills the **Village Hat Shop,** 3821 Fourth Ave. (© 619/683-5533; www.villagehatshop. com), whose best feature may be its mini-museum of stylishly displayed vintage hats.

Lovers of rare and used books will want to poke around the **used bookstores** on Fifth Avenue, between University and Robinson avenues. Though their number has decreased with the advent of online shopping, you can always find something to pique your interest. This block is also home to **Off the Record,** 3865 Fifth Ave. (© 619/298-4755), a new and used music store known for an alternative bent and the city's best vinyl selection. A few doors down is **Wear It Again Sam,** 3823 Fifth Ave., south of Robinson (© 619/ 299-0185; www.wearitagainsamvintage.com). It's a classy step back in time, with vintage clothing—for both females and males—in styles from the first half of the 20th century.

A half-mile east of Hillcrest is the start of San Diego's self-proclaimed **Antique Row.** It lies north of Balboa Park, along Park Boulevard (beginning at University Ave. in Hillcrest) and on Adams Avenue (extending from Park east to around 40th St. in Normal Heights). Antique and collectible stores, vintage-clothing boutiques, and dusty used-book and record stores line this L-shaped district, providing hours of treasure hunting. There are plenty of coffeehouses, pubs, and small restaurants to break up the excursion. For more information and an area brochure with a map, contact the **Adams Avenue Business Association** (© 619/282-7329; www. GoThere.com/AdamsAve).

OLD TOWN & MISSION VALLEY

Old Town Historic Park is a restoration of some of San Diego's historic sites and adobe structures, a number of which now house shops that cater to tourists. Many have a "general store" theme, and carry gourmet treats and inexpensive Mexican crafts alongside the obligatory T-shirts, baseball caps, snow domes, and other souvenirs. New, but maintaining the park's old Californio theme, is **Plaza del Pasado,** 2754 Calhoun St. (© 619/297-3100; www.plazadelpasado. com), which incorporates 11 specialty shops, 3 restaurants, and a boutique hotel. Costumed employees, special events and activities, and strolling musicians add to the festive flavor.

Mission Valley is the epicenter of San Diego's suburban mall explosion. There are two major and several minor shopping centers here (see "Malls," p. 156).

Mission Bay & the Beaches

The beach communities offer laid-back shopping in typical California fashion, with plenty of surf shops, recreational gear, casual garb, and college-oriented music stores. If you're looking for something more distinctive than T-shirts and shorts, you'd best head east to Mission Valley.

For women in need of a new bikini, the best selection is at **Pilar's,** 3745 Mission Blvd., Pacific Beach (*©* **858/488-3056**), where choices range from stylish designer suits to hot trends like suits inspired by surf- and skate-wear. There's a smaller selection of one-piece suits, too. Across the street is **Liquid Foundation Surf Shop,** 3731 Mission Blvd., Pacific Beach (*©* **858/488-3260**), which specializes in board shorts for guys.

San Diego's greatest concentration of antiques stores is found in the **Ocean Beach Antique District,** along the 4800 block of Newport Avenue, the community's main drag. Most of the stores are mall-style, featuring multiple dealers under one roof. The hundreds of individual sellers cover the gamut—everything from Asian antiquities to vintage watches to mid-20th-century collectibles. Although you won't find a horde of pricey, centuries-old European antiques, the overall quality is high enough to make it interesting for any collector. Highlights include **Newport Avenue Antiques,** 4836 Newport Ave. (*©* **619/224-1994**), which offers the most diversity: Its wares range from Native American crafts to Victorian furniture and delicate accessories, from Mighty Mouse collectibles to carved Asian furniture. **Ocean Beach Antique Mall,** 4847 Newport Ave. (*©* **619/223-6170**), has a more elegant setting and glass display cases filled with superb American art, pottery, and china. Names like Roseville, McCoy, and Royal Copenhagen abound, and there's a fine selection of quality majolica and Japanese tea sets. The **Newport Avenue Antique Center,** 4864 Newport Ave. (*©* **619/222-8686**), is the largest store, and has a small espresso bar. One corner is a haven for collectors of 1940s and 1950s kitchenware (Fire King, Bauer, melamine); there's also a fine selection of vintage linens. Most of the O.B. antiques stores are open daily from 10am to 6pm, with somewhat reduced hours Sunday.

LA JOLLA

Shopping is a major pastime in this upscale community. Women's clothing boutiques tend to be conservative and costly, like those lining Girard and Prospect streets (**Ann Taylor, Armani Exchange,**

Polo Ralph Lauren, Talbots, and **Sigi's Boutique**). But you'll also find less pricey venues like **Banana Republic** and **Dansk.**

Recommended stores include **Island Hoppers,** 7844 Girard Ave. (© 858/459-6055), for colorful Hawaiian-print clothing from makers like Tommy Bahama; the venerable **Ascot Shop,** 7750 Girard Ave. (© 858/454-4222), for conservative men's apparel and accessories; and **La Jolla Shoe Gallery,** 7852 Girard Ave. (© 858/551-9985), for an outstanding selection of Echo, Clark's, Birkenstock, Mephisto, Josef Siebel, and other shoes built for walking.

Even if you're not in the market for furnishings and accessories, La Jolla's many home-decor boutiques make for great window shopping, as do its ubiquitous jewelers: Swiss watches, tennis bracelets, precious gems, and pearl necklaces sparkle in windows along every street.

CORONADO

This rather insular, conservative navy community doesn't have a great many shopping opportunities; the best of the lot line Orange Avenue at the western end of the island. You'll find some scattered housewares and home-decor boutiques, several small women's boutiques, and the gift shops at Coronado's major resorts.

Coronado has an excellent independent bookshop, **Bay Books,** 1029 Orange Ave. (© 619/435-0070). It carries a nice selection in many categories, plus volumes of local historical interest, and books on tape. **La Provençale,** 1122 Orange Ave. (© 619/437-8881), is a little shop stocked with fabric, tablecloths, pottery, and tableware items from the French countryside; nearby, **In Good Taste,** 1146 Orange Ave. (© 619/435-8356), has a staggering selection of gourmet and food gift items—in addition to a tempting display of luscious truffles and sweets. And, if you're in pursuit of swimwear, poke your head into **Dale's Swim Shop,** 1150 Orange Ave. (© 619/435-7301), a tiny boutique jam-packed with suits to fit all bodies, including rare European makers seldom available in this country.

The Ferry Landing Marketplace   As you stroll up the pier, you'll find yourself in the midst of souvenir and other shops filled with gifts, jewelry, and crafts. You can get a quick bite to eat or have a leisurely dinner with a view, wander along landscaped walkways, or laze on a beach or grassy bank. Open daily 10am to 9pm. There's a farmer's market every Tuesday from 2:30 to 6pm. 1201 First St. (at B Ave.), Coronado. © 619/435-8895. Take I-5 to Coronado Bay Bridge, to B Ave., and turn right. Bus: 901. Ferry: From Broadway Pier.

ELSEWHERE IN SAN DIEGO COUNTY

San Diego's best outlet mall is 40 minutes north, at the **Carlsbad Premium Outlets,** 5620 Paseo del Norte (✆ **760/804-9000**), and includes the usual outlet shops and upscale retailers like Barneys New York, Donna Karan, Crate & Barrel, Wilson's Leather, Dooney & Bourke, and Polo Ralph Lauren. The **Cedros Design District** ✆, along the 100 and 200 blocks of South Cedros Avenue in Solana Beach (30 min. north of downtown San Diego), is an outstanding place for designer interior decorating goods. The strip is located just northwest of the Del Mar racetrack; reach it by taking the Via de la Valle exit off the I-5 and going right on Cedros Ave. The Coaster station is next to the district.

2 Shopping A to Z

Large stores and shops in malls tend to stay open until about 9pm on weekdays, 6pm on weekends. Smaller businesses usually close at 5 or 6pm or may keep odd hours. When in doubt, call ahead.

ANTIQUES

See also the "Hillcrest/Uptown" and "Mission Bay & the Beaches" sections in "The Top Shopping Neighborhoods," earlier in this chapter.

The Cracker Factory Antiques Shopping Center   Prepare to spend some time here, exploring three floors of individually owned and operated shops filled with antiques and collectibles. It's across the street from the Hyatt Regency San Diego, a block north of Seaport Village. 448 W. Market St. (at Columbia St.). ✆ **619/233-1669.** Bus: 7. Trolley: Seaport Village.

ART

The *Arts Down Town* guide is available at the Museum of Contemporary Art; it's a handy color brochure/map for exploring downtown galleries and exhibits.

The Artists Gallery   This gallery features 30 regional artists in a variety of media, primarily paintings. 7420 Girard Ave., La Jolla. ✆ **858/459-5844.**

Fingerhut Gallery   Fingerhut is a Southern California minichain offering fine-quality lithographs and etchings from masters like Picasso, Chagall, and Matisse. This branch, however, is notable for the "secret" art of La Jolla's own Theodor Geisel (aka Dr. Seuss), whose whimsical-yet-provocative unpublished works explode with the same color and exuberance of illustrations from his famous books. 1205 Prospect St., La Jolla. © **800/774-2278** or 858/456-9912. www. fingerhutart.com/lajolla.htm.

Scott White Contemporary Art This gallery, in a grand space once occupied by the I. Magnin department store, specializes in modern and contemporary painting, sculpture, and photography. Andy Warhol, Roy Lichtenstein, and Mark Rothko are among the names. 7661 Girard Ave., Suite 200, La Jolla. © **858/551-5821**.

Taboo Studio This impressive shop exhibits and sells the work of jewelry designers from throughout the United States. The jewelry is made of silver, gold, platinum, and inlaid stones, in one-of-a-kind pieces, limited editions, or custom work. The gallery represents 65 artists. 1615½ W. Lewis St., Mission Hills. © **619/692-0099**. www.taboo studio.com.

BOOKS

Barnes & Noble The San Diego branch of this book discounter sits amid one of Mission Valley's smaller malls, Hazard Center. Open daily 10am to 9pm. 7610 Hazard Center Dr., Mission Valley. © **619/220-0175**.

Borders This full-service book and CD store just west of the Mission Valley shopping center offers discounts on many titles. There's an adjoining coffee lounge. Open Monday to Thursday 9am to 11pm; Friday and Saturday 9am to midnight; Sunday 10am to 10pm. 1072 Camino del Rio N., Mission Valley. © **619/295-2201**.

Obelisk Bookstore San Diego's main gay and lesbian bookstore is where Clive Barker and Greg Louganis do their book signings. Gay-themed videos and DVDs are also available. Open Monday to Thursday 10am to 10pm; Friday and Saturday 10am to 11pm; Sunday 11am to 10pm. 1029 University Ave., Hillcrest. © **619/297-4171**.

Warwick's Books This popular third-generation-owned bookstore is a browser's delight, with more than 40,000 titles, a large travel section, gifts, cards, and stationery. Authors come in for readings several days each week. Open Monday to Saturday 9am to 6pm; Sunday 11am to 5pm. 7812 Girard Ave., La Jolla. © **858/454-0347**. www.warwicks.com.

DEPARTMENT STORES

Macy's There are several branches of this comprehensive store, which carries clothing for women, men, and children, as well as housewares, electronics, and luggage. Macy's also has stores in the Fashion Valley (clothing only), Mission Valley Center (housewares only), University Towne Center, and North County Fair (Escondido) malls. Open Monday to Friday 10am to 9pm; Saturday 10am to 8pm; Sunday 11am to 7pm. Horton Plaza. © **619/231-4747.** Bus: 2, 7, 9, 29, 34, or 35.

Nordstrom A San Diego favorite, Nordstrom is best known for its outstanding customer service and fine selection of shoes. It features a variety of stylish fashions and accessories for women, men, and children. Tailoring is done on the premises. There's a full-service restaurant on the top floor, where coffee and tea cost only 25¢. Nordstrom also has stores in the Fashion Valley, University Towne Center, and North County Fair (Escondido) malls. Open Monday to Friday 10am to 9pm; Saturday 10am to 8pm; Sunday 11am to 7pm. Bus: 2, 7, 9, 29, 34, or 35. Horton Plaza. © **619/239-1700.** Bus: 2, 7, 9, 29, 34, or 35.

FARMERS' MARKETS

We love our open-air markets. In **Hillcrest,** the market runs Sundays from 9am to noon at the corner of Normal Street and Lincoln Avenue, several blocks north of Balboa Park. The atmosphere is festive, and exotic culinary delights reflect the eclectic neighborhood. For more information, call the **Hillcrest Association** at © **619/299-3330.**

In **Ocean Beach,** there's a fun-filled market Wednesday evenings between 4 and 8pm (until 7pm in fall and winter) in the 4900 block of Newport Avenue. In addition to fresh-cut flowers, produce, and exotic fruits and foods laid out for sampling, the market features llama rides and other entertainment. For more information, call the **Ocean Beach Business Improvement District** at © **619/224-4906.**

Head to **Pacific Beach** on Saturday from 8am to noon, when Mission Boulevard between Reed Avenue and Pacific Beach Drive is transformed into a bustling marketplace.

In **Coronado,** every Tuesday afternoon the Ferry Landing Marketplace hosts a produce and crafts market from 2:30 to 6pm; see p. 152 for a full review.

FLEA MARKETS

Kobey's Swap Meet *Value* Since 1980, this gigantic open-air market positioned at the west end of the Sports Arena parking lot has been a bargain-hunter's dream-come-true. As many as 3,000 vendors fill row after row with new and used clothing, jewelry, electronics, hardware, appliances, furniture, collectibles, crafts, antiques, auto accessories, toys, and books. There's produce, too, along with food stalls and restrooms.

Insider's tip: Although the market is open Friday through Sunday from 7am to 3pm, the weekend is when the good stuff is out— and it goes quickly, so arrive early. Sports Arena, 3500 Sports Arena Blvd. ✆ 619/226-0650 for information. Admission Fri 50¢; Sat–Sun $1; children under 12 free. Take I-8 west to Sports Arena Blvd. turnoff or I-5 to Rosecrans St. and turn right on Sports Arena Blvd.

MALLS

See p. 148 for details on **Horton Plaza.** See "The Top Shopping Neighborhoods: Elsewhere in San Diego County," p. 153, for information on the **Carlsbad Premium Outlets** factory outlet mall.

Fashion Valley Center   The Mission Valley corridor, running east-west about 2 miles north of downtown along I-8, contains San Diego's major shopping centers. Fashion Valley is the most attractive and most upscale, with four anchor stores, **Neiman Marcus, Nordstrom** (which keeps longer hours), **Saks Fifth Avenue,** and **Macy's,** plus 140 specialty shops and an 18-screen AMC movie theater. Other noteworthy shops include **Z Gallerie, Smith & Hawken,** and **Bang & Olufsen.** Open Monday to Friday 10am to 9pm; Saturday 10am to 6pm; Sunday 11am to 6pm. 352 Fashion Valley Rd. ✆ 619/297-3381. Hwy. 163 to Friars Rd. W. Bus: 6, 16, 25, 43, or 81.

Mission Valley Center   This old-fashioned outdoor mall predates sleek Fashion Valley, and has found a niche with budget-minded stores like **Loehmann's, Nordstrom Rack,** and **Target,** as well as **Macy's Home Furnishing.** There's a 20-screen AMC movie theater and about 150 other stores and places to eat. Across the streets to the north and west are other complexes that feature **Sak's Off Fifth Avenue** (an outlet store), **Borders,** and more. Open Monday to Friday 10am to 9pm; Saturday 10am to 6pm; Sunday 11am to 6pm. 1640 Camino del Rio N. ✆ 619/296-6375. I-8 to Mission Center Rd. Bus: 6, 16, 25, 43, or 81.

University Towne Center (UTC)   This outdoor shopping complex has a landscaped plaza and more than 150 stores, including some big ones like **Nordstrom, Sears,** and **Macy's.** It is also home to a year-round ice-skating rink and the popular On Tap Bistro and Brewery. Open Monday to Friday 10am to 9pm; Saturday 10am to 7pm; Sunday 11am to 6pm. 4545 La Jolla Village Dr. ✆ 858/546-8858. I-5 to La Jolla Village Dr. and go east, or I-805 to La Jolla Village Dr. and go west. Bus: 50 express, 34, or 34A.

MUSIC

In addition to the mega chains like Tower Records and the Warehouse, you'll find a good crop of independent outlets. Probably the best place for serious collectors is **Lou's Records,** 434 Hwy. 101 in Encinitas, about 30 minutes north of downtown (© 760/753-1382; www.lousrecords.com). Here you'll find one building devoted to new CDs (the imports are pricey), another to used CDs and vinyl, and a new store next door catering to DVD fanatics. More central is **Off the Record,** 3849 Fifth Ave., Hillcrest (© 619/298-4755; www.otrvinyl. com), which has a good selection of indie releases and used CDs, but I can't stand how cases are plastered with stickers and security tags. Die-hard headbangers should make the trek to **Blue Meanie Records,** 916 Broadway in El Cajon, 20 minutes east of downtown (© 619/442-5034), where a head-shop ambience adds to the selection of metal and punk albums, T-shirts, and posters. Last but not least is **Folk Arts Rare Records,** 3611 Adams Ave. in Normal Heights (© 619/282-7833), which is nirvana for serious jazz and blues collectors. Situated in an old house, the store hasn't caught up with the CD era yet, but you'll find first-edition rarities on vinyl and 78s, most of them fairly priced.

TOYS

Freddy's Teddies & Toys   With shelves stacked literally from floor to ceiling, this Coronado shop's comprehensive inventory defies its cozy size and truly has something to interest anyone who steps inside. Open daily 10am to 5pm. 930 Orange Ave. © 619/437-0130. www.coronadotoys.com.

TRAVEL ACCESSORIES

Along with the stores listed below, try **Eddie Bauer** in Horton Plaza (© 619/233-0814) or **Traveler's Depot** (© 858/483-1421) for travel gear.

John's Fifth Avenue Luggage   This San Diego institution carries just about everything you can imagine in the way of luggage, travel accessories, business cases, pens, and gifts. The on-premises luggage-repair center is an authorized airline repair facility. There is also a store in the Fashion Valley mall, with extended hours. Open Monday to Friday 9am to 5:30pm; Saturday 9am to 4pm. 3833 Fourth Ave. © 619/298-0993.

Le Travel Store   In business since 1976, Le Travel Store has a good selection of soft-sided luggage, travel books, language tapes, maps, and lots of travel accessories. The long hours and central location make this spot extra handy. Open Monday to Saturday 10am–7pm; Sunday noon to 6pm. 745 Fourth Ave. (between F and G sts.). *C* **619/544-0005**. www.letravelstore.com. Bus: 2, 7, 9, 29, 34, or 35. Trolley: Gaslamp.

The Map Centre This shop, recently relocated to this shopping plaza across I-5 from Old Town, has the whole world covered—in maps, that is. Open Monday to Friday 10am to 5:30pm; Saturday 10am to 5pm. 3191 Sports Arena Blvd. (west of Rosecrans). *C* **619/291-3830**. www.mapcentre.com.

8

San Diego After Dark

San Diego's cultural scene has never been second-rate, but it's always lounged in the shadows of Los Angeles and San Francisco, content to take a back seat to the beach, the zoo, and the meteorologically inspired state of affairs. But the dot-com wave brought new blood and new money into the city, and arts organizations have felt the impact. The city's opera, live theaters, and other arts organizations are thriving as new ears and eyes claim San Diego's art scene as their own.

For a rundown of the week's performances, gallery openings, and other events, check the listings in "Night and Day," the Thursday entertainment section of the *San Diego Union-Tribune* (www.union trib.com), or the free *San Diego Weekly Reader* (www.sdreader.com), published on Thursday.

The local convention and visitors bureau's *Art + Sol* pamphlet is published every 6 months and provides a calendar of events and profiles of 11 member institutions; get a free copy by calling ☎ **800/270-WAVE,** or check www.sandiegoartandsol.com. The San Diego Performing Arts League produces *What's Playing?*, a performing arts guide, every 2 months. You can pick one up at the ARTS TIX booth or write to 701 B St., Suite 225, San Diego, CA 92101-8101 (☎ **619/238-0700;** www.sandiegoperforms.com).

Half-price tickets to theater, music, and dance events are available at the **ARTS TIX** booth in Horton Plaza Park, at Broadway and Third Avenue. The kiosk is open Tuesday through Thursday at 11am, and Friday through Sunday at 10am. The booth stays open till 6pm daily except Sunday, when it closes at 5pm. Half-price tickets are available only for same-day shows except for Monday performances, which are sold on Sunday. Only cash is accepted. For a daily listing of offerings, call ☎ **619/497-5000** or check www.sandiegoperforms.com; the website also sells half-price tickets for some shows. Full-price advance tickets are also available; the kiosk doubles as a Ticketmaster outlet, selling seats to concerts throughout California.

1 The Performing Arts

THEATER

These listings focus on the best known of San Diego's many talented theater companies. Don't hesitate to try a less prominent venue if the show appeals to you.

The Globe Theatres ☆☆ This complex of three performance venues is located inside Balboa Park, behind the Museum of Man. Though best known for the 581-seat Old Globe—fashioned after Shakespeare's—it also includes the 225-seat Cassius Carter Centre Stage and the 612-seat open-air Lowell Davies Festival Theatre. Between them, they mount 14 plays year-round, from world premieres of such subsequent Broadway hits as *Into the Woods* to the excellent summer Shakespeare San Diegans have come to expect from "their" Globe. Balboa Park. © 619/239-2255. Fax 619/231-5879. www. theglobetheatres.org. Tickets $19–$50. Senior, student, and military discounts available. Bus: 7 or 25. Free parking in the park's public lots.

La Jolla Playhouse ☆☆ Boasting a Hollywood pedigree (founded in 1947 by Gregory Peck, Dorothy McGuire, and Mel Ferrer), and a 1993 Tony Award for outstanding American regional theater, the Playhouse stages six productions each year (May–Nov) at two fine theaters on the UCSD campus. *The Who's Tommy* and *Big River* also premiered at the Playhouse before going on to great acclaim on Broadway. For each show, one Saturday matinee is a "pay what you can" performance, and any night, all unsold tickets are available for $12 each in a "public rush" sale 10 minutes before curtain. 2910 La Jolla Village Dr. (at Torrey Pines Rd.). © 858/550-1010. Fax 858/550-1025. www.lajolla playhouse.com. Tickets $35–$55. Parking $3. Bus: 30, 34, or 34A.

Lamb's Players Theatre The season for this professional repertory company runs from February to December. Shows take place in the 340-seat theater in Coronado's historic Spreckels Building, where no seat is more than seven rows from the stage. Recent productions include *Godspell,* Noel Coward's *Private Lives,* and Anton Chekhov's *Uncle Vanya.* 1142 Orange Ave., Coronado. © 619/437-0600. www.lambsplayers.org. Tickets $20–$40. Street parking is usually available nearby. Bus: 901, 902, or 904.

San Diego Repertory Theatre The Rep mounts plays and musicals at the 550-seat Lyceum Stage and the 250-seat Lyceum Space in Horton Plaza. Situated at the entrance to Horton Plaza, the two-level subterranean theaters are tucked behind a tile obelisk. 79

Broadway Circle, in Horton Plaza. ℭ **619/544-1000**. www.sandiegorep.com. Tickets $23–$40. Free validated parking at Horton Plaza Shopping Center. Bus: All Broadway routes.

CLASSICAL MUSIC

La Jolla Chamber Music Society ★★ This well-respected organization has been bringing marquee names to San Diego since 1968. Past performers include Pinchas Zukerman, Emanuel Ax, Joshua Bell, the American Ballet Theatre, and other world-class artists. Most of the 40-plus annual shows are held October through May in the beautiful, 500-seat Sherwood Auditorium at the Museum of Contemporary Art. The annual highlight is SummerFest, a 3-week series of concerts, forums, open rehearsals, talks, and artist encounters—it's held in early August and is broadcast nationally live on National Public Radio (NPR). At Sherwood Auditorium, 700 Prospect St., La Jolla. ℭ **858/459-3728**. Fax 858/459-3727. www.ljcms.org. Tickets $15–$75. Bus: 30 or 34.

San Diego Symphony ★ Like a phoenix from the ashes, San Diego's symphony is on the verge of major triumph. The organization floundered for a decade starting in the late 1980s, in conjunction with a local recession, inept management, and the malaise that gripped many fine orchestras around the country. In 1998, the symphony emerged from bankruptcy, and in 2002, enduring financial stability, arrived with a $120-million bequest by Joan and Irwin Jacobs (founder and CEO of Qualcomm). The bequest allows the organization to lure top talent, including new resident conductor, Jahja Ling. The symphony's home is the Fox Theatre, a 1929-era French rococo–style downtown landmark, restored and now known as Symphony Hall. The season runs October through May. A Summer Pops series, with programs devoted to big band, Broadway, and Tchaikovsky, is held weekends from late June through August on Navy Pier at the Embarcadero—always bring a sweater and possibly a blanket for these pleasantly brisk evenings. 750 B St., at Seventh Ave. ℭ **619/235-0804**. www.sandiegosymphony.com. Tickets $10–$80. Bus: 1, 3, or 25. Trolley: Fifth Ave.

OPERA

San Diego Opera ★★ The San Diego Opera has grown into one of the community's most successful arts organizations. The annual season runs from late January to mid-May, with five offerings at downtown's 3,000-seat Civic Theatre, ranging from well-trod warhorses like *Madama Butterfly* to new productions such as

Thérèse Raquin, all performed by local singers and big-name talent from around the world. The company also hosts several recitals each year at La Jolla's Sherwood Hall, featuring heavy-hitters like Marilyn Horne. The annual lineup is announced around April, and non-subscription tickets go on sale by December. At the Civic Theatre, 202 C St. *(C)* **619/570-1100** (box office) or 619/232-7636. www.sdopera.com. Tickets $20–$140. Standing room, student, and senior discounts available. Bus: 2, 7, 9, 29, 34, or 35. Trolley: Civic Center.

DANCE

The **San Diego Dance Alliance** is the umbrella organization for the local dance community (*(C)* **619/230-8623;** www.sandiegodance. org). The alliance puts on the **Nations of San Diego International Dance Festival,** held each January and spotlighting the city's ethnic dance groups and emerging artists. The website provides links to 22 local dance outfits. Among San Diego's major dance companies are the **California Ballet** (*(C)* **858/560-5676;** www.californiaballet. org), a classical company that produces four shows annually at the Civic Theatre downtown, including *The Nutcracker.* **San Diego Ballet** (*(C)* **619/294-7378;** www.sandiegoballet.org) and **City Ballet** (*(C)* **858/274-6058;** www.cityballet.org) also focus on classical dance pieces.

2 The Club & Music Scene

LIVE MUSIC

SMALL VENUES

The Belly Up Tavern *(R) (Finds)* This club in Solana Beach, a 30-minute drive from downtown, has played host to critically acclaimed and international artists of all genres. The eclectic mix ranges from Duncan Sheik to Etta James to Frank Black to The Roots. A funky setting in recycled Quonset huts underscores the venue's uniqueness. Look into advance tickets, if possible, though you can avoid excessive Ticketmaster fees by purchasing your tickets at the box office. 143 S. Cedros Ave., Solana Beach (1½ blocks from the Coaster stop). *(C)* **858/481-9022** (recorded info) or 858/481-8140 (box office). www.bellyup.com.

The Casbah It may have a total-dive ambience (and black-walled bathrooms grimy enough to make you clench muscles you didn't even *know* you had), and passing jets overhead sometimes drown out ballads, but this blaring Little Italy club has a well-earned rep for showcasing alternative and rock bands that either are, were, or will

No Smoking

In 1998, California enacted legislation that banned smoking in all restaurants and bars. As a rule, don't light up in any public area indoors. If you're looking to light up in clubs, lounges, and other nightspots with outdoor terraces, check with the staff or watch to see what the locals are doing first.

be famous. Past headliners at the 200-capacity club have included the Yeah Yeah Yeahs, Will Oldham, The White Stripes, and local act Rocket From the Crypt. Look into advance tickets if possible; live music can be counted on at least 6 nights a week. Every month or two the Casbah turns into Jivewire, with wall-to-wall bodies on the small dance floor and ear-to-ear new wave, disco, and hip-hop classics on the sound system. 2501 Kettner Blvd., at Laurel St., near the airport. ℭ 619/232-HELL. www.casbahmusic.com.

Croce's Nightclubs   Croce's is the cornerstone of Gaslamp Quarter nightlife: a loud, crowded, and mainstream gathering place around the corner from Horton Plaza. Two separate clubs operate a couple doors apart: You'll find traditional jazz at Croce's Jazz Bar 7 nights a week (8:30pm–12:30am), and rhythm and blues at Croce's Top Hat Friday and Saturday (9pm–1am). The music blares onto the street, making it easy to decide whether to go in or not. The clubs are named for the late Jim Croce and are owned by his widow, Ingrid, who was a vital component of the Gaslamp's revitalization. The cover charge is waived if you eat at the restaurant. 802 Fifth Ave. (at F St.). ℭ 619/233-4355. www.croces.com. Cover $5–$10.

4th & B   Located in a former bank building downtown, 4th & B is a no-frills music venue made comfortable with haphazardly placed seating (balcony theater seats, cabaret tables on the main floor) and a handful of bar/lounge niches—one actually inside the old vault. The genre is barrier-free; everyone from Fishbone to Toto to They Might Be Giants to Lisa Marie Presley has shown up here, along with regular bookings of the San Diego Chamber Orchestra. 345 B St., Downtown. ℭ 619/231-4343. www.4thandB.com.

LARGER VENUES

There's a worthwhile concert just about any night of the week—you just need to know where to find it. The free *San Diego Weekly Reader,* published on Thursdays, is the best source of concert information, listing dozens of shows in any given week; check the website at www.sdreader.com for an advance look. Tickets typically go on sale 4 to 10 weeks before the event—on-sale dates are usually announced in the Thursday *Reader* or the Sunday *San Diego Union-Tribune*. Depending on the popularity of a particular artist or group, last-minute seats are often available through the box office or **Ticketmaster** (© 619/220-8497; www.ticketmaster.com). You can also go through a broker like **Advance Tickets** (© 858/581-1080; www.advancetickets.com) if you're willing to pay a higher price for prime tickets at the last minute.

Among the special venues is **Humphrey's** ✦, 2241 Shelter Island Dr. (© 619/523-1010; www.humphreysconcerts.com), a much-beloved 1,300-seat outdoor venue on the water. It has ideal acoustics, and Humphrey's seasonal lineup covers the spectrum of entertainment—rock, jazz, blues, folk, and comedy. Although there's not a bad seat in the house, you can often snag one in the first eight rows by buying the dinner/concert package ($47 extra) for the adjoining restaurant of the same name—the food's nothing special, but if sitting up front is of value to you, it's a good deal. Concerts are held mid-May through October only, and tickets for most shows go on sale in early April. (Seats are also available through Ticketmaster.)

The **Open Air Theater** (© 619/594-6947), on the San Diego State University campus, northeast of downtown along I-8, is a 4,000-seat outdoor amphitheater. It has great acoustics—if you can't get a ticket, you can sit outside on the grass and hear the entire show. **Cox Arena** (© 619/594-6947), also located at SDSU, has equally superb acoustics in an indoor, 12,000-seat facility that is used for bigger draws—for both of these facilities, parking is tight.

The **Spreckels Theatre,** 121 Broadway (© 619/235-9500), and **Copley Symphony Hall,** 750 B St. (© 619/235-0804), are wonderful old movie houses which also are used by touring acts throughout the year; past shows have included Annie Lennox, Margaret Cho, and *Forever Tango*. For both venues, tickets are available at the box office or through Ticketmaster.

Many of the big-name touring acts play at one of our big venues. The best is **Coors Amphitheatre** (© 619/671-3600), a slick facility located seemingly a stone's throw north of the Mexican border, in Chula Vista. Built in 1999, the 20,000-seat venue has excellent acoustics and good sightlines, and it lures many of the summer tours. The drawbacks: overpriced snacks and drinks, and the location is 25 to 45 minutes south of downtown (depending on traffic).

The **San Diego Sports Arena** (☎ **619/225-9813;** www.sandiego arena.com) is located west of Old Town. Built in 1967, the 15,000- to 18,000-seat indoor venue has lousy acoustics, but many big-name concerts are held here because of the seating capacity and availability of paid parking.

COMEDY CLUBS

The Comedy Store   Yes, it's a branch of the famous Sunset Strip club in Los Angeles, and yes, plenty of L.A. comics make the trek to headline Friday and Saturday shows here. Less prominent professional comedians perform live Wednesday and Thursday, and Sunday's open-mic night can be hilarious, horrendous—or both. 916 Pearl St., La Jolla. ☎ 858/454-9176. Cover $5–$20 (plus 2-drink minimum).

DANCE CLUBS & CABARETS

Olé Madrid   Loud and energetic, this dance club features a changing lineup of celebrated DJs spinning house, funk, techno, and hip-hop. The adjoining restaurant has terrific tapas and sangria. Open Tuesday through Saturday. 751 Fifth Ave., Gaslamp Quarter. ☎ 619/ 557-0146. Cover $10 after 10pm.

Sevilla   This Latin-themed club is the spot for salsa lessons Tuesday through Thursday and Sunday at 8pm, followed by live bands at 10pm. Friday and Saturday is a Latin/Euro dance club and Monday is Rock en Español. Sevilla also has a tapas bar. 555 Fourth Ave., Gaslamp Quarter. ☎ 619/233-5979. www.cafesevilla.com. Cover $5–$10.

CRUISES WITH ENTERTAINMENT

Bahia Belle 🅰   Cruise Mission Bay and dance to live music under the moonlight aboard this stern-wheeler. Passengers are picked up from the dock of the Bahia Hotel, 998 W. Mission Bay Dr., on the half-hour from 6:30pm to 12:30am, and at the Catamaran Resort Hotel, 3999 Mission Blvd., on the hour from 7pm to midnight. 988 W. Mission Bay Dr. ☎ 858/539-7720. www.sternwheelers.com. Tickets $6 adults, $3 children under 12. Operates nightly July–Aug; operates Fri–Sat only Sept–June. Children accompanied by an adult allowed until 9pm; after 9pm, 21 and over only (with valid ID).

Hornblower Cruises   Aboard the 151-foot antique-style yacht *Lord Hornblower,* you'll be entertained—and encouraged to dance— by a DJ playing a variety of recorded music. The three-course meal is standard-issue banquet style, but the scenery is marvelous. Boarding is at 6:30pm, and the cruise runs from 7 to 10pm. 1066 N. Harbor Dr. (at Broadway Pier). ☎ 619/725-8888. www.hornblower.com. Tickets Sun–Fri $55; Sat

$60 adults (children ages 4–12 are 40% off). Price does not include sodas or alcoholic beverages. Bus: 2. Trolley: Embarcadero.

San Diego Harbor Excursion   This company offers nightly dinner on board the 150-foot, three-deck *Spirit of San Diego,* with two main courses, dessert, and cocktails. A DJ plays dance music during the 2½-hour cruise. Sometimes there's also a country-western band or even a karaoke singalong. Boarding is at 7pm, and the cruise lasts from 7:30 to 10pm. 1050 N. Harbor Dr. (at Broadway Pier). ✆ **800/44-CRUISE** or 619/234-4111. www.harborexcursion.com. Tickets $50 adults ($69 with alcoholic beverages), $30 children ages 3–12, free for children under 3; all prices $5 higher on Sat. Bus: 2. Trolley: Embarcadero.

3 The Bar & Coffeehouse Scene
BARS & COCKTAIL LOUNGES

The Beach   Currently very "in" among trendoids, the Beach is the rooftop bar of the W hotel. What makes it truly unique is that most of the floor is sand—you can take your shoes off even in winter since the sand is heated and the drinks are served in plastic. A gas fire pit adds to the ambience, as do the cabanas lining one wall. Don't forget your flip-flops, shovel, and pail. The hotel's two other bars, the Living Room Coffeehouse and Magnet, are also smart. 421 B St. (at State St.), Downtown. ✆ **619/231-8220.**

The Bitter End   With three floors, this conceited, Brit-themed Gaslamp Quarter hot spot manages to be a sophisticated martini bar, after-hours dance club, and relaxing cocktail lounge all in one. On weekends you're subject to velvet rope/dress code nonsense. 770 Fifth Ave., Gaslamp Quarter. ✆ **619/338-9300.** www.thebitterend.com. Cover Thurs $5 after 9:30pm, Fri–Sat $10 after 8:30pm.

Cannibal Bar   Attached to the lobby of the Polynesian-themed Catamaran Hotel, the Cannibal Bar thumps to the beat of a different drum machine—though you *can* get a mean mai tai at the bar. Party central at the beach for thundering DJ-driven music, the Cannibal also books some admirable bands now and then. 3999 Mission Blvd., Pacific Beach. ✆ **858/539-8650.** Cover Wed–Sun $5–$6.

Lips   Drag review, with or without dinner. There's a different show nightly, like Bitchy Bingo on Wednesday and celebrity impersonations on Thursday. Shows start at 7 or 7:30pm Sunday through Thursday; Friday and Saturday have two seatings at 6 and 8:30pm. 2770 Fifth Ave. (at Nutmeg St.), Hillcrest. ✆ **619/295-7900.** www.lipsshow.biz. Cover $3; dinner reservations guarantee seating.

Martini Ranch The Gaslamp Quarter's newest crowd-pleaser is this split-level bar boasting 30 kinds of martinis (or martini-inspired concoctions). Downstairs resembles an upscale sports bar playing videos, cartoons, and sports simultaneously across the room. If the sensory overload addles your brain, traipse upstairs to relax in scattered couches, love seats, and conversation pits. 528 F St. (at Sixth Ave.), Gaslamp Quarter. ✆ **619/235-6100.** www.martiniranchsd.com. Cover $10 Fri–Sat after 8:30pm.

The Onyx Room Hipsters dive into this cutting-edge underground (literally) club where the atmosphere is lounge, the drinks are up, and the music is cool. Live jazz is featured on Tuesdays. Upstairs is **Thin,** run by the same crew and open Tuesday through Friday from 4pm, Saturday and Sunday from 7pm. 852 Fifth Ave., Downtown. ✆ **619/235-6699.** www.onyxroom.com. Cover Fri–Sat $10 (admission to both bars), Thurs $5 for Onyx.

Ould Sod Irish through and through, this little gem sits in a quiet neighborhood of antiques shops northeast of Hillcrest, hosting a very local crowd. On Tuesdays, the tavern features low-key folk or world-music performances; you'll find various other live bands and karaoke Wednesday through Saturday. 3373 Adams Ave., Normal Heights. ✆ **619/284-6594.** Cover Wed $3.

Princess Pub & Grille A local haunt for Anglophiles and others thirsting for a pint o' Bass, Fuller's, Watney's, or Guinness, this slice of Britain (in Little Italy . . . go figure) also serves up overpriced bangers 'n' mash, steak-and-kidney pie, and other pub grub. The after-work crowd can be festive, and if you drink enough, the food starts to taste good. 1665 India St., Little Italy. ✆ **619/702-3021.** www.princesspub.com.

Top Of the Cove At this intimate piano bar in one of La Jolla's most scenic restaurants, the vibe is mellow and relaxing on Fridays and Saturdays after 8:30pm. The music—mainly standards and show tunes—is piped into the outdoor patio. 1216 Prospect Ave., La Jolla. ✆ **858/454-7779.**

Turf Supper Club *Finds* Hidden in one of San Diego's old, obscure, and newly hip neighborhoods (about 10 min. east of downtown), the gimmick at this retro steakhouse is cheap, "grill your own" dinners. Steaks are delivered raw, but seasoned, on a paper plate—you do the rest. *Tip:* Don't be afraid to ask for grilling suggestions from the staff. The decor and piano bar (on Sun) are pure 1950s, and wildly popular with the cocktail crowd; the volume level other nights is not always conducive to intimate dining. 1116 25th Ave., Golden Hill. © 619/234-6363.

Late-Night Bites

Late-night meals aren't a big part of San Diego life outside downtown, but there are a few good choices. See chapter 5 for complete listings on most of the following restaurants.

Downtown The kitchen at **Croce's,** 802 Fifth Ave. (© 619/233-4355), stays open till midnight all week. You can order appetizers from the eclectic menu, or opt for a full (expensive) meal. **Kansas City Barbecue,** across the street from the Hyatt, serves meals until 1am nightly. The stylish coffeehouse **Café Lulu,** a block from Horton Plaza, stays open till 1am Sunday through Thursday and 3am Friday and Saturday. It serves healthy foods featuring bread from Bread & Cie.

Hillcrest/Uptown The relentlessly 1950s-themed **Corvette Diner** serves up terrific coffee shop–style food and a page-long menu of fountain favorites; it stays open till midnight Friday and Saturday. Or satisfy your sweet tooth with a sublime creation from **Extraordinary Desserts,** which also serves imported teas and coffees along with not-so-sweet scones and tea cakes. **Crest Cafe** is a friendly neighborhood joint for burgers, pastas, and sandwiches; it's open till midnight Sunday through Thursday, till 1am Friday and Saturday.

Elsewhere In Old Town, the irrepressible **Old Town Mexican Cafe** stays open for basic Mexican and tasty margaritas until 11pm Sunday through Thursday, and serves until "about" midnight on Friday and Saturday. Day or night, it's hard to top the Chinese seafood delicacies found at **Emerald Restaurant** in Kearny Mesa, and it's open until midnight daily. In Pacific Beach, **Nick's at the Beach,** 809 Thomas Ave. (© 858/270-1730), is open until 1am nightly and serves laid-back seafood; nearby **Saska's,** 3768 Mission Blvd. (© 858/488-7311), stays open till 12:45am Sunday through Thursday, till 1:45am Friday and Saturday, serving steaks, fish, and pasta.

COFFEEHOUSES WITH PERFORMANCES

Claire de Lune Coffee Lounge *(Finds)*   Every Tuesday is poetry night: It's one of the biggest in the country, drawing 200 to 300 people. The third Thursday of the month is live belly dancing; Friday and Saturday feature varied bands. 2906 University Ave. (at Kansas), North Park. (C) 619/688-9845. www.clairedelune.com.

Twiggs Tea and Coffee Co. *(Finds)*   Tucked away in a peaceful neighborhood, this popular coffeehouse has an adjoining room for live music Thursday through Sunday, poetry readings every other Monday, and an open-mic night on Wednesday. 4590 Park Blvd. (south of Adams Ave.), University Heights. (C) 619/296-0616. www.twiggs.org. Sometimes a $6–$12 cover for higher profile acts.

4 Gay & Lesbian Nightlife

For what's happening at the gay clubs, pick up the weekly *San Diego Gay & Lesbian Times.*

The Brass Rail   San Diego's oldest existing (since 1960) gay bar, this Hillcrest institution is loud and proud, with energetic dancing every night, bright lights, and a come-as-you-are attitude. Thursday and Saturday are Latino Night, hip-hop reigns on Friday and Sunday, and Wednesday is Women's Night. 3796 Fifth Ave. (at Robinson St.), Hillcrest. (C) 619/298-2233. Cover Fri–Sat $7 ($4 with gym card or military ID).

Club Montage   This state-of-the-art dance club has all the bells and whistles: laser-and-light show, 12-screen video bar, pool tables, and arcade games. Three levels of dancing, four oversize bars, a video bar, and a rooftop smoking patio with views of downtown draws a mixed (gay and non-gay) crowd on Fridays. 2028 Hancock St. (C) 619/294-9590. www.clubmontage.com. Cover charge varies.

The Flame   The city's top lesbian hangout has a large dance floor and two bars. It's packed on Saturdays. A mixed crowd attends Friday's Goth Night; gender reversal takes place for Wednesday's "Drag King" contest. 3780 Park Blvd. (C) 619/295-4163. Cover Wed $3, Sat $8.

Flicks   The first video bar in town, Flick's airs *Six Feet Under* and *Queer as Folk* live and offers various theme nights to supplement the rotating music and comedy clips. Tuesday is Fish Tank for lesbians. 1017 University Ave., Hillcrest. (C) 619/297-2056. Cover Mon $2, Fri $4.

Kickers   This country-western dance hall next to the ever-popular Hamburger Mary's restaurant attracts an equally male-female crowd for two-stepping and line-dancing Thursday through Saturday; free dance lessons are part of the mix. Sunday is busiest, with a high-energy tea dance and a $2 cover. Monday through Wednesday feature theme nights. 308 University Ave. (at Third Ave.), Hillcrest. ℂ 619/491-0400.

Numbers   It's a predominantly male crowd at this busy dance emporium, with three bars, two dance floors, and go-go boy dancers. Friday is Ladies' Night. Open daily from 1pm. 3811 Park Blvd. (at University Ave.), Hillcrest. ℂ 619/294-9005. www.numbers-sandiego.com. Cover $3–$5.

Rich's   High-energy and popular with the see-and-be-seen set, Rich's offers house music and monster tribal rhythms, and a small video bar. Open Thursday through Sunday only. 1051 University Ave. (between 10th and Vermont). ℂ 619/497-4588. www.richs-sandiego.com. Cover some nights.

Six Degrees   Mellower than the Flame, this casual lesbian gathering place north of Little Italy has a small dance floor, occasional live entertainment, and popular Sunday barbecues. 3175 India St. (at Spruce St.). ℂ 619/296-6789.

Top of the Park   The penthouse bar of this lodging, which is adjacent to Balboa Park, is a very popular social scene on Friday evenings from 5 to 10pm. 525 Spruce St. (at Fifth Ave.), Hillcrest. ℂ 619/ 291-0999. www.parkmanorsuites.com.

5 More Entertainment

CINEMA

A variety of multiscreen complexes around the city show first-run films. My favorite venue, from a sheer presentation standpoint, is Pacific's **Gaslamp Stadium,** Fifth Avenue at G Street, downtown (ℂ 619/232-0400); the 15 theaters all offer stadium seating with large screens and great sound systems. The AMC chain operates swarming complexes in both the **Mission Valley** and **Fashion Valley** shopping centers (ℂ 858/558-2AMC); both have free parking but popular films sell out early on weekends. Current American, independent, and foreign films play at Landmark's five-screen **Hillcrest Cinema,** 3965 Fifth Ave., Hillcrest, which offers 3 hours of free parking (ℂ 619/299-2100); the **Ken Cinema,** 4061 Adams Ave., Kensington (ℂ 619/283-5909); and the four-screen **La Jolla Village,** 8879 Villa La Jolla Dr., La Jolla, also with free parking (ℂ 858/453-7831).

The **Museum of Photographic Arts** in Balboa Park (ℂ 619/238-7559; www.mopa.org) has a well-chosen revival series featuring

American and foreign classics, shown Friday and Saturday and some weeknights. The **OMNIMAX** theater at the Reuben H. Fleet Science Center (✆ **619/238-1233**), also in Balboa Park, features IMAX movies in the early evening projected onto the 76-foot tilted dome screen (later screenings on weekends). Planetarium shows are held the first Wednesday of the month.

PERFORMANCE ART

Sushi is San Diego's preeminent performance art gallery, a 3,000-square-foot facility for interactive, visual art, music, dance, and other shows, attended by up to 200 people. Thought-provoking performances by Karen Finley, John Fleck, Tim Miller, and others have kept Sushi on the map. Performances are usually at 8pm, and prices range from $5 to $15. Sushi is located at 320 Eleventh Ave., between J and K sts., in the downtown warehouse district (✆ **619/235-8466;** www.sushiart.org).

CASINOS

Native American tribes operate seven casinos in east and north San Diego County. The leader is probably **Barona Valley Ranch Resort and Casino,** located at 1000 Wildcat Canyon Rd., Lakeside (✆ **888/7-BARONA** or 619/443-2300; www.barona.com), 40 minutes from downtown. The casino features 2,000 Vegas-style slots, 54 table games, and a 125-seat off-track betting area. The resort (which

---

Finds **Running with the Grunion**

The **Grunion Run** is a wacky local tradition that few visitors experience. But if someone invites you to hustle down to the beach for a late-night fishing expedition, armed only with a sack and flashlight, do not be afraid. Grunion are 5- to 6-inch silvery fish that wriggle out of the water to lay their eggs in the sand. They make for decent eating (coated in flour and cornmeal, then fried), providing you don't mind catching them barefoot, but it's fun just to watch the action. April through early June is peak spawning season in Southern California (which, with Baja California, is the only place you'll find grunion)—anywhere from a few dozen to thousands of grunion can appear during a run. You do need a valid state fishing license to catch grunion (see "Fishing" under "Outdoor Pursuits," p. 140). If you'd like more information, the little critters have their own website: **www.grunion.org**.

---

includes 397 guest rooms and an 18-hole championship golf course) is alcohol-free, but not smoke-free (Indian reservations are exempt from California's nonsmoking laws).

Sycuan Casino & Resort is outside El Cajon, 30 min. from downtown, at 5469 Dehesa Rd. (© **800/2-SYCUAN** or 619/445-6002; www.sycuan.com). Sycuan features 1,800 slots, 65 game tables, a bingo palace, an off-track betting area, and a 450-seat theatre which features name touring acts. Sycuan acquired the neighboring Singing Hills Country Club, which includes 11 tennis courts, two 18-hole championship golf courses, and a 102-room lodge.

The **Viejas Casino** is at 5000 Willows Rd., in Alpine (© **800/ 84-POKER** or 619/445-5400; www.viejas.com), about 40 min. from downtown. Here you'll find 2,000 slots, 80 table games, an off-track betting room, a 1,500-seat Bingo pavilion, five restaurants, and a showroom. Across the road is the **Viejas Outlet Center,** which features the usual suspects: Eddie Bauer, Liz Claiborne, Polo Ralph Lauren, and others.

Index

See also Accommodations and Restaurant indexes below.

Frommer's® National Park Guides

Algonquin Provincial Park
Banff & Jasper
Family Vacations in the National
  Parks

Grand Canyon
National Parks of the American West
Rocky Mountain

Yellowstone & Grand Teton
Yosemite & Sequoia/Kings Canyo
Zion & Bryce Canyon

Frommer's® Memorable Walks

Chicago
London

New York
Paris

San Francisco

Frommer's® With Kids Guides

Chicago
Hawaii
Las Vegas
New York City

Ottawa
San Francisco
Toronto

Vancouver
Walt Disney World® & Orlando
Washington, D.C.

Suzy Gershman's Born to Shop Guides

Born to Shop: France
Born to Shop: Hong Kong, Shanghai
  & Beijing

Born to Shop: Italy
Born to Shop: London

Born to Shop: New York
Born to Shop: Paris

Frommer's® Irreverent Guides

Amsterdam
Boston
Chicago
Las Vegas
London

Los Angeles
Manhattan
New Orleans
Paris
Rome

San Francisco
Seattle & Portland
Vancouver
Walt Disney World®
Washington, D.C.

Frommer's® Best-Loved Driving Tours

Austria
Britain
California
France

Germany
Ireland
Italy
New England

Northern Italy
Scotland
Spain
Tuscany & Umbria

The Unofficial Guides®

Beyond Disney
California with Kids
Central Italy
Chicago
Cruises
Disneyland®
England
Florida
Florida with Kids
Inside Disney

Hawaii
Las Vegas
London
Maui
Mexico's Best Beach Resorts
Mini Las Vegas
Mini Mickey
New Orleans
New York City
Paris

San Francisco
Skiing & Snowboarding in the W
South Florida including Miami &
  the Keys
Walt Disney World®
Walt Disney World® for
  Grown-ups
Walt Disney World® with Kids
Washington, D.C.

Special-Interest Titles

Athens Past & Present
Cities Ranked & Rated
Frommer's Best Day Trips from London
Frommer's Best RV & Tent Campgrounds
  in the U.S.A.
Frommer's Caribbean Hideaways
Frommer's China: The 50 Most Memorable Trips
Frommer's Exploring America by RV
Frommer's Gay & Lesbian Europe

Frommer's NYC Free & Dirt Cheap
Frommer's Road Atlas Europe
Frommer's Road Atlas France
Frommer's Road Atlas Ireland
Frommer's Wonderful Weekends from
  New York City
Retirement Places Rated
Rome Past & Present